JAMES AGEE: SELECTED JOURNALISM

JAMES AGEE
SELECTED JOURNALISM

EDITED, WITH AN INTRODUCTION,
BY PAUL ASHDOWN

THE UNIVERSITY OF TENNESSEE PRESS

The paper in this book meets the guidelines for permanence
and durability of the Committee on Production Guidelines
for Book Longevity of the Council on Library Resources.
Binding materials have been chosen for durability.

Library of Congress Cataloging in Publication Data

Agee, James, 1909–1955.
Selected journalism.
Bibliography: p.
I. Ashdown, Paul, 1944–   .   II. Title.
PS3501.G35A6   1985   814'.52   85-710
ISBN 0-87049-466-X (alk. paper)

FOR BARBARA AND LANCE

CONTENTS

ILLUSTRATIONS

ACKNOWLEDGMENTS

Many people offered encouragement and assistance in the production of this book, whether they knew it or not. Those to whom the editor would like to extend special thanks are: David McDowell, Rhonda Chapman, Nancy Buchanan, Tom Denk, Michaele Orlowski, David Madden, James Crook, Kelly Leiter, Donald Hileman, Erik Wensberg, Ross Spears, Paula Tyler, Harriet Beeler, Susan Strickler, Dan Yearout, Gina Pera, James Andreas, James Justus, David Herwaldt, Margo Keltner, Isabel Kouri, Carolyn Davis, John Hill, Victor Kramer, Bettie Mason, and especially Carol Orr and the staff of the UT press.

Time Inc. graciously granted permission to publish the articles as they appeared in *Fortune* and *Time*. Permission to publish photographs was granted by David Herwaldt, Time Inc., the Library of Congress, St. Andrew's-Sewanee, Harvard University, John Hill and the Estate of Walker Evans, and the Tennessee Valley Authority.

INTRODUCTION

James Agee spent most of his professional life on the payroll of *Time* and *Fortune*, but what he had to say about journalism was vitriolic. "The very blood and semen of journalism is a broad and successful form of lying," he wrote in his anti-journalistic manifesto, *Let Us Now Praise Famous Men*. "Remove that form of lying and you no longer have journalism."[1] Of those at *Fortune* who sent him to Alabama in 1936 to write about cotton tenantry, he wrote:

> It seems to me curious, not to say obscene and thoroughly terrifying, that it could occur to an association of human beings drawn together through need and chance and for profit into a company, an organ of journalism, to pry intimately into the lives of an undefended and appallingly damaged group of human beings, an ignorant and helpless rural family, for the purpose of parading the nakedness, disadvantage and humiliation of these lives before another group of human beings, in the name of science, of "honest journalism" (whatever that paradox may mean), of humanity, of social fearlessness, for money and for a reputation for crusading and for unbias which, when skillfully enough qualified, is exchangeable at any bank for money (and in politics, for votes, job patronage, abelincolnism, etc.) and that these people could be capable of mediating this prospect without the slightest doubt of their qualification to do an "honest" piece of work, and with a conscience better than clear, and in the virtual certitude of almost unanimous public approval.[2]

To oppose such crass mendacity Agee had written a prayer in homage to "those who in all times have sought truth and who have told it in their art or in their living."[3] Yet despite his harsh judgment about the veracity of journalism, he could turn it to his own high-minded purposes; truth was not precluded. He assured his friend and former teacher, Father James Harold Flye, that the "cruelty" he recounted in one *Fortune* article was used "to inspire pity in readers who never feel it when it is asked in another's behalf directly."[4] He wrote Father Flye in 1945 that an article *Time* assigned him on Europe "interests me as much as any piece of personal writing I could possibly be doing . . . and really seems hopeful of some good result."[5] The short prose masterpiece he wrote for *Time* after the bombing of Hiroshima and Nagasaki "in the aftershock of a great wound" conveyed his outrage at what he saw as the blasphemous cleaving of the atom. Such pieces, his friend Robert Fitzgerald said, were news stories "to which no one else could do justice" and in which he often was able "to dignify the reporting of events."[6]

Nor did Agee dislike the work of journalism as much as he implied. Perhaps more significantly, he was very good at it. Mia Agee recalled that her husband "enjoyed having to write long mechanical process captions as he did for *Fortune*. . . . These tasks had some of the intriguing characteristics of certain games and puzzles, and in Jim's hands they became small poems."[7] Of one assignment for *Fortune*, he told Father Flye: "The only writing I do which approaches decency is on this job—and on other stuff I seem to be pretty well congealed."[8]

Agee "quickly raised the quality of some of the feature stories that magazine carried to a level never again achieved by a publication of that sort in America,"[9] contends Thomas Daniel Young, in assessing Agee's *Fortune* material. Moreover, journalism provided Agee "the broad audience for which he had always secretly longed,"[10] Genevieve Moreau has pointed out. Robert Bingham notes that "Agee chose journalism, and all in all it didn't treat him badly."[11] John Updike furthermore concludes that "the poignant fact about Agee is that he was not badly suited to working for Henry Luce."[12]

Yet it has become obligatory in the cultic literature written about Agee since his death at age forty-five in 1955 to denigrate the energy he expended on journalism. While critics have seen in Hemingway's reportage the origins of a singular literary style and have commented favorably on the discipline it imposed, they have tended to see in Agee's journalism only the vestigial talents

of a spent poet draining himself on the ephemeral and the spu-
rious. "Enough, and perhaps more than enough, has been said
by various people about the waste of Jim's talents in journalism,"
Robert Fitzgerald said.[13]

As Updike's words can also be applied to another literary figure
with a journalistic career, Ernest Hemingway, a brief comparison
of Agee's journalistic endeavors with Hemingway's is perhaps in
order. Robert Phelps, in his introduction to the *Letters of James
Agee to Father Flye*, asks why Agee did not write, as he said he
wanted to, a dozen "Chekhov-Shakespeare novels" instead of a
quarter of a million unsigned words for *Time* and *Fortune*. Updike, reviewing the collection, counters that argument, saying
that the question betrays "a very sick literary situation. . . . The
study of literature threatens to become a kind of paleontology of
failure, and criticism a supercilious psychoanalysis of authors. I
resist Agee's canonization by these unearthly standards." As to
the value of the unsigned words, Updike argues that "surely a
culture is enhanced, rather than disgraced, when men of talent
and passion undertake anonymous and secondary tasks. Excellence in the great things is built upon excellence in the small."[14]

Hemingway's much larger corpus of journalistic writing has
been widely anthologized, most notably by William White in *By-
Line: Ernest Hemingway*. But Agee's journalism, although a considerable portion of the body of his work, is neglected. Hemingway, too, was diffident about the quality of his journalism even if,
like Agee, he continued to produce it throughout his career.
White contends that Hemingway's journalism is important at a
number of levels. First, it is good journalism. Second, much of it
is reworked and appears later in his fiction. And third, journalism
provided Hemingway with a literary apprenticeship and contains
the elements of his mature style.[15]

Although they developed their craft in quite different circumstances—Hemingway as a general assignment reporter on the
Kansas City *Star*, a space-rate feature writer on the Toronto *Daily
Star* and later a magazine free-lance writer, and Agee as a New
York magazine staff writer—each discovered early that journalists
and novelists are both essentially storytellers. Hemingway's lead
for a news story he wrote for the Toronto *Daily Star* on September 25, 1923 emphasizes this storytelling role:

> There are no names in this story.
> The characters in it are a reporter, a girl reporter, a quite beautiful daughter in a Japanese kimono, and a mother.

So, too, does Agee's lead, written when he was about the same age, for "The American Roadside," published in the September 1934 issue of *Fortune*:

> The characters in our story are five: this American continent; this American people; the automobile, the Great American Road, and— the American Roadside.

As journalism has continued to move toward greater professionalism, however, its adepts, sometimes uncomfortable with the conception of journalism as a branch of literature, have tried to define it as a social science. Such a definition, though, is contrary to a long and worthy tradition. As the British journalist and novelist Malcolm Muggeridge points out in an essay about the journalist G. K. Chesterton:

> It is often contended that Chesterton wrote too much and too hastily; that his financial exigencies and polemical inclinations led him to prefer journalism to literature. This, in my opinion, is highly dubious. In the first place, I question the hard and fast distinction between the two categories of writing. . . . Between them lies a vast no-man's-land in which most writers, from Johnson to H. G. Wells and Shaw, have been content to forage, if not to reside.[16]

Both Agee and Hemingway fall within such a tradition. Some of their best journalism is difficult to categorize, as for example Agee's metaphysical discourse on "Smoke," published in the June 1937 issue of *Fortune*, or Hemingway's "Remembering Shooting-Flying: A Key West Letter," which appeared in *Esquire* in February 1935. Like Hemingway, Agee was interested in truth more than fact. "And though he wrote as he saw things, his writing shows most vividly how he felt about what he saw," White said of Hemingway. "If the details were sometimes slighted, the picture as a whole—full of emotional impact of the events on people— was clear, lucid and full. For the picture as a whole was what Hemingway the artist cared about."[17]

Agee, however, slighted few details and was less intrusive in his journalism than Hemingway, perhaps because of the nature of the publications for which he wrote. Hemingway's familiar first and second person perspective was very different from the voice of the narrator of Agee's unsigned pieces. Moreover, difference in subject matter usually required considerable difference in treatment. As a journalist, Agee reported no trials, covered no battles, witnessed no executions, interviewed no world leaders, caught no trout, shot no ducks, cabled no dispatches, and ran with no bulls at Pamplona. Agee's pieces were usually considerably longer, such as the TVA articles he wrote for *Fortune*, or considerably shorter, like the capsule news summaries for *Time*. In their journalism Hemingway and Agee bear significant comparison only in descriptive or impressionistic writing or observations of spectacles or popular pastimes: for example, Hemingway's "Bull Fighting Is Not a Sport—It Is a Tragedy" in the Toronto *Star Weekly* on 20 October 1923 or his "Bullfighting, Sport and Industry" in the March 1930 issue of *Fortune*, and Agee's "Cockfighting" in the March 1934 issue of *Fortune*. And, of course, Agee's essays were never subjected to the discipline of the newspaper copy desk, which would have deleted much of his expansive prose and sometimes gratuitous introspection.

Agee probably always retained his youthful enthusiasm for Hemingway, the emblematic American celebrity-writer. He had written Father Flye of Hemingway in 1927, describing as "terrific, and fine" the short stories in *Men Without Women*.[18] Ten years later, Agee was in the Carnegie Hall audience that heard Hemingway speak on the Spanish Civil War.[19]

But Agee's prose owed far more to the King James version of the Bible, *The Book of Common Prayer*, to James Joyce, and to his poetic imagination than to Hemingway or to any newspaper or popular magazine tradition. The photographer Walker Evans noted that Agee's prose "was hardly a twentieth century style; it had Elizabethan colors."[20] An Agee sentence could become a filigree of images, a Gregorian chant, and it is the intensity of this power that has created and sustained the Agee cult. Furthermore, his works have been adapted for theater, opera, cinema, and television drama. "Knoxville: Summer of 1915," which later appeared as the prelude to *A Death in the Family*, was set for soprano and orchestra by Samuel Barber. This setting is particularly responsive to the musical quality of Agee's prose as well as to the opportunities the text affords the composer for vivid word-painting. Agee's own musical gifts were observed from early childhood when his aunt Paula Tyler gave him his first piano lessons.[21]

Agee was, as Robert Phelps described him, a sovereign prince of the English language.[22] To read Agee is to feel "a kind of smiling universal milky silence, not fog, or even the lightest kind of mist, but as if the whole air and sky were one mild supernal breath"; to touch curtains scalloped "like the valves of a sea creature"; to serve "at the altar at earliest lonely Mass, whose words were thrilling brooks of music and whose motions, a grave dance: and there between spread hands the body and the blood of Christ was created among words and lifted before God in a threshing of triplicate bells."[23]

Agee's descriptive power is reminiscent of James Joyce's. Robert Fitzgerald recounts that Joyce engrossed Agee and "got into his blood so thoroughly that in 1935 he felt obliged . . . to master and get over that influence if he were ever to do anything of his own."[24] Joyce could make the reader feel snow falling over Ireland "on every part of the dark central plain, on the treeless hills, falling softly upon the Bog of Allen and, farther westward, softly falling into the dark mutinous Shannon waves. . . . His soul swooned slowly as he heard the snow falling faintly through the universe and faintly falling, like the descent of their last end, upon all the living and the dead."[25] Agee could just as readily draw a curtain across a darkling South: "All over Alabama, the lamps are out. Every leaf drenches the touch; the spider's net is heavy. . . . Beneath, . . . the lower American continent, lies spread before heaven in her wealth. The parks of her cities are iron, loam, silent, the sweet fountains shut, and the pure facades, embroiled, limelike in street light are sharp, are still."[26] Such lyric power harnessed in the explication of the mysteries of American capitalism and culture in all its incarnations produced journalism stunning in its effect.

This is exactly what Henry Luce had in mind when he conceived a new magazine that would supplement his successful venture with *Time*. Luce had learned through the success of *Time*, according to the popular historian Frederick Lewis Allen, that "there was money to be made . . . by the sharp presentation of facts, and particularly of facts about America."[27] *Time's* distinctive manner elicited a clever parody that Agee edited while he was at Harvard; it was later to come to the attention of the new editors of *Fortune*. By 1930 *Time* had become an artifact. Luce envisioned something radically different for *Fortune*. In this venture, pictures and words were to be conscious partners. But this partnership was to place great demands upon both the photographer and the writer. Mere technicians would not be able to convey the impression Luce wanted; he decreed that *Fortune* would put poets and fabulists rather than scriveners and accountants to the task of telling the story of American commerce. He believed poets could be taught to write about business, even though there was no precedent for such a marriage of poetry and business journalism. A new style would have to be created. Thus the cadre of *Fortune* staff writers and contributors would come to include Hemingway, Stephen Vincent Benét, Hart Crane, Archibald MacLeish, Dwight Macdonald, Russell Davenport, James Gould Cozzens, and others charged with weaving a rich tapestry of beautiful words. The results, however, were mixed.

The imperious Cozzens, for instance, resigned after ten months. He disliked the monthly deadlines and late night conferences. He also disliked the research. For an article on the Fuller Brush Company he reluctantly attended salesmen's pep meetings and accompanied a door-to-door brush peddler on his rounds. He disliked the magazine's style. He resisted the editors' demands for multitudes of similes in each paragraph: "The truth is that a simile is a boob trap," he wrote. "What it amounts to is that the writer, unable to think clearly enough or write well enough to say what he means, gets around the impasse by cutely changing the subject."[28] Hemingway took Luce's check for $1,000 for his 2,500 word contribution on bullfighting, but only after he had expressed skepticism about "the romance of business" and questioned his friend Archibald MacLeish's involvement with such a magazine.[29]

Agee had reservations, too, but he put them aside as he struggled to identify a workable style. In learning to weave his texts around the photographic essays that accompanied some of his articles, Agee experimented with cinematic techniques such as panorama, flashback, montage, and closeup in his writing. His work with superb photographers such as Walker Evans eventually

led to *Let Us Now Praise Famous Men*, a new form of documentary
journalism. Avoiding the stale similes, he produced vividly original metaphors and clever analogies. But a greater challenge for
Agee and for all the *Fortune* poets was assimilating a rising social
consciousness into the framework of a business magazine.
The very nature of such a publication in the context of the economic conditions during which it was published seemed certain
to confound the interests of what now would be called "upscale"
readers and the objectives of creative writers and editors. Certainly Agee's savage response to his employers in *Let Us Now
Praise Famous Men* suggests he never resolved the conflict pre-
sumably exacerbated by the brutal contrast between the cupidity
of the advertising in the magazine and the conditions he recounted in such pieces as "Drought" and the TVA articles. Yet, as
Allen suggested, *Fortune*, which although edited by liberals for
the benefit chiefly of the rich, . . . trimmed its sails so skillfully
to the winds of conservatism that it . . . subtly broadened reac-
tionary minds."[30]
    This skillful balancing of liberal sympathies with awareness of
conservative tastes is nowhere shown to better advantage than in
Agee's best descriptive writing and reflection about the Tennessee Valley Authority. James Agee was born in the Tennessee
River valley, in Knoxville, in 1909 and there he spent the first 16
years of his life. The valley figures in most of his best poems, his
longer fiction, and in parts of *Let Us Now Praise Famous Men*.
The great tension in Agee's prose, as in his life, arose in the conflict between the attitudes of his Tennessee mountain forebears
on his father's side and the sensibilities of his mother's family, the
Tylers, who had come to Knoxville from the Midwest. Within
these families, and within Agee, there was a clash of social and
religious values, from which emerged *The Morning Watch* and
the Pulitzer Prize-winning *A Death in the Family*. These autobio-
graphical novels tell the story of the death of Agee's father in 1916
and Agee's subsequent coming of age at an Anglo-Catholic boy's
school in the Cumberland Mountains.
    It was at St. Andrew's School near Sewanee, Tennessee, that
Agee came under the influence of Father James Harold Flye, the
remarkable priest who became his mentor and lifelong confidant.
A graduate of Yale who later attended the University of Virginia,

Father Flye teaching at St. Andrew's School in 1940. Photograph
courtesy of David Herwaldt.

Flye joined the Episcopal Church while he was teaching in Florida. He became a candidate for Holy Orders in the Diocese of Atlanta and enrolled in the General Theological Seminary in New York. Once ordained, he spent two years at an Episcopal church in Milledgeville, Georgia, and was then called by the Order of the Holy Cross to teach history at St. Andrew's. Father Flye seems to have served as a surrogate parent for Agee; their close relationship is documented in the long letters they exchanged over three decades.

Agee left Tennessee in 1925 to attend Phillips Exeter Academy in New Hampshire and then Harvard. He began his career with *Fortune* in 1932, returning to Knoxville in 1933 on an assignment from *Fortune* at the suggestion of Archibald MacLeish which gave him an opportunity to confront the changes under way as the TVA transformed the valley into a New Deal showcase. Agee put himself into the project with characteristic energy, though undoubtedly a good deal of apprehension, for he quickly realized that TVA was attempting nothing short of fashioning a new civilization through "a decentralization of industry, regional planning on a large scale, a well-wrought and well-controlled balance between the Jeffersonian dream of an agrarian democracy and the best characteristics of what so many people like to call the Power Age." But he also saw that in "this enormous machine the balance wheel is human." Its main target would have to be the mountaineer, "the strong backbone of the Tennessee Valley. His forefathers settled this country in the 1700's when the effete civilization east of the Alleghenies stuck in their craws." TVA's task was to tame these mountaineers, among whom were numbered living members of Agee's family, and teach them responsibility to society.

He wrote Father Flye that Luce had told him the article "was one of the best pieces of writing he'd seen in *Fortune*." But Luce also chided him for his lack of knowledge about business. Luce promised to feed him "tough business stories thick and fast: I must do my best to learn the business ropes: they shan't expect anything wildly fast out of me, but the idea is this: that I really am interested in doing well with this job: in making it part of my career."[31]

Much has been made of the conditions under which Agee worked at *Fortune*. In his office on the fifty-second floor of the Chrysler Building, Agee often worked all night fortified by cigarettes and whiskey, accompanied by a phonograph played at full volume. He digressed on this practice in *Let Us Now Praise Famous Men* and in a letter to Father Flye: "Something attracts me very much about playing Beethoven's Ninth Symphony there—with all New York about 600 feet below you, and with that swell ode, taking in the whole earth, and with everyone on earth supposedly singing it."[32] A friend is alleged to have entered Agee's office on one occasion only to find him dangling outside a window—an enactment of a metaphoric fascination with death from a great height that he had conveyed in a letter to Father Flye.[33] He also is reported to have lived in a Brooklyn garret with a goat while working on one assignment. In front of the house someone scrawled: THE MAN WHO LIVES HERE IS A LOONY.[34]

In various ways these and other stories and descriptions suggest the actions of a compulsive neurotic, supposedly tortured by wasting his talents on hack writing. Indeed, Agee's psyche has been so amply discussed by a great range of acquaintances, scholars, critics, confidants, cultists, and a biographer that there is a danger of later generations regarding him—as seems to be the case with Hemingway—largely as a posturing, eccentric, self-destructive aesthete, or a sort of literary James Dean. This "supercilious psychoanalysis" has led to many simplifications about both these writers and overlooks the fact that a writer needs a clear head and at least an occasionally stable personality in order to write against a deadline, or to write anything at all.

His first tough business story was about the monopolistic price of steel rails, and Luce himself apparently tried to teach Agee some basic economics. Agee was, however, by no means ignorant of the subject. As a student at Exeter, he had won a prize by writing an essay on international trade. But Luce despaired of Agee's interest in the subject and the article was turned over to Dwight Macdonald for completion. The opening sentences, a description of the rails transecting "the green breadth of America . . . under the maleficent influence of that disorderly phosphorous which all steel contains," are characteristically Agee's.[35] Released from the formal strictures of the dismal science, Agee went on to write distinctive articles on broader social, economic and cultural issues and human interest subjects.

But this was by no means a relegation of his talents to subject matter of secondary importance. Although *Fortune* articles were devoted to corporate moguls and major industries, the editors recognized that capitalism was also sustained and explained by a multitude of individual transactions, and that commerce was affected as much by the smallest of social changes as by major shifts in production and consumption. For while New Dealers were essentially inventing the national economy, at the personal level life was still a contest of chance and necessity. And Agee saw in these transactions elements of both class struggle and an essential egalitarianism. Thus the cockfighters, "gentlemen, breeders, yokels, gangsters—society's highest and its lowest," would meet at illegal pits, gaming like "members of some sinister secret order" at a blood sport dating from antiquity, with its own codes and sacraments. This "minor and surreptitious pleasure of the rich, secret passion of the poor" would not figure into the gross national product of the Keynesian economic planners, or submit to the zeal of reformers who had made it illegal and disreputable. The future would come to show a vast underground economy of surreptitious transactions. As in the TVA articles, Agee sensed the resistance of the individual to collectivism, and the endurance of pagan blood rituals brought from across the sea to the western hemisphere's tenebrous brooding forests and mountains and their urban counterparts. Agee realized that cockfighting contained deeper meaning than mere brutality, even to the ritualistic consumption of the sacrificial birds.

For many issues, *Fortune* assigned its entire staff to cover all aspects of a single subject. Such was the case with an issue in 1934 devoted to Mussolini's Italy. Agee's topic was the desiccated society of Rome, with one foot in Fascism and another in the ancient Empire. This gave him an opportunity to develop a theme that would reappear often in his writing—the essential decadence of the modern world. "Quietly in his marble-skinned and magnificent and cold palazzo, Prince Doria waits for death to take him," he began. And this death, when it came, would be like unto the death of "all the Princes of Rome and their proud families . . . and that entire Roman aristocracy of which these families are the crests." He saw—as many others of his time did not—that Mussolini was creating an evil religion, and that inevitably one earthly kingdom must give way to "fresh blood and power."

Another of Agee's prescient essays, "The American Roadside" anticipated the vast changes being wrought by the automobile and the emerging highway system, along which "this people casually moves in numbers and by distances which make the ancient and the grave migrations of the Celt and the Goth look like a smooth crossing on the Hoboken Ferry." He also saw that a great industry, already grossing some $3 billion in 1934, would develop along the roads and transform the American economy. He understood before it was clear to many others that "the conjunction of confused bloods, history and the bullying of this tough continent to heel, did something to the American people— worked up in their blood a species of restiveness . . . for the plain unvarnished hell of it." Already the economy was being tethered to the automobile and the petroleum industries, and the habits being formed on the American highways of the 1930s would contribute forty years later to a world economic crisis centered in the Middle East.

In "Drought," he went beyond economic statistics measured in bushels of wheat and corn to the wretchedness of starving livestock and displaced farmers. "The U.S. Commercial Orchid" was an especially tantalizing subject. He envisioned it as "a clear & inescapable small study of snobbism: but I can't catch it on the hip in the right way. The flower itself isn't responsible: but people's reactions to it have been and are so vile that I hate its very guts along with theirs." [36]

He wrote Father Flye that the orchid "is more completely endowed with snob-appeal, and with nothing else, than any other commodity I know of. And then for that matter I just privately don't like the plain looks of the flower." The way he wanted to write the article, he told Father Flye, was like this:

The orchid gets its name from the Greek *orchis*, which means testicle; and there are those who condemn that title as understanding the case, since to them the flower resembles nothing printable

Fortune cover art by Antonio Petruccelli. Reproduced by permission of *Fortune*.

so much as a psychopathic nightmare in technicolor. It has also been favorably compared in sexual extravagance to the south apse of an aroused mandrill, and it sports a lower lip that qualifies to send the Bourbon Dynasty into green visceral spasms of invidious love's labors lost.

"And so," he continued,

> though not a single promotive gesture had been made over the orchid through all the centuries up to 1929, the orchid was already, in the minds of many select ladies and gentlemen who could afford to have the idea, a very definite if sort of special last word, if it was a last word you wanted to touch off the establishment of a young woman as at liberty for marriage, or most gracefully and with most conspicuous expense to assert your opinion of her as something pretty nice to be seen with, or to set her off at her virginal sweetest as she was wedded in unsunderable wedlock, or indeed to lend Class to any occasion of social or sentimental stature such as the celebration, by snotting one's neighbor along Fifth Avenue, of the embarrassment and ultimate destruction of Death through the glorious resurrection of Jesus Christ.[37]

He doubted that this passage would be included in the published version. It wasn't. Moreau, making much of this incident as an early indication of Agee's disenchantment with *Fortune*, characterizes it as a deliberate attempt to provoke his employers.[38] Undoubtedly Agee resisted a conventional treatment of the subject and found it difficult to render the subject in purely objective prose. But the finished product shows his ability to say more than the words alone might suggest. He makes his point with humor and skill. In addition he displays a shrewd understanding of the human side of economics which he was to do repeatedly with his *Fortune* assignments. Certainly his frustration exploded with *Let Us Now Praise Famous Men*, but there is considerable evidence that he enjoyed the challenge of writing within the *Fortune* format, carefully testing the waters of creative license.

In 1935 Agee returned again to the Tennessee Valley and wrote part of a twenty-two-month reassessment of the entire TVA project. This brought him even closer to the heart of his own mystery. He passed through the autochthonous valleys and mountains of his deep memory, right to his father's home in LaFollette, not far from the Norris Dam and the land of his ancestors—soon to be flooded by TVA. It may well have been his own uncle, thinly disguised as the tippling undertaker Ralph in *A Death in the Family*, who provided for the article an assessment of TVA: "A LaFollette undertaker to whom has fallen the job of removing several hundreds of the coffins, at $20 a shot, from the Norris Reservoir area, holds that TVA is doing a fine work."

He saw the Norris Dam under construction across the Clinch River. On the Campbell County side of the Clinch at the fork of the Clinch and the Powell rivers stood the town of Agee, named for his great-great-grandfather James H. Agee, a former state senator. Before the town and much of the surrounding valley was flooded in 1936, TVA resettled about 14,000 people and more than 5,000 graves. [39]

The movement of the graves, some of which sheltered the bones of his ancestors, touched Agee deeply. "There are all kinds," he wrote. "Nameless graves and unsurvived." Here he betrayed the cadences of Ecclesiasticus, Chapter 44, from which he drew the title of his most famous book. He told the story of a woman "who stood very silent, not crying, in the rain, in rain-sagged calico, and watched the walnut coffin raised and fitted into its new board box: and who lifted her wet skirt to take her tears only when the box was crayoned with 'TVA.'"

Yet he could see some humor in the intransigence of those who resisted relocation for profit, or for excess of devotion, as in the story of an old man who made a solemn vow:

> His forefathers had brought fire into the valley 150 years before; it had never been allowed to go out; he would by God not budge an inch unless TVA took it safely with him. On further questioning the old man granted that maybe once or twice when he'd been gone a couple of weeks it had needed right smart cheering up when he got back; yes, it might have went out in the meantime. Once he was gone a whole summer. Yes, it stood to reason it might have.

That same soft paraphrased mountaineer idiom would reappear throughout *A Death in the Family* and *Let Us Now Praise Famous Men*. One of Agee's greatest gifts, his deep respect for nuances of native speech, appeared first and was tested in the laboratory of his journalism.

In all his writing, but especially his TVA articles, Agee revealed the Southern and essentially Celtic romantic reverence for the land. "We have wrung the very blood from the land, shipped its health to market and seaward by the sewers and left it exhausted and misplanted for the rain to do the rest," he wrote. "Left to its own devices and the rains, that whole land could be desert before another century had passed."

Despite the considerable achievement of his TVA article, Agee wrote Father Flye that he found it "glib, superficial and limited. Some half good prose." [40] Here, ostensibly, was another sign of the continuing frustration that led him to the strange melancholy frenzy of *Let Us Now Praise Famous Men*. That lavish documentary work, undertaken with Walker Evans as a *Fortune* assignment in 1936, was a reaction against everything Agee thought he found objectionable in journalism. "Feel terrific personal responsibility toward story; considerable doubts of my ability to bring it off; considerable more of Fortune's ultimate willingness to use it as it seems (in theory) to me," he wrote Father Flye. [41]

As he expected, *Fortune* indeed did not use the extraordinary manuscript, which Evans and Agee finally published in 1941. What is intriguing, however, is the response of his employers. What writer could be expected to remain in the employ of an organization whose directors he had slandered as liars and exploiters of the destitute? If Agee's blast at his employers was not included in the original manuscript he submitted to them (and it likely was not) they had the opportunity to read it in the published book. Yet Time, Inc. continued to employ Agee and gave him additional responsibilities. His editor at *Time*, T. S. Matthews, has testified that he was puzzled and to some extent repulsed by Agee's eccentricities, and urged him on occasion to resign and get on with his own writing. But at the same time Matthews told Agee "he could always be sure of getting his job again." [42] The only possible conclusion is that Agee was so well respected as a writer that his employers would suffer almost any indignity to accommodate him. This was, according to Robert Bingham, not uncharacteristic of the Luce empire, in which "great pains are taken to get the best out of each employee by making allowances for his individual needs and difficulties." [43] And the depth of Agee's own animosity must also be considered. If he indeed thought as little of journalism and the Luce organiza-

tion as he said he did in *Let Us Now Praise Famous Men*, why did
he return?

Through this much admired and much analyzed work, Agee
certainly tried to exorcise a demon that had troubled him throughout his literary life. But it is a demon that troubles all journalists
who seek a deeper reality in their work. What was unusual was
not the problem itself but his ability to define it. "If I could do it,
I'd do no writing at all here," he wrote in a memorable passage.
"It would be photographs; the rest would be fragments of cloth,
bits of cotton, lumps of earth, records of speech, pieces of wood
and iron, phials of odors, plates of food and of excrement."[44] He
wanted to do anything other than what was understood as an objective analysis, a sociological treatise, a clinical report of the
conditions of tenant farmers. He wanted the reader actually to
participate in the farmers' humanity. This presented great difficulties for a classically educated product of aristocratic schools.
Like George Orwell, he tried to make himself over as a pro-
letarian. But this also was a form of intrusive deception, nor did
it automatically pull him to the heart of the matter. He wrote Father Flye: "My trouble is, such a subject cannot be seriously
looked at without intensifying itself toward a centre which is beyond what I, or anyone else, is capable of writing of: the whole
problem and nature of existence."[45] This is what he had been
trying to do in his *Fortune* articles and, of course, he failed. According to his own criteria, he also failed in *Let Us Now Praise
Famous Men*.

As Alfred T. Barson points out, Agee's journalism was often
most successful "when he could work his subject around to a
moral evaluation" to provide "a leverage upon his sensibility."
Such an attempt to respond to what has been reported he places
in the tradition of Stephen Crane's "The Open Boat" and Hemingway's *The Green Hills of Africa*, a quality of extrapolating universal significance from isolated experience.[46] This "New Journalism," as a later generation would call it, has been attempted
by Truman Capote, Tom Wolfe, Norman Mailer, Hunter Thompson, and others.

It was natural for Agee to try to do this. He would have drawn
from his Anglicanism the congruence of the physical and spiritual
worlds. This point has not been sufficiently recognized, although

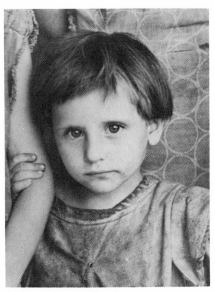

Agee saw in the sad countenances of Alabama tenant farmers and their families the images of "an undefended and appallingly damaged group of human beings." Photographs by Walker Evans, courtesy of Estate of Walker Evans. Prints from the Library of Congress.

it was manifest to Fitzgerald, Matthews and others who either knew him well or studied his works carefully. "A sense of the breathing community immersed in mystery, exposed to a range of experience from what can only be called the divine to what can only be called the diabolical, most intelligent in awe and most needful of mercy—a religious sense of life, in short—moved James Agee in his best work," Fitzgerald wrote.[47] The very structure of many of his poems, especially "Dedication," and prose works, especially *The Morning Watch*, "A Mother's Tale," and *Let Us Now Praise Famous Men*, portions of the TVA articles, "Smoke," and "Victory: The Peace," suggest extended prayers and portions of the Mass and other Episcopal services. When he writes that TVA's "prime ultimate objectives" are only "the outward and visible signs" of a social and industrial utopia, he uses language familiar to him from St. Augustine and from the catechism in *The Book of Common Prayer*.

> *Question.* What meanest thou by this word *Sacrament*?
> *Answer.* I mean an outward and visible sign of an inward and spiritual grace given unto us.[48]

Agee was immersed in this catechism at the monastery school he attended as a child. There, under the tutelage of the Holy Cross Fathers, "classes, meals, scholastic work, houskeeping and outdoor work were strictly scheduled according to a liturgical conception of the day as a succession of work rituals. The humblest gestures were assigned an ecclesiastical significance, and the moral import of every action was emphasized."[49] Common objects became outward and visible signs. Life became a series of canticles and lamentations. Events revealed synchronicity. There too he would have developed his sense of cosmic irony which appears throughout his work.

Such irony is evident, for example, in his structuring of a simple news item in *Time* about a test flight (published in this collection as "Great Britain: Beyond Silence"). Captain Geoffrey De Haviland "shut himself into what was probably the most advanced piece of air machinery ever to get beyond the blueprinting stage, and took off into the darkening sky." Observers saw "the strange machine's magnificent trajectory" and, later, scraps of wreckage. Agee speculates that in setting a new record,

The Chapel at St. Andrew's School as it looked during the years Agee
was in attendance. The liturgical drama that occurred within
permeated his later works, especially *The Morning Watch*. Photograph
courtesy of St. Andrew's-Sewanee.

Captain De Haviland may have experienced "more of the new problems of aeronautics than is known to any living man." Quoting Hamlet, he proposes that in crossing the sonic threshold, Captain De Haviland had only located *The undiscovered country from whose bourn / No traveler returns.*

The High Church tradition in which Agee was immersed, derived from The Oxford Movement within the Church of England, placing exceptional emphasis on the Christian Platonism of the early Greek Fathers. The great Anglo-Catholic theologian John Keble explained that

> everything to them existed in two worlds: in the world of sense, according to its outward nature and relations; in the world intellectual according to its spiritual associations. And thus did the whole scheme of material things, and especially those objects in it which are consecrated by scriptural allusion, assume in their eyes a sacramental or symbolic character.[50]

In Agee's cosmology, nothing would have been excluded from this dichotomy, neither atomic bombs, nor cocks, nor desiccated Romans, nor Alabama farmers. His best journalism became a kind of sacramental celebration of actuality, a metaphysical journalism that drew energy from the ordinary. "Cockfighting," as Genevieve Moreau suggests, is not mere spectacle, but sacrament, "the cock itself the symbol of a mortal though triumphant individualism."[51] Michael Vincent Little develops this interpretation in his brilliant study, comparing Agee's stance toward reality to the actualization of Teilhard de Chardin's "Omega Point" in the present.[52]

The point at which integrated consciousness breaks through and transcends time would have been comprehensible to Agee, if not in Teilhardian terms, then in terms of the imagery of the Mass and the Church Year. Time, in this conception, is very different from the timeliness of event-bound periodical journalism. It is the time that is beyond time, the conception of time that once caused Russian peasants to proclaim the resurrection on Easter morning as if it had only just occurred. This sense of time lends itself to the reporting of transitory conditions and events as fables and parables, portents and presentiments. Those afflicted, or perhaps gifted, with such an unconscious ordering of reality would not be tranquil.

"A wild yearning violence beat in his blood, certainly, and just as certainly the steadier pulse of a saint," was the way Agee's editor, T. S. Matthews put it. "He wanted to destroy with his own hands everything in the world, including himself, that was shoddy, false and despicable; and to worship God, who made all things,"[53]

But this sort of journalism may have its perils. In 1980 *New York Times* writer Howell Raines talked with some of the sharecroppers Agee anointed in *Let Us Now Praise Famous Men*. He contended that some were still unhappy over being in the original book. Some found Agee's approach intrusive and patronizing, or imagined they had been cheated out of a fortune.

Once Agee got the tenant farmers out of his system, his writing became more controlled and more forceful. He turned one of his next assignments into a philosophical treatise on smoke and the industrial revolution. He knew a great deal about smoke because the Knoxville neighborhood in which he grew up was full of it. In *A Death in the Family* he describes his father holding him from a viaduct "to inhale the burst of smoke from a switch engine which passed under."[55] In his *Fortune* article smoke becomes the fulminating breath of a monster, a diabolical and killing miasma upon the green and verdant land.

His bitter "Havana Cruise," based on a six-day journey from New York to Cuba on the steamship *Oriente* is a critique of middle-class values. An editor's note accompanying the story said the "anonymous reporter" *Fortune* sent on the cruise "came back with this human document that has little to do with the profound economic problems of the merchant marine." Most of the issue was devoted to the shipping industry. Moreau thought the article read like good fiction.

> The central character, the tourist in his many guises, is taken from the beginning to the end of his voyage in the space of a few pages. All the experiences and emotions of a pleasure cruise—excitement, curiosity, boredom, torpor, flirtations, drunkenness, newfound friends, disappointment—are captured in the course of the narrative. And Agee raises his piece to the level of profound social criticism when he describes the tourist as the helpless, anony-

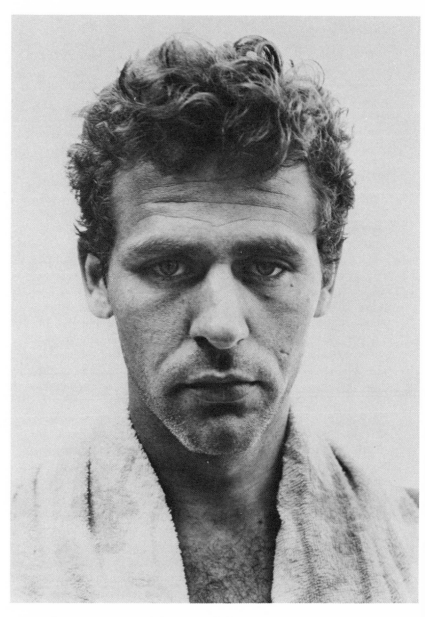
Walker Evans captured the visage of a languorous James Agee on Long Island Beach in 1937. Photograph courtesy of the Fogg Art Museum, Harvard University.

mous, middle-class victim of the unscrupulous tourist industry, whose main motive, of course, is profit. It is the essential emptiness of middle-class life that makes the exploitation possible, Agee suggests, and it is this lesson that the tourist inevitably learns on board as he attends his "school of disenchantment." [56]

In 1939 Agee began writing regular book reviews for *Time*. This led to film reviews, the critical journalism that has won Agee the most unequivocal praise. Robert Bingham thought him "the best film critic there ever was." [57] Had he written nothing other than the film reviews and scripts collected in two volumes as *Agee on Film*, a distinguished niche in American letters would have beeen assured. While writing reviews for *Time*, Agee reviewed many of the same films for *The Nation*. These reviews sometimes tended toward the baroque, while his capsule *Time* reviews were more precise and more journalistic. This exercise in compression taught Agee to be less mannered and precious. By 1945 *Time* was calling upon Agee to write special news and feature articles. The eight beautifully written pieces included in this collection illustrate the degree to which he succeeded.

Moreau comments on his first assignment, "Europe: Autumn Story," that Agee "blended the themes of hope and disillusionment and introduced a diffuse symbolism of the seasons man's life passes through. He also returned to an idea already expressed in *Famous Men*, that the goodwill and generosity of Americans might be more damaging than helpful, bringing little comfort to a long-suffering people." [58] His best article, "Victory: The Peace," shows Agee quick to realize that dropping the atomic bomb on Nagasaki and Hiroshima had brought about a profoundly spiritual change because it "split open the universe and revealed the prospect of the infinitely extraordinary." His was an early and prophetic warning of the Faustian bargain that had been struck.

By 1948 Agee had ended his association with *Time*, although he continued to write occasional profiles and special articles for *Life*. The final period of his career saw him complete, or nearly complete, a magical television screenplay based on the life of Abraham Lincoln, two novels, short stories and portions of the scripts for *The African Queen*, *The Night of the Hunter* (an eerie descant to *A Death in the Family* and subsequent themes in his own life) and other films. His death in the midst of this productivity cut short a life of singular achievement and, as those interested in his work have endlessly pointed out, even greater promise. He had simply worked himself to death.

A sense of unfulfilled promise is what has led many of Agee's admirers to see his journalistic work as a betrayal of his potential as a poet and a novelist. "The trouble with Agee as a journalist was that he couldn't be just workmanlike," Dwight Macdonald wrote. "He had to give it everything he had, which was not good for him." [59]

But it is precisely because he gave it everything he had—and what he had was genius—that his neglected journalism needs rediscovery. If Agee chose to devote his best and most intense efforts through some sixteen years to what Updike called anonymous and secondary tasks, it seems disingenuous to suppose that the result is not an essential part of his achievement. Is it seriously to be supposed that Agee's literary achievements, most manifestly displayed in *Let Us Now Praise Famous Men*, would have been forthcoming without his journalistic apprenticeship? Or is it likely that the author of such extraordinary works would not have brought to journalism an equal portion of ability and insight? Could it not also be said that Agee wasted his energy on poetry, novels, and short stories at the expense of film scripts, criticism, and journalism? The answer is in the texts that follow. Unsigned, they nonetheless bear the signature of one of America's greatest writers.

Further scholarship might wish to draw a distinction between those articles in which Agee functioned as a reporter and gathered his own primary information on the scene and those that were primarily rewritten from facts gathered by others. The former would include, for example, most of the TVA pieces, "Saratoga," and "Havana Cruise." The latter would include "Roman Society" and most of the *Time* articles. Many articles, however, fall into both categories. Agee was adept with either technique. He was a gifted observer and listener, but this talent also allowed him to sift through and select raw information collected by others.

Both skills are required of journalists, as any city desk rewrite specialist or wire service correspondent could affirm. It might be suggested that the authorship of rewritten material could hardly be attributed to the writer. Indeed, the wire services do draw a distinction between a field correspondent—whose by-line appears with the story—and the bureau writer whose task it is to assemble a news story from a series of facts cabled or, more often, phoned into a bureau. In the case of these magazine articles, however, the writer played a much larger role in gathering and organizing the material. As both *Time* and *Fortune* made researchers available to their writers, some of the articles are undoubtedly to some degree collaborative ventures, a kind of group journalism. And all journalism, of course, is subject to revision by editors. But this situation is not unique to journalism: many questions have been raised, for example, about the extent to which Maxwell Perkins shaped the writing of Thomas Wolfe. A writer of Agee's meticulousness would maintain a larger measure of editorial control of his material. After his death many unfinished projects remained. But, for example, the Audio-Visual Center of Williamsburg, Virginia was unable to find a writer to complete a script Agee had been working on because he had given it too personal a direction.[60] All his writing projects took a personal direction, and he would not have been an easy collaborator. In most of his work, his style is singular enough for the reader readily to recognize his hand. Robert Fitzgerald says that whatever Agee wrote for *Time* "was so conspicuous that it might as well have been signed."[61] In articles such as "Havana Cruise" his authorship is doubly unquestionable: the identifying editor's note and the statements of those who accompanied him on the voyage. Portions of those articles that contain great blocks of technical information or timely facts probably involved an associate. But many novelists employ research assistants. Memoirs and biographies are often the product of a team of fact gatherers. Ultimately, however, it falls to the writer to cull and assimilate those facts into the framework of a story.

Identifying these unsigned pieces was made possible by Genevieve Moreau's bibliographic research into the assignment files of *Time* and *Fortune*.[62] Martha Skinner Thomas obtained from the publisher's office of *Fortune* a list of the articles assigned to Agee, and the publisher's office confirmed the same information in a letter to the editor of these selections.[63] Agee made many references to his articles in his letters to Father Flye. Moreau does draw a distinction between articles that are clearly identifi-

able as Agee's and those such as "Steel Rails" which are believed
to have been completed by another writer. Robert Fitzgerald,
Dwight Macdonald, T. S. Matthews, and others who worked with
Agee at *Time* and *Fortune* also refer to the articles. Additional
references to them appear in numerous books, theses and dis-
sertations dealing with aspects of Agee's career or the Luce
publications.

What has been attempted in the selection of articles for this
collection is a representation of Agee's best or most interesting
writing for the two publications. The reader may consult Moreau's bibliography for a complete list. Any such journalistic anthology involves some subjectivity. William White solved a similar problem in *By-Line: Ernest Hemingway* by selecting 29
articles from Hemingway's 154 in the Toronto *Daily Star* and *Star
Weekly*; 17 of his 31 contributions to *Esquire*; and assorted articles from *Vogue, Collier's, PM, Holiday, True, Look* and other
publications. A greater portion of Agee's work is included here. It
might have been possible, although perhaps not sensible, to include all of Agee's journalism in a very large single volume, but
this would seem to be an unwarranted attempt to obtain inclu-
siveness merely for its own sake. Interested readers should find
these selections sufficient. If not, the remaining articles can be
obtained with only moderate difficulty in a good research library.

The texts appear in their entirety. The only omissions have
been references to illustrations that do not appear in the book, or
editors' teasers about previous articles in the same magazine.
The omissions have not been indicated by ellipses, which were
thought to be intrusive. Where an ellipsis appears, it was used by
Agee. There has been no attempt to standardize punctuation or
style, or even to correct the few errors in the original texts. In
some cases some curious phrasing would appear to be an oversight. Agee's sentences frequently were irregular. That is part of
the delight in reading them. Subheadings have been omitted.
Titles often differed from the tables of contents in the magazines
when they were used as headlines accompanying the articles.
The titles that appear in this book do not always conform to Moreau's bibliographical references.

A limitation of this collection is the omission of many of the
photographs and illustrations that appeared with the *Fortune* ar-

ticles. They were omitted either because they could not be located, because permission to reproduce them could not be obtained, or because they would not fit the format of this book. Those photographs that do appear were among those that accompanied the original articles and carry portions of the original cutlines. Agee was a most visual writer, and *Fortune* a most visual magazine; readers are encouraged to examine the beautiful graphics and illustrations that accompanied these articles. Especially impressive are the paintings by Sanford Ross that accompanied the article "Saratoga" and those by John Steuart Curry that accompanied "The American Roadside."

A final question remains to be considered: how Agee might have responded to the publication of these articles, for in every sense this is James Agee's book. Would he have agreed with Hemingway that no one has the right to dig up the writing a writer did under deadline and hold it up for comparison against his other work? No one can say. But all good journalism has a predictive quality about it, and in the course of time some of those predictions are affirmed and others are denied. There is a great charm in the early writings of superannuated journalists, and a tender diffidence in their reflections on their earlier work. Malcolm Muggeridge illustrates this point in his epilogue to *Things Past*, Ian Hunter's anthology of a half century of Muggeridge's journalism, by likening his reaction to reading the selections to the way Macbeth felt about Banquo's ghost:

> The time has been,
> That, when the brains were out, the man would die,
> And there an end; but now they rise again . . .
> And push us from our stools.

But then he goes on to point to the accumulated evidence that a great theme recurred throughout his life's work that he had not altogether perceived. For Muggeridge, this was the Christian faith, and he was delighted to discover "some early intimations of this realization, thereby confuting the widely held belief that my transcendental aspirations afflicted me suddenly in old age when I was past appreciating fleshly pleasures, and had altogether wearied of trying to make sense of the hopes and desires of this world and of the ideas pertaining to them."[64]

Would Agee have found in these selections the same golden thread, following it "backward beyond remembrance and beyond the beginning of imagination" to the God of the void he had sought so desperately throughout his life?[65] Much would have depended on how he might have come to terms with his own beginnings. Perhaps he might have passed some of his last days in the Knoxville neighborhood he knew as a child, where the streetcars climbed the hills in the light of mother-of-pearl, and where at last he might have found the peace which passeth all understanding.

NOTES

1. James Agee and Walker Evans, *Let Us Now Praise Famous Men* (Boston: Houghton Mifflin, 1960), 235.

2. Ibid., 7.

3. James Agee, *Permit Me Voyage* (New Haven: Yale Univ. Press, 1934), 16.

4. James Agee, *Letters of James Agee to Father Flye*, 2nd ed. (Boston: Houghton Mifflin, 1971), 97.

5. Ibid., 149.

6. James Agee, *The Collected Short Prose of James Agee*, ed. Robert Fitzgerald (Boston: Houghton Mifflin, 1968), 51–52 passim.

7. Mia Agee, with Gerald Locklin, "Faint Lines in a Drawing of Jim," in *Remembering James Agee*, ed. David Madden (Baton Rouge: Louisiana State Univ. Press, 1974), 154.

8. Agee, *Letters*, 56.

9. Thomas Daniel Young, *Tennessee Writers* (Knoxville: Univ. of Tennessee Press, 1981), 88.

10. Genevieve Moreau, *The Restless Journey of James Agee* (New York: William Morrow, 1977), 207.

11. Robert Bingham, "Short of a Distant Goal," *The Reporter*, 25 Oct. 1962, p. 56.

12. John Updike, "No Use Talking," *New Republic*, 13 Aug. 1962, p. 12.

13. Agee, *Collected Short Prose*, 52.

14. Updike, 12.

15. Ernest Hemingway, *By-Line: Ernest Hemingway*, ed. William White (New York: Scribner's, 1967), xi–xiv passim.

16. Malcolm Muggeridge, *Things Past*, ed. Ian Hunter (New York: William Morrow, 1979), 146.

17. Hemingway, xii.

18. Agee, *Letters*, 31.

19. Agee, *Collected Short Prose*, 36–37.

20. Agee, *Famous Men*, x.

21. Letter from Paula Tyler (James Agee's aunt), 29 July 1978.

22. Agee, *Letters*, 1.

23. James Agee, *The Morning Watch* (Boston: Houghton Mifflin, 1950), 13; *A Death in the Family* (New York: McDowell, Obolensky, 1957), 80; *Famous Men*, 89.

24. Agee, *Collected Short Prose*, 27.

25. James Joyce, *Dubliners* (New York: Modern Library, 1971), 287–88.

26. Agee, *Famous Men*, 44–45.

27. Frederick Lewis Allen, *Since Yesterday* (New York: Bantam, 1965), 274.

28. Matthew J. Bruccoli, *James Gould Cozzens, A Life Apart* (New York: Harcourt Brace Jovanovich, 1983), 139–40.

29. Carlos Baker, *Ernest Hemingway, A Life Story* (New York: Scribner's, 1969), 205–206.

30. Allen, 274–75.

31. Agee, *Letters*, 66.

32. Agee, *Famous Men*, 15–16; *Letters*, 60.

33. Moreau, 119–20; Agee, *Letters*, 68.

34. Agee, *Collected Short Prose*, 38; Moreau, 171.

35. Agee, *Collected Short Prose*, 18; Dwight Macdonald, *Against the American Grain* (New York: Random House, 1962), 165.

36. Agee, *Letters*, 77.

37. Ibid., 81–82.

38. Moreau, 130.

39. Carson Brewer, "Town's History Rises Through Waters of TVA," *Knoxville News-Sentinel*, 15 May 1983.

40. Agee, *Letters*, 74.

41. Ibid., 92.

42. T. S. Matthews, "Agee at *Time*," in *Remembering James Agee*, ed. Madden, 116.

43. Bingham, 55.

44. Agee, *Famous Men*, 13.

45. Agee, *Letters*, 104–105.

46. Alfred T. Barson, *A Way of Seeing* (Amherst: Univ. of Massachusetts Press, 1972), 45.

47. Agee, *Collected Short Prose*, 23.

48. *The Book of Common Prayer*, Standard Book of 1928 (New York: Thomas Nelson, 1944), 581.

49. Moreau, 45.

50. Quoted in Geoffrey Rowell, *The Vision Glorious* (New York: Oxford Univ. Press, 1983), 25.

51. Moreau, 118.

52. Michael Vincent Little, "Sacramental Realism in James Agee's Major Prose," Diss. Univ. of Delaware 1974, passim.

53. Matthews, 118.

54. Howell Raines, "Let Us Now Revisit Famous Folk," *New York Times Magazine*, 25 May 1980, passim.

55. Agee, *A Death in the Family*, 24–25.

56. Moreau, 157–58.

57. Bingham, 57.

58. Moreau, 210–11.

59. Macdonald, 165.

60. Moreau, 309.

61. Agee, *Collected Short Prose*, 51.

62. Genevieve Fabre, "A Bibliography of the Works of James Agee," *Bulletin of Bibliography*, 24, May-Aug. 1965, pp. 145–48, 163–66.

63. Martha Skinner Thomas, "James Agee: A Bio-Bibliography," Thesis, Univ. of Tennessee, 1967, p. 5.

64. Muggeridge, 247–50 passim.

65. Agee, *Collected Short Prose*, 143.

JAMES AGEE: SELECTED JOURNALISM

TENNESSEE VALLEY AUTHORITY

T he Tennessee River system begins on the worn magnificent crests of the southern Appalachians, among the earth's oldest mountains, and the Tennessee River shapes its valley into the form of a boomerang, bowing it to its sweep through seven states. Near Knoxville the streams still fresh from the mountains are linked and thence the master stream spreads the valley most richly southward, swims past Chattanooga and bends down into Alabama to roar like blown smoke through the floodgates of Wilson Dam, to slide becalmed along the crop-cleansed fields of Shiloh, to march due north across the high diminished plains of Tennessee and through Kentucky spreading marshes toward the valley's end where finally, at the toes of Paducah, in one wide glass golden swarm the water stoops forward and continuously dies into the Ohio. The watershed encompasses some 44,000 square miles, a valley about the size of England and within a day's journey of all between Boston, Duluth, Key West, a valley whose climate is excellently mild (the mean annual temperature is 60 degrees), a valley which is the heart of the Southeast. Within that valley are—a number of things. Four cities: *Asheville*—in the eastern mountainous land of summer resorts, a city which has never quite got over the shock of Mr. Thomas Wolfe's novel *Look Homeward Angel* (he was a local boy and should have done more kindly by them). *Knoxville*—at the head of the Tennessee, girdled with mines and quarries and timber, the first capital of the state of Tennessee, the seat of the University of Tennessee, the erstwhile (1931) twenty-eighth most murderous city, big or little, in the U.S. *Chatta-*

nooga—self-styled Dynamo of Dixie and great center for religious publications, whose 400 factories more or less and hospitable attitude toward Yankee industrialists and whose strategic location as a distributor do much to give point to the Dynamic epithet but hardly explain the more typically native boast of more churches per capita than any other city in the U.S. *Paducah*—set among the western lands of Kentucky tobacco and among the great tobacco buyers (American Tobacco and Axton-Fisher have "interests" there).

There are also the towns up-and-coming like Bristol and Kingsport and Johnson City and the villages down-at-heel like Dayton of blessed memory and Jacksboro and Tracy City. And but for the fine soft slur of speech in the streets and the still goodly number of Model T Fords and the few deciduous southern mansions with their hitching posts and the "niggertowns" with their clay beaten down by bare heels and the whitewashed clapboard shacks and the odd predilection of the valleyite for "lawing,"* these towns might as easily be in Massachusetts or Minnesota with Main Street much the same the country over. And there's the Negro, too, who might be better off in Charleston or in Harlem. And here and there a Southern Gentleman of the old school, who still nuzzles "burbon" juleps and quotes Horace and talks "hosses" and loves his country as the greatest battleground of all the war, next to Virginia. And here and there a farmer prosperous enough to spend five to ten thousand a year on fertilizer alone. And the mountaineer, of whom more later. And the crops, which are varied and which are often as not poor in the bargain. And many a mine and knitting mill and lumber camp in the valley and a smattering of the outposts of big companies like International Harvester at Chattanooga and Aluminum Co. of America near Knoxville—all to remind you that in the past two generations men came in from the North and men came to in the South and a New South grew up and twisted its roots through the Old. These industries and these companies are of less significance to TVA by title and size and balance sheet than for what they have done for

---

*Valley vernacular for hanging about the courthouse on one's own—or others'—legal business. No dispute is too small to "go to law over." Of the valleyman's indoor sports, "lawing" is among the most popular.

the valley. There are these things among many others and there is the open country itself by the millions of acres—some of the loveliest and most somber and some of the cruelest and most haggard you will find in all America. There are also, all told, some 2,000,000 people.

This is the Tennessee Valley you might see as a visitor. It is more or less the valley you'd know if you lived there. It is the valley that is newly TVA's to have and to hold for better, for worse. To TVA there are things about the valley still more important and not so easily seen. The mountains are profoundly muscled with some forty of the minerals most useful to man. Coal and iron ore and limestone (which, properly handled, add up to spell "Ruhr") are there in huge quantities and are convenient to the river; there is much copper and zinc and marble and bauxite (the ore of aluminum) and lead; immense deposits of manganese scarely touched (the natives condition their rutty roads with it) and phosphate rock in huge abundance and asphalt rock; even traces of silver and gold. Of chestnut oak and oak pine there are excellent stands, billions of board feet, and there are dense forests of the temperate trees. The soil is as varied as the stones under it. The river is a powerful and far-falling river constant in its course, and its bed of limestone and tough clay is in general a good bed for big dams. Indeed, nature set the stage for something of a Utopia. And if you believed only the Chambers of Commerce and the first signs you saw on every road you might believe that 2,000,000 people haven't done so badly. From the forests of the seven states which the valley involves, 7,000,000,000 board feet are cut each year. In sixty years Tennessee has produced nearly a quarter of a billion tons of coal. The yearly value of natural resources (exclusive of timber) in Tennessee alone is $38,500,000. Fine figures, these. You could paint the whole valley with such figures. You might find business pretty bad but they'd be nice figures just the same, and the picture a good clear-cut picture of the sort it is nice to look at.

But here is the other side of the picture: careless fires and unregulated cutting have ruined and are ruining great stands of timber on watersheds where trees should have stood forever. Because natural resources which should have sustained local industries indefinitely have been shipped away in crude form and exhausted, whole communities have been and are being pauperized, abandoned. Where the forests are no more, where the farms are steep, where the land is light, where copper fumes wander, vast acreages of farmland are rapidly being totally laid waste by erosion. The waste land descends unimpeded into the river slowly but surely to choke the channels and to fill in great natural reservoirs that cannot be replaced. Scarcely under control and highly capricious in its flow, the Tennessee River floods the bottom lands and does an estimated $1,780,000 damage every year and adds its more than mite to the springtime disorders of the Mississippi. The river is poorly developed for navigation. Its power possibilities have scarcely been touched. Muscle Shoals was a try; it cost the government some $150,000,000 and, as everyone knows, is now a muscle-bound white elephant.

Of the 2,000,000 inhabitants perhaps one in six lives in a large city. But more important to TVA are the small-towners, still more important are the farmers. Over half the people live on farms. Some of the soil is good. Some of the best is in danger of flood. Much more, thanks to erosion, is being slaked of its life. Still more is light and sandy and inherently unfit for cultivation. The farmer in the mountains who takes apart the long sick land between the tilted racks of stone calls eight bushels of wheat and ten of corn to the acre a right good crop.* The farmers are backward in their methods; machinery in these times even less used than ever; fertilizer is expensive; power is unavailable to the poorer people at reasonable prices, virtually unheard of on many farms and for that matter in many communities; families are large; food is poor; pellagra and hookworm and dysentery are general among the mountain people. To these farms, from the factories of stricken midland cities, jobless prodigals have returned by the tens and scores of thousands in no hope of work but with some hope for mere existence.

There are, to be sure, prosperous men who till good lands but where TVA has looked it has found the typical valley farmer and his family getting along on $100 cash a year.

---

*Between 1918 and 1927 Iowa farmers averaged a yield of 39.8 bushels of corn to the acre; the average yield of Kansas wheat was thirteen bushels. Averages for Tennessee for the same period were: for corn, twenty-four bushels; for wheat, 10.6 bushels.

When the farmer lives up the shadowy coves and deep among the mountains on farms so steep that, in native parlance, a man "falls outen his own garden" and "swings in his back door on a grapevine," in a country so wild that he "keeps possums for house cats," he is more and less than a farmer: he is a mountaineer. He is the strong backbone of the Tennessee Valley. His forefathers settled this country in the 1700's when the effete civilization east of the Alleghenies stuck in their craws. They whipped the Britishers and Loyalists at King's Mountain. They kept much to themselves and their great-grandsons do likewise and live in much the same way, while slowly the sawmills and the mines and the railways and the highways and now TVA burn seclusion from about them. Many of them are illiterate; many are lawless in the bad sense and the good of that word. They never heard of Margaret Sanger and they have little interest in Mazda bulbs and little respect for this century of progress. Homespun and feuds and "mountain dew" are not so rife among them as some dreamy souls would have you believe, but you would find them all if you looked around a bit. Their language is pidgin-Elizabethan and some of their songs are still of the sea and of England and strong in their blood is a species of rugged individualism which makes the Gary brand look more pallid than usual. In short, for all the cheap romancing the fact has had, they are of that incomparably pure American stock which produced such men as Lincoln and Chief Justice Marshall and, for that matter, Cordell Hull. TVA has a deep but realistic respect for what it calls the native culture of the valley and, far more directly than the citizen of Knoxville, the mountaineer is a part of TVA's plans.

Such is the laboratory for a great experiment. Such are the raw materials good and ill from which TVA prepares to fashion a civilization which, in a certain important way, is new and is significant to all the U.S. That important way is well enough known: the past four years have filled the air with it in various forms. Most simply, it is this: the Tennessee Valley and the continent as a whole had many riches in common when, in 1492, those riches began to be suspected. And the development of the valley up to the present has had much in common with the development of the U.S., the opening up of any rich, new land in the westward course of empire. It has been praised as a pioneer development.

Other salient characteristics are these: it has been consistently shortsighted, wasteful, uncoordinated. Far and wide the opinion—sound, bad, and indifferent—grows that we are approaching a turning point in civilization, that among other things an ancient human habit must be corrected. Man must learn to cooperate with his surroundings instead of disemboweling and trampling and hoping to discard them. On the crest of this wave of talk and overrapid action TVA is the first American attempt to tackle the problem specifically and bit by bit to build at the pace which scientific advancement requires. If TVA succeeds in its valley, it will be of significance not merely to the whole Southeast and not merely as a classic model for similar work in other valleys* but ultimately of importance to all the U.S. At least that is the way the Authority looks at it.

Of TVA's experiment these, briefly stated, are the prime ultimate objectives:

To regulate river flow. To develop navigation to a maximum. To eliminate flood. To develop and use electric power as a yardstick to gauge the practices of private power companies. To distribute as much power as possible as cheaply as possible to as many people as possible. To try to develop cheap fertilizers. To control soil erosion. To classify and improve the soil and put it to its best uses. To promote better farming methods. To conserve the forests. To develop all resources in the valley in good relation to one another.

These are the outward and visible signs of something else again. Apparently it isn't quite possible to undertake such comprehensive responsibilities without a somewhat Utopian gleam in the eye: at any rate TVA has it. The coordination TVA seeks is social as well as industrial. In other words, it involves human beings. The TVA vision runs something like this: the natural forces and resources in the valley will be developed with one eye on the

---

*The valleys of the great Columbia and Missouri rivers have been mentioned as eligible for similar treatment. And last August California's Governor Rolph signed legislation establishing a state water project Authority which will have charge of a $170,000,000 development to which, it is expected, the federal government will contribute $48,000,000. Chief objectives: to build Kennett Dam (as great in bulk as Boulder Dam); to impound the flood waters of the Sacramento; to pump excess water into dryish San Joaquin Valley; to develop and sell electric power.

long future and the other on the immediate welfare of the people. Farmers will till only the good and tillable soil. The rich resources of the valley will be developed by relatively small industrial groups; production will be governed more by local than by outside demand. The factories will be not in the cities but in the open valley. The leaders, by preference, will be valley men—the workers must be—until unemployment is no more in the valley. Not only will farmers and villagers earn a prospering penny; people will move out from the cities and work the land and the machine as well. In short, a number of familiar phrases flow readily to mind: what TVA is after is a decentralization of industry, regional planning on a large scale, a well-wrought and well-controlled balance between the Jeffersonian dream of an agrarian democracy and the best characteristics of what so many people like to call the Power Age.

In this enormous machine the balance wheel is human. And here TVA becomes almost mystical in its earnestness and speaks of preserving and developing the native culture. For what that means, you must look again at the man and woman who sit on their front porch. These mountaineers must be raised and reconciled to such higher standards of living as obtain in more prosperous parts of the valley. They must also be taught responsibility to society. On the other hand the more prosperous valleyites must be raised to that high standard of Americanism which is peculiarly the mountaineer's.

It is no easy task and it is not easily definable, but it is important to TVA and it is therefore to be considered. How seriously, if not indeed fanatically, TVA is taking these social issues its employment policies will serve to show. From the very first the stand has been notably firm against political appointments, to the slight irritation of Postmaster General Jim Farley, and just as firm, though more kindly, against unemployed "outsiders." TVA's work is indeed to be of, by, for the valley people. As for the valleyite who applies for work, he is faced with a peculiarly searching questionnaire, is asked much in detail about his schooling and his relationship with spirituous liquors during the past outlawed decade. To gather such strange if valuable data requires, to say the least, tact—if you wish an independent countryman to take your job rather than starve in protest. Evidently TVA has tact, too, for men are taking jobs. The men who build Norris Dam will live in the carefully pioneer-style model town which will rise at Cove Creek. They will work only three days a week. (Three days' wages will go far in mountain families used to getting along on $100 and less a year—and will go to twice as many families.) On the free days these workmen may, if they like, attend vocational school and learn plumbing and masonry and carpentry and other crafts. Not, as TVA points out, for the purpose of annoying the trades unions, but primarily to supply good handymen to remote neighborhoods which have had none before.

All of which is very fine. It has an epic quality—and a quality more easily put in words than in deeds. Who are the men who are to translate it? They are more important to the plan than their titles suggest, for like many another Rooseveltian conception, the Tennessee Valley Authority can be visualized only in terms of the men he chose to administer it.

The TVA is a corporation created by the Tennessee Valley Authority Act, which in turn was created by warlike little Senator Norris of Nebraska and by a President who saw more in it than "putting the Government into the power business" (which had brought two prompt Republican vetoes) and by careful study of the legal set up of Port of New York Authority and—like any great and farsighted idea—by a number of men who also ran. To the extent of having a corporate name and seal, the right to sue and be sued, to make contracts, to adopt bylaws, to purchase or lease property, it is an independent corporation. It is under no government department but it is entitled to the help and advice of any federal office, including the Patent Office. It is armed with the right of eminent domain. Fifty million dollars of the President's $3,300,000,000 recovery program is at its disposal to begin with, and there are possibilities of additional income from the sale of power and fertilizer. For future work the Board is authorized to issue, on the credit of the U.S., $50,000,000 in 3½ per cent bonds having a fifty-year maturity. (So far as power is concerned, there will be so subsidy. TVA must sell its power at a rate which will not only return all operating costs but will also, over a term of years, retire the capital invested.) The task has no deadline. TVA has only to submit an annual report to the President and to

Congress. From time to time the President may recommend additional legislation. He it is who appoints and may at any time remove the Directors.

The Directors are three: two elderly college presidents named Morgan and a very lively young lawyer named Lilienthal. As Chairman of the Board, Roosevelt promptly appointed Dr. Arthur Ernest Morgan, self-taught President of Antioch (Work-and-Study) College, which in ten years he has built up from an obscure experiment. His first official act was to submit a careful inventory of his personal properties, a thing no U.S. public officer had ever thought of doing before. Dr. Morgan is as well known among hydraulic engineers as among educators. It was he who put the wild Miami River in its place after the Dayton (Ohio) flood in 1913; it was he who lent an authoritative hand to the drafting of the drainage codes of half a dozen states. President Roosevelt was impressed by something more when he first read Dr. Morgan's *Antioch Notes*. Dr. Morgan's friends know him as a man of considerable human wisdom, of breadth and integrity and originality of mind.

The other Morgan is a college president too. He is Dr. Harcourt Alexander (no kin to Dr. A. E.) Morgan, who leaves behind fourteen years' service as President of the University of Tennessee. He is an authority on artichokes, bugs, cats, dogs, eggs, fish, geraniums, hay, iguanas, jam, and so down the alphabet. He is also, by dint of years of study, an authority on agriculture and industry in his valley. To balance industry and agriculture is his assigned task.

David E. Lilienthal, Director and General Counsel, is more the "wonder boy" type. He has a brilliant past at thirty-four, especially as a legal authority on public utilities. At Harvard Law he was (like a few other headliners today) one of Felix Frankfurter's star pupils. Later he became the friend and associate of Donald Richberg, was Special Counsel for the city of Chicago in the telephone-rate controversy which Chicagoans will well remember. At thirty-two he left Chicago to help Wisconsin's Governor Philip La Follette reorganize the State Railroad Commission. His revision of the public-utility statutes of Wisconsin has already served as a model for several other states.

The Directors serve nine-year terms (staggered to begin with

at nine, six, and three at a $10,000-a-year salary—less, for the
time being, the government's 15 per cent cut in basic salaries.
Each is entitled to one of the numerous empty government houses
on the Muscle Shoals reservation where by requirement of the
creative act, official TVA headquarters must be. They also get
traveling expenses.

Preliminaries are if anything harder than the job itself. It takes
time to learn just where such a corporation stands in relation to
the statutory framework of seven states and many municipalities.*
It takes time to make your own definitive studies geological, social, and industrial; time to know all there is to know about every
square mile of a great valley.

Granting all these points, eyebrows have yet been raised at the
record of the Authority's first months in its valley. TVA's reluctance
to issue detailed statements, its practice of giving such items as
employment figures in round and sometimes conflicting numbers
(even when asked to specify), the fact that not until August 10 did
TVA allocate specific duties to its three Directors to execute pre-
liminary projects "with the least possible delay"—at such small
straws in a large wind, no few people have looked askance, have
suggested that two elderly academicians, however at home with
round phrase and round idea, have limitations when confronted
with a mass of cold hard detail demanding stern organization.
They have at any rate been less specific than gentlemen handling
the public's money usually are. By the end of the summer, TVA
had begun to assert itself as we shall presently see. But with
much theory still to be translated into practice, it is perhaps as
well to bear these criticisms in mind.

The critics, however, mislead if they imply that valley workers
are idle, have no immediate plans. Many a valley venture hums.
On September 1, after 200 men had spent the summer taking in-

*Late in August a situation arose which will force a definition of TVA's position and
powers. Southern Industries & Utilities, Inc. applied to the Federal Power Commission for a fifty-year permit, against the issue of which Counsel Lilienthal, in
the name of TVA, made formal protest. S.I.& U.'s proposed development: a dam
and powerhouse at Aurora (near Paducah), an immense valley-gulfing reservoir
167 miles long. Grounds for protest: Congress granted TVA exclusive jurisdiction
in all developments on the Tennessee. The matter is to be settled at a public
hearing.

ventory, TVA inherited Muscle Shoals and sixty (sometimes called eighty) Shoals men from the War Department (and in all is absorbing between 400 and 600 men from the War and other departments). The Authority will arrive at its own valuation of this property through "an appraisal by disinterested engineers." What will be done with the Shoals nitrate plants is yet to be decided. As they stand, they're pretty useless and outdated. But TVA, experimenting in cooperation with agricultural colleges and farmers' organizations, hopes in time to learn how to make fertilizers which will sell at about a third their present cost. Perhaps on the "four-county" plan—a central plant to each four counties, each to serve the needs of its limited territory. TVA doesn't know yet. In the mountains northwest and southeast of Knoxville, two CCC camps and 400 men are beginning the great task of reforestation and erosion control which in time, Dr. Morgan estimates, will absorb 5,000 workers at the very least. In a secluded laboratory a onetime Alabama Rhodes Scholar is developing a new method of transmitting power over long distances—a method which may make today's transmission as obsolete as a wooden plow. What the method and who the man are TVA's secrets. In Knoxville's Sprankle Building, in 106 offices, TVA draftsmen are busied over plans; in the wild country twenty miles above Knoxville, where Cove Creek steps into the Clinch River, more men on the TVA payroll explore the countryside. In these last two activities center TVA's most immediate, most important present undertaking: the Norris Dam.

The wild honeycomb of caves upstream has been found safe against reservoir leakage, and now TVA's men are laying out highway and railway connections, clearing the three miles of land where a model and permanent town will rise to house the workers. An able body of able-minded men is going over the plans for Norris Dam, among them Colonel George R. Spalding (St. Louis office of the War Department), Mr. S. M. Woodward of the University of Iowa (whom Chairman Morgan describes as "one of the ablest men the United States ever produced in hydraulics"), Mr. J. L. Savage (designer of the Boulder and Madden dams), and Mr. Savage's colleagues in the Denver office of the Reclamation Bureau. Who will boss the job of building, TVA can't tell. Some other government agency snitched from under the TVA nose the able gentleman chosen (his name is withheld), and all the Authority can say is that Norris Dam will *not* be built by public contract. However that may be, construction will start early in 1934. The 250-foot Norris Dam and the powerhouse will take four years to build and, together with the transmission line that will link the development with Muscle Shoals, will cost nearly $45,000,000. The deep tangle of valleys above the dam will brim with a ragged lake of some eighty-three square miles, impounding 140,000,000,000 cubic feet of water.*

The average March–October flowage ratio of the Tennessee River at Muscle Shoals has been estimated at ten to one (peak divergence was fifty-three to one). The Norris Dam, with its immense storage, will go far toward bringing this flow into balance. Which will mean:

For navigation:

At present, navigation is governed by the seasons, and the channels are poor. Every year 2,000,000 tons of cargo ply the river below and the river above Muscle Shoals, but only 12,000 tons use its locks. Water storage and the clearing of a nine-foot, 650-mile channel will give this tonnage free passage from Knoxville to Paducah. In time to come the valley's raw materials will have cheap passage by water, and cheaply by water valley products may reach any port on earth.

Flood:

Norris Dam will greatly reduce; subsequent dams will eliminate.

Power:

At present Muscle Shoals can count on only about 120,000 horsepower of "firm" (constant, year-round) waterpower—and only firm power is worth talking about. The powerhouse at Norris Dam will generate 220,000; by balancing the flow of the Tennessee is sure to raise Muscle Shoals well toward its ultimate capacity of 610,000 horsepower. Subsequent dams not yet scheduled will do still more. The ultimate horsepower possible to wrench out of the river is estimated at 3,000,000.

---

*From ninety-two cemeteries to drier territory, tactful TVA will transfer the occupants of 4260 graves, "with signal honor to the dead and with due deference to the living."

What TVA could do with this power is what scared Presidents
Coolidge and Hoover into vetitive spasms. Nine power companies under two great holding corporations, Commonwealth &
Southern and Electric Bond & Share, now serve 550,000-odd
valley customers with power at an average production and transmission cost estimated at nine mills per kilowatt hour.* Wholesale
power to other utilities and to manufacturers is generally cheap,
but it is alleged that domestic users and small municipalities have
been known to pay six to eighteen times the average production
cost.

These private companies, combined, are equipped to supply
33 per cent more power than the valley is using.

Within a very few years, thanks to TVA, excess production will
jump to 66 per cent. And TVA hopes to sell its power at a uniform
switchboard rate considerably lower (how much, nobody can be
sure) than rates have a habit of being. How on earth the valley is
to absorb all this excess power and what on earth it will mean to
the power companies and a $400,000,000 investment in private
power (the figure is Wendell L. Willkie's President of Commonwealth & Southern), powermen would like very much to know.

Many an interested party was trying to find out during the
summer months—while TVA issued broad missionary statements
and while TVA's Directors kept dumb and looked wise. Not even
yet, not for years to come, may powermen or TVA or any human
agency know all it wants to know about TVA's power problems, yet
when, on August 25, the Authority put its cards on the table,
powermen recognized a New Deal and a strong hand indeed.

Lawyer David Lilienthal, in charge of TVA's electric power, will
act on these basic policies: "Private and public interests in the
business of power are of a different kind and quality and should
not be confused. The right of a community to own and operate its
own electric plant is undeniable . . . one of the measures which
the people may properly take to protect themselves against unreasonable rates. Such a course of action may take the form of

*This, as applied to all nine companies, is the merest estimate-derived-from-an-
estimate. Carl D. Thompson's "Confessions of the Power Trust" contains, among
much else, a study of Alabama Power Co. (subsidiary of Commonwealth & Southern) as a representative company, and Alabama Power's average production cost is
therein estimated at .882 cents a kilowatt hour.

acquiring the existing plant, or setting up a competing plant, as circumstances may dictate. The fact that (TVA) action . . . may have an adverse economic effect upon a privately owned utility . . . a matter for the serious consideration of the Board in framing and executing its power program . . . is not the determining factor. The most important considerations are the furthering of the public interest in making power available at the lowest rate consistent with sound financial policy, and the accomplishment of the social objectives which low cost power makes possible." (Power is indeed the lifeblood of TVA's social-industrial-agrarian scheme; of the local industries and of the well-run farms TVA hopes to foster. And already more than fifty towns have applied for power service.)

"To provide a workable and economic basis for operations," TVA plans first "to serve certain definite regions" (those in the vicinity of Muscle Shoals and Norris Dam, and the belt of land that will lie near the transmission line connecting these dams) "and to develop its program in those areas before going outside." Later, the development will include the whole Tennessee Valley and "to make the area a workable one and a fair measure of public ownership . . . several cities of substantial size (such as Chattanooga and Knoxville) and ultimately, at least one city of more than a quarter million . . . such as Birmingham, Memphis, Atlanta, or Louisville."

Although TVA's present intention is to develop its power program in the valley before thinking of going outside, it may go outside "if there are substantial changes in general conditions . . . government policy . . ." or if the private companies "do not cooperate in the working out of the program."

And, possibly more sinister still to powermen, since conceivably it foreshadows a great buying-over campaign: "Every effort will be made . . . to avoid the construction of duplicate physical facilities, or wasteful competitive practices. Accordingly, where existing (transmission) lines of privately owned utilities are required to accomplish the Authority's objectives . . . a genuine effort will be made to purchase such facilities . . . on an equitable basis."

Accounting will show "details of costs, and will permit of comparison of operations with privately owned plants, to supply a 'yardstick' and an incentive to both private and public managers."

TVA's power accounts and power records "will always be open to inspection by the public." Powermen bitterly recall that day in War-time when Alabama Power forked over the site of Muscle Shoals—on which it had already spent some $5,000,000—to the government. All that for $1. They remember, too, what happened later when for publicity purposes Alabama Power reproduced that $1 check: Alabama Power was fined $500 for reproducing a government document. Nowadays even louder and funnier things are afoot. Tossing reminiscences aside, the same gentlemen as bitterly observe that (through a 3 per cent tax on the gross revenues from sales of energy both commercial and domestic, through the $1 tax on every $1,000 worth of capital stock which, as NRA boys, they must hand over) they along with thousands of investors in private power and along with U.S. citizens by the millions the country over, are forced to pay for TVA's program. Bitterly they agree with Professor Richard J. Smith, legal authority on utilities (who, in the *Yale Law Journal*, June 1933, points out that municipal control and state regulation of private power have often as not been merely negative in properly directing the expansion of the industry), and again bitterly they expand upon his observations, cry that if the government *must* take the utilities in hand there's a sounder, wiser way of doing it than by TVA's proposed policy of serving isolated municipalities, or breaking down the great transmission systems whereby the load may be balanced and the rates may be kept down. That wiser way, say the powermen, is by out-and-out, comprehensive acquisition of such systems. And as for that, Wendell L. Willkie recalls the offer he made before a House Committee last April when TVA was imminent: to absorb all power TVA might generate and to sell it over his own lines at rates congruent with such savings as TVA might effect. Not a move was made about that but Mr. Willkie's offer still stands.

As for what can be done about it, powermen will remind you of certain rights which are theirs according to the Fourteenth Amendment. And will observe that TVA cannot enter into direct competition without nullifying the franchise which grants a utility exclusive right to operate within its given territory. And will remark that even in these dizzy times there are courts where, perhaps, such matters will be granted a fair hearing.

In fact, TVA has swung a bold foot through a beehive of problems both practical and ethical, of significance not merely in themselves but as they apply to the whole theory of relationships between private and public interests. These are problems and this is a theory which have yet to be solved and defined. Meanwhile, one corner is quite clear of doubt: in very truth, the U.S. government is "in the power business."

Such is the program of the Tennessee Valley Authority. (And be it observed that power, important though it is, is to be the mere spine of the whole living animal.) Such are the mere first inklings of the action which must, through years to come, carry it out. And such are a few of the problems yet to be solved by the men who have committed themselves by oath to a belief in "the feasibility and wisdom" of TVA's program. Meanwhile, nothing is built and all is planning and a ruffling of blueprints. Not until 1938, when Norris Dam stands tall and solid to the memory of the men who fought for it, when the great hive-shaped dynamos down the river begin to whine their hearts out, will TVA begin to realize returns. Not until then will the world be qualified to begin to judge the men now busy with beginnings.

COCKFIGHTING

You are a gentleman. You have a taste for sport (most likely horses), leisure to indulge it, and an estate. One quiet morning you walk down to your stables. As you come around the side of the barn, you hear a soft but violent fluttering of wings, an agitated hissing, a passionate exclaiming of low voices. You look down, and there are your Negroes (if you happen to be a southern gentlemen) crouched in a wide circle on the ground, leaning on bent knuckles, peering into the center of the ring. They are watching two birds, large and brightly colored, that cling together beak to beak with arched necks, dancing up and down, while their wings whir and they slash at each other viciously, rapidly, with their spurs. The birds are gamecocks, most ferocious of all domestic creatures, and their dance is fatal—it can end only in death. And you are present at one of the many new births of man's most ancient sport, legally extinct in at least forty of the United States, frowned on in all, minor and surreptitious pleasure of the rich, secret passion of the poor, purpose of the Heel Tap Club, most exclusive in the world: cockfighting.

Since 1879* there has been next to no open pitting of gamecocks in the U.S. Breeders who engage in it, hangers-on who watch it, may be subject to fines or imprisonment, their accessories seized; the birds themselves may be "arrested" and destroyed. Rarely, an obscure paragraph or two may appear in your newspaper: a cockfight has been raided, a few anonymous gentlemen fined. But for all the public knows, this sport, which kings

---

*When the last public main (between Georgia and Kentucky) was held at the old Spanish cockpit in New Orleans, scene of America's most famous cockfights.

and presidents have favored, might be as obsolete as dueling. Only its few devout followers can hint at the number of matches fought yearly in the U.S. (perhaps a few hundred, perhaps a few thousand) or the amount of money which changes hands in fees and purses (from $5,000,000 up); and neither gentleman nor gangster, whose codes after all have much in common, will reveal where these mains are fought or who fights them. But cockers will tell you this: that the American Society for the Prevention of Cruelty to Animals (which gets a slice of all fines imposed by its initiative in most states) collects thousands of dollars every year. And slaughters hundreds of thoroughbred cocks.

Around cockfighting, centuries older than most other sports, has grown a host of rules, customs, and traditions, but in essence it is the simplest of combats. Two breeders or their handlers, cocks under their arms, step into the pit (a twenty-foot circle inclosed within a low wall), set the birds down face to face on the ground, and stand back, attentive. The cocks do the rest—fly at each other and fight until one is dead or unconscious. For weapons they use gaffs, slender, curving needles of murderous steel fitted to their legs over the filed stumps of their natural spurs. The gaffs may be long or short (one and one-quarter to two and one-half inches); with them the cock slashes forward and upward, turning his leg as a boxer turns his arm in an uppercut, using his beak to bite and hold and balance. The longest gaffs give the shortest, bloodiest fights. They are used chiefly in the South, where heat, sloth, and sudden temper discourage lengthy argument among cocks as among men. Little can be done to aid the fighters. If a blood clot forms in a cock's throat, his handler may (when the referee calls time out on some technicality) suck at the cock's beak to remove it; if he is wounded (blind or paralyzed) so that he cannot fight, he may rest while his opponent's handler scoops up his own cock and runs through a complicated count; then, if he is still helpless, he forfeits the match.

There are three ways of pitting cocks. Most frequently, on impulse or to settle a discussion of their birds' merits, two breeders may set their favorite cocks against each other informally and bet on the result: such a fight is a "hack." Formal cockfights require weeks of training and preparation. Two promoters may collect teams of cocks, their own and/or their friends', match them by weight in an odd number of fights, and so make a "main" to which come spectators from miles around. Besides the betting on individual performances, there is usually a big wager on the outcome of the main. Greatest events of the cocking world are tournaments held annually where enthusiasts are thickest. To these travel breeders who come hundreds of miles for the chance to win a purse and a championship, perhaps to make their strains famous, and so valuable commercially. An entry fee is charged each contestant, the sum divided into purses for the winners. Such tournaments may last for several days, and the winning cocks meet in elimination matches from which emerge the champions. To U.S. Breeders, the Orlando (Florida) and Jersey Breeders' tournaments are the Kentucky Derby and Preakness of cockfighting.

If you doubt the color and gravity of these spectacles, read one of the four national magazines devoted exclusively to fighting cocks. *Grit and Steel, Feathered Warrior, Knights of the Pit,* and *Game Fowl News* are the four, with a combined circulation of some 25,000 copies a month. Correspondents in all parts of the country report the outcome of important mains and tournaments; exciting matches, valorous birds are described; breeders advertise the courage and cunning of their fowl. For (obscure and furtive as it is) cockfighting is a sport and a business, with thousands of followers who give their lives and fortunes to it. Absent though it may be from the sports columns of the New York *Times* or the Chicago *Tribune*, it has its definite place in the sporting life of the nation. The tout who haunts the race tracks, the gangster who feeds on boxing and wrestling matches, the gentleman who hunts with thoroughbreds at Warrenton or Radnor—all these are likely to be found around the pit when two fine cocks are matched.

Those who love the sport are not discouraged by its clandestine nature. With the fanatic fervor of all enthusiasts, they gather covertly in dark, deserted places, from Christmas until Independence Day, to see their birds win a main or two, then die. The pit may be erected in a neighbor's barn, in an abandoned shed, a basement, or a gymnasium—sometimes even in gloomy, unrented lofts of Manhattan office buildings. In all parts of the country (but chiefly in rural districts) news of a coming main passes among the devotees discreetly, by word of mouth. Like members of some sinister secret order, they meet silently on the appointed day;

gentlemen, breeders, yokels, gangsters—society's highest and its lowest, seldom those in between who comprise the Public. A file of cars follows its leader down a road, turns off, halts in a field beside some ominous black building yawning against the night sky. The headlights vanish; the obscure company melts through a doorway. Then, within, the cautious mumbling of their voices may be heard, and the sport begins.

Like members of a secret order, too, these sportsmen have their unwritten code of honor. Nothing unites them but their common passion and the peril of the Law. They sign no legal contracts, give no tokens of good faith; none are needed. Their bets are made verbally and paid without question. They expect no trickery in the pit, for a gamecock fights eagerly to the finish, without aid or urging, and such prearranged decisions as grace the prize ring and the track are next to impossible. The cocking clan has also its High Moral Purpose: its value of the gamecock as an example of ideal courage. They love to quote the speech Themistocles made to his Athenian army in 480 B.C., on the way to Salamis: "These animals fight not for the gods of their country, nor for the monuments of their ancestors, nor for glory, nor for freedom, nor for their progeny, but for the sake of victory, and that one may not yield to the other." Rugged individualists are these rooster worshipers, and they will remind you that the eagle was chosen to symbolize the U.S. by only two votes over the cock.

What makes a *game* cock is courage. It is a superlative kind of courage, blind, stubborn, and uncompromising, which has only two ends: victory or death. And therein lies the fascination of this spectacle—it is the most primitive combat a man may be privileged to see in these times. The birds are bred for gameness alone; they are delicately cared for, fed, and conditioned, with no purpose except to die in battle. Other cocks, bred for poultry or for exhibition, may be as pure in blood, but to a cocker they are only "dunghills." A dunghill cock will fight for supremacy in the poultry yard, sometimes to the death; but in the cocking pit, armed with gaffs, he will turn and run. His business is to eat and to reproduce his kind. A gamecock, confronted by any rival rooster, will ignore the most alluring hens, the most delicious food, while he glares with beady hatred at his instinctive enemy for days on end; restrained from fighting, he will fall dead of hunger and exhaustion.

There is an axiom among breeders: "A cock is as good as he proves himself in the pit." The purest ancestry, the best training and handling are no guaranty that a cock will be truly game. For gameness, in this sport, is an absolute quality, not a comparative one; and there is no certain proof of gameness except death. That they may judge as best they can the quality of a bird for the pit, breeders have only one test. They take two stags (to a cock what pups are to a dog—after their first molting, when they are about a year old, they become cocks) and let them spar with muffs fitted over their spurs.* But such a trial is little more than a test of form and tactics.

And there's another axiom of the pit, following logically from the first: "You can't *buy* a gamecock. You can borrow or steal it, or it may be given to you." For the cost of fine cockflesh is an indeterminate matter. Fresh from a victory in the pit, after winning a $5,000 stake, a bird may be worth $5,000. A few weeks later, after losing his next fight, he may be worth nothing. The breeder who owns a fine cock values him beyond any cash reckoning. Those cocks which *are* sold may sell for as little as twenty-five dollars. They are the birds you see advertised in the cocking journals or changing hands among the grooms in your stable. What their genealogy is, nobody can say, but they are likely to be sufficiently pure in blood, sufficiently game. Other cocks, or notable strains which have produced good fighters for four or five generations, may now and then be had privately from friendly breeders for a few hundred dollars.

The cost of raising a cock is almost negligible. You can breed two hundred for little more than the cost of breeding two. To compete in an ordinary main you may hatch as many as a hundred eggs and select from them as many as twenty-one promising cocks. That will take you about a year and a half, at an average expense of $5 a week—in all, $350. If you hire a man to train and diet them for the pit, you will pay $75 for his work. All your

---

*From this practice, in 1725, Jack Broughton got the idea of boxing gloves for prizefighters.

equipment, including gaffs, can be bought for another $25 or less. That brings your total expenses to less than $500. Each of your twenty-one cocks has cost you about $20—to breed a thorough-bred yearling for the Futurity would take $5,000—and a winner may bring you anywhere from $50 to $5,000, or more: whatever stake has been agreed upon. Or you can compete in the tournament at Orlando, which costs $1,000 to enter, and win from $1,500 to $8,000 in prizes. Its rich patrons put big money into cockfighting. But it's a game a poor man can afford to play.

If this were the normal margin of profit in cockfighting it would be easy money indeed. There is this catch, however: unlike human fighters, cocks rarely lack courage, never lay down. Their gameness is absolute. And so, if his birds are properly trained, a breeder can count himself normally lucky to win his 50 per cent of the fights he enters. To win six times out of ten is an astonishing average, and few exceed it. There is the case of the prosperous plumber. He bred some gamecocks for his own amusement and found that he had a genius for handling them, as some men have for handling bees. So he gave up plumbing and went in for cockfighting in earnest. His string of victories was considered extraordinary, but in 1930 he made only $8,500. And 1930 was his banner year. To a plumber that may be a mighty good income; to a boxing promoter it would look trifling. Obviously a man doesn't take up cocking for the money in it. Illegal or not, it couldn't be called a racket.

Actually the only real money to be gained from the pit is in bets. And that may be as much or as little as the better's purse allows. There is no sport more purely dependent on chance than cockfighting. To the rich (who are careless of money) it is a game above suspicion; to the poor (who have none) it is a game they can afford. Racing or boxing or baseball may be the national pastimes of the masses in all great U.S. cities. But in the little towns and the lonely rural stretches which are still America, cockfighting is the people's sport. Especially in the South; no spectacle excites a Negro like a cockfight. That's why, until some remote time when the nation turns wholly urban, in countless barnyards the game-cock will remain a telltale evidence of lawbreaking, as (until lately) was the whiskey bottle. You cannot have fine poultry without a cock or two. And where there are cocks you will surely come upon your servants some fine morning, gathered in a ring to watch them fight. Being a gentleman, you will as surely pause to watch yourself.

The genealogy of the gamecock is as vague and anonymous as the genealogy of the masses who have bred him. Where he first came from is a fruitless inquiry: farmers, slaves, and soldiers have had their fighting birds for as long as man remembers. In Persia cockfighting was ancient when Alexander the Great made his conquest; Japanese game fowls are as old as the Japanese imperial family (First Family of the World); and the Spaniards, most passionate of all cockfighters,* found cocks before them in Mexico and Peru. Because in early times voyages were long and fresh stores necessary to efficient soldiers, where armies went the hen (and therefore the cock) was likely to go also. Is that how roosters came into Britain, with Caesar's legionaries? Or were they there already? There, at any rate, they were; and the British watched them assassinate each other in 55 B.C., were still watching them in 1655 A.D. when already they were drifting into the American colonies. First sport of the New World (after boxing, for which a man required no accessories) was cockfighting.

U.S. gamecocks have an honorable but confused ancestry. Until the Revolution most were of pure English blood. Such were the birds General Washington imported from New Orleans and asked Thomas Jefferson over to Mount Vernon to see. Such also were the valiant cocks Andrew Jackson bred even after he got to the White House. But after the Revolution American seamen began to bring back outlandish fowls from the Orient and turn them loose in native barnyards. There were some odd results. From a red Malay cock (now stuffed in the Peabody Academy of Science), brought home to Salem in 1846 by Captain Richard Wheatley, and a hen of English blood sprang the first Rhode Island reds. Other miscegenetic unions produced breeds with exotic names known only in the cockpit: Crazy Snakes, Kansas Sluggers, Roughhouse Blues, Strychnine Greys, Stone Fences, White Mules, many another as threatening. Some 250 native strains have been distinguished, but interbreeding has so mingled them that few

*In all Spanish-speaking countries cocks share with bulls the honor of dying most often to amuse the people.

are pure. Intermixture makes them no less aristocratic. Game fowl crossed with dunghill blood soon disappear from the pit, and so rarely corrupt the noble strains. Famous U.S. names (which mean little): Warhorses, Whitehackles, Shufflers, Roundheads. How to breed gamecocks is a question steeped in controversy and superstition. But from the lore of all breeders, whether intuitive or scientific, three simple and universal rules emerge. They are these:

The blood must be kept fresh. Almost all American cockers agree that inbreeding has brought ruin upon English, Scotch, and Irish fowl. A certain amount of inbreeding is practiced, to fix new strains, to keep famous strains pure, especially to reproduce in their children the qualities of great and valorous sires. Some line breeding (matings between nephews and aunts, which to a cocker are not incest) is necessary—how much depends upon the breeder's own discretion, perhaps more upon the purity of the strain itself. Some cockers claim to have produced fine birds after forty years of strict inbreeding. But the majority seek fresh blood after four incestuous generations at most.

The blood must be kept game. The fierce valor of fighting cocks hangs upon a delicate thread of training and selection. A single drop of dunghill blood, as all breeders agree, will destroy it for all time, produce birds fit only to strut about the barnyard.

The hen must be as game as the cock. Oldtime breeders used to say that "one good hen is worth a dozen cocks." Few modern breeders, though they grow lyrical over the strength and spirit of a fine hen, go quite so far. They do grant that sire and dam may have equal influence on the heredity of their young; the sisters of great fighters are prized, and mated with fine cocks.

Cocks differ in the pit as boxers differ in the ring. Each has his own personality, readily felt by a true devotee of the sport, and the methods of no two are quite alike. But, like boxers too, they may be divided by temperament into two rough classes: shufflers and single strokers. A shuffler is a swift, aggressive fighter; he strikes as fast and as often as he can move his legs; he gives his enemy no rest. Single-strokers are powerful, slower and more cunning; they wait for an opening, then thrust accurately and deep, conserving their strength. In the long northern matches these cocks are deadly: they are the Gene Tunneys of the pit.

Shufflers do better in the short, violent matches of the South: like Jack Dempsey, they are killers. But the greatest cocks are those which know both methods. To live long, a cock should crowd his opponent when he can, trying for a quick death, but dawdle when he must and wait for a chance to strike.

Because among most game birds there is little to choose in courage, and because victory depends as much on chance as on skill, physical condition is of first importance in the pit. They are matched by weight, usually within a limit of two ounces; so that any needless fat is a big handicap. And either too much weight or too little is likely to hurt the cock's wind, his greatest asset, whether in a short, violent fight or in a long, exhausting one. Once it took six weeks to feed and train a cock for the pit; now ten or twelve days is considered enough. He is kept alone in a small coop, his weight and vitality closely watched. Daily his feeder puts him on a cushioned table for exercies, tosses him up, lets him fall with flapping wings. The cock finds it very pleasant.

Talented feeders and handlers command great respect among their own kind, high and low. Usually they work under the patronage of wealthy sportsmen; sometimes their reputation grows until they can afford to work for whom they please. Greatest figure in U.S. cocking, now grown almost legendary, was Michael Kearney, who came over from Ireland in 1875 with his birds under his arm. Strains which he developed first for August Belmont and other sportsmen, later for Herman Duryea, biggest gentleman breeder of his time, still dominate American pits. Duryea and Kearney fought their cocks in England and France, won some twenty mains, lost none. In thirty years of breeding they lost only one main, to John Hoy. Today Harry Kearney, Michael's son, is considered a fine handler.

Andrew P. O'Conor, born in America of Irish parents, is a famous handler who has fought cocks for more than forty years. O'Conor's banner years were 1905–06, when he made a triumphal tour abroad, handling for the Earl of Clonmell, who became his friend and patron. Out of three mains, he won two, the third was a draw; a quarter of million dollars changed hands in purses and bets. When O'Conor was in his prime, Dr. H. B. Clarke of Indianapolis was also a notable figure, fighting his own cocks abroad. Dr. Clarke still makes an occasional match. Because so

many strains have lost their identity few breeders today achieve
the fame of Kearney, O'Conor, and many others thirty years ago.
Currently most successful are Peter Horrocks of Cleveland, Col.
John H. Madigin of Buffalo, and Thomas W. Murphy of Pough-
keepsie. Col. Madigin has won four purses (two of them firsts) in
the Orlando tournament, where meet the finest cocks in the
South.

Nobody will tell you who are the eight top breeders (socially) of
gamecocks in the U.S. And for a very good reason: all but one are
rich, all are prominent socially and members of that small, se-
cretive society of cockers: The Heel Tap Club. Founded in 1922,
the club centers its roving headquarters about Boston and New
York. To its tournaments each season came the eight members
with their friends and retainers and their retainers' friends, bringing their own birds which they handle themselves. Once a year it
meets as a club, at a dinner given by one member for the other
seven.

The names of these reticent enthusiasts, like the name of Yah-
weh, may not be spoken; nor are their names, for all this silence,
high in the councils of government or business. Five are Bosto-
nians. Mr. A and Mr. B are relatives by marriage, both hunting
enthusiasts; Mr. A sells insurance, Mr. B is a dog fancier. Mr. C is
a partner in a prominent brokerage firm. Mr. D has a woolen tex-
tile business. Two others do nothing but manage their estates.
Mr. E was a pioneer breeder of polo ponies, Mr. F races horses,
is a famous shot. Mr. G is one of the oldest members of the New
York Stock Exchange, but none too active on it. His only sporting
interest is cockfighting. Only Southerner in the club is Mr. H, a
Virginian of the old planter tradition, without money, but a lover
of cocks and horses: a typical southern sportsman.

Mysterious this roster may be; but mystery has become a necessity (at least in the North) among cock lovers whose social
prominence would otherwise bring them under the spotlight of
the Law. Only in the rural South has the Law remained so feudal
that it knows better than to molest gentlemen. And even there,
publicity outside of their own circle is avoided by these sportsmen. But they protest. Many a Courtesy Colonel grows apoplectic over his julep, reflecting on the indignity offered by animal
cruelty laws to an old, honorable, and patrician pastime. It is the

timid, weakspirited bourgeoisie, they say, who take away cock-fighting from both their inferiors and their betters.

"What happens to the dunghill chicken?" a cocker will exclaim. "At best, his neck is wrung to fit him for the family dinner. At the worst, he is mutilated and fattened, then sent off to a poultry house where pickers with sharp knives slash the roof of his mouth, so that he may bleed to death slowly while he is stripped of his feathers."

To the sportsman a gamecock's death is triumphant and exalted. Even cockers grant that the bird is stupid. Probably he feels no pain—only an irresistible urge to annihilate the enemy who stands for an abstract challenge to his supremacy. Out of the pit, he is well fed and housed, parades at his ease in a small universe of his own. Perhaps three times in a season he fights, and if he is powerful enough to survive, his taste for battle is only whetted. He may live four years (some cocks have lived and fought to be eight) before age and boredom make a victim of him. Then he dies, still in such fury of hatred that no spectator can pity him. And a score or so of gamblers and poor farmers, a sprinkling of fine gentlemen, are happy. To all this the A.S.P.C.A. makes no answer. But faithfully, each year, it gathers up its unrepentant horde of blue-blooded birds. Sometimes (in the great cities) it puts them to die in lethal chambers. More often it turns them over to the police, who wring their necks to feed prisoners or the poor. Many a sergeant who knew no better has locked his sullen flock of criminals in a cell overnight, returned in the morning to find them dead. For gamecocks love nothing better than to fight: like sailors ashore, they can imagine no happier paradise than one in which rages an endless free-for-all, ending constantly in death.

ROMAN SOCIETY

Quietly in his marble-skinned and magnificent and cold palazzo, Prince Doria waits for death to take him. He isn't what you'd call old—only fifty-two—but he is an invalid and, more significantly, he is a Roman Prince. Waiting is the best he can do. As the big world wags today, his will not be a momentous death, for in this world he has done small harm, and small good. He has lived according to his lights, and as a Roman Prince lives in this time. His piety is proverbial in Rome. He is one of the greatest of Italian landowners, and he was busy at land reclamation long years before Mussolini had given it a second thought. A few years back, when taxes were beginning to be bitterly high, he made news of a sort when he dared put before Mussolini a complaint in the form of a carefully itemized expense account. He had pinched and economized, but Mussolini merely scrawled across the report: "Too extravagant. Cut down." Lately he made mild news again when he signed over a large and handsome villa to the Holy See.

Whether he did it in piety or in thrift, no man can say. Few men know Prince Doria well. He has no wish to make news, or friends. He lives aloof from his time and State, an invalid, quite alone except for the hard, good, homely, Scottish nurse whom he finally married, and but for Orietta their young daughter; he has only one sister, and has never had a brother. Neither a prominent nor a powerful citizen, Prince Doria. And yet when death comes to take him it will take a good deal from this world. It will take an eight-hundred-year-old and princely name and all that centuries have bestowed upon it: Filippo-Andrea Prince Doria-Pamphili-Landi, Seventh Prince of the Holy Roman Empire von Torriglia, Thirteenth Prince of Melfi, Seventh Prince of San Martino and of

Valmontone, Prince of Naples, Nobile Romano Coscritto, Patrician of Genoa, Lord of Turbigo, of Ceriseto, of Rocca Massima
and Colleterro, of Castigliochetta, and of the Grottoes of St.
Stephen . . .

And so dies not Prince Doria merely, but all the Princes of
Rome and their proud families (princely because in their time
these families put or sustained a Pope upon his throne), and that
entire Roman aristocracy of which these families are the crests.
And a whole Italian aristocracy. Consider it in Rome alone and
you will behold that death, and the gestures of living that are essentially death throes.

Witness first of all how they are meaningless and incapable in
this new Italy, in the Fascist State, and even in those fields where
once they shone. For generations past, the only fields that the
aristocrats have held worthy of them have been the military service, statesmanship, the Church. Today, a hardy peasantry supplies the College of Cardinals with its ablest members; the bourgeoisie does the same for the Cabinet. In College and Cabinet
alike, noble names are few and third string; the old and princely
and semiroyal names are nil. Time was, before the War, when the
nobility could at least be proud of its cavalrymen. The old glamour still obtains, and some of the noblest Romans still do exhibition riding no centaur would scorn. But for all that, even the
horsiest Roman must realize that the automobile is here to stay—
and the airplane with it. And despite some few tryhards, no
Roman nobleman has specially distinguished himself in the new
glories of the air. Nor does the average aristocrat seem to be capable, either by background or by native intelligence, of making
much headway in the new and vital and rising—though as yet virtually nameless—aristocracy of Fascism.

There are, to be sure, exceptions. The Roman Church can
name, at least, the aged Prince Boncompagni-Ludovisi. He is the
only Prince of this time to take holy orders (though there are
plenty of high-born nuns); and his Church honored him as best it
might under the circumstances (he had begotten children) with
the title of Vice Camerlengo. His son, who was once a bank president, is now Governor of Rome. The ambitious and able but relatively nouveau Prince Potenziani (whose father's name was Gra-
binski and who, with his daughter as hostess, was Italy's master of

ceremonies at the Chicago Fair last year) has also held that office. Don Piero Colonna, who has declared of his cousin Prince Colonna that he "seems to think Roman society is his private property," is an official of Rome. Don Piero is perhaps the most dynamic of Roman noblemen and, a lover of Americanisms, he calls his wife Baby. As for nobility in business, the half-American son of Princess Jane di San Faustino (née Jane Campbell of New York, U.S.A.) works for Fiat. But mention these few and you have told of just about the only responsible noblemen in Rome.

Aldobrandini, Altieri, Antici-Mattei, Boncompagni-Ludovisi, Borghese, Caetani, Chigi della Rovere-Albani, Colonna, del Drago, Doria, Giustiniani-Bandini, Massimo (Lancellotti), Odescalchi, Orsini, Palestrina (Barberini), Rospigliosi, Ruspoli, Sacchetti, Salviati: such are the resonant and the proud-hearted names whose owners you might pass in any street in Rome and never know you had passed them. To the Holy Roman Church in its great time of temporal power most such families gave at least one Pope (to say nothing of whole shoals of Cardinals); and from Siena and from Florence and from Milan and from Genoa they followed him in flocks to Rome. Upon his nephews and upon those "nephews" who were sons, every such Pope bestowed the titles and the dignities and the vast wealth of land which none of their posterity that survives can forget. As the power of the Church waned, so waned the power of these great families. So far had it waned by 1922 that the March on Rome meant fairly little in their lives; the one historical event within centuries that made much difference to the Noble Roman occurred in 1870, and that, though its significance has faded, is still a red-letter year to him.

In 1870, after a couple of decades of turmoil, after Cavour and Garibaldi, a King was enthroned in Rome, the Pope's temporal realm was wrested from him, and he himself was relegated to the Vatican. And in Roman aristocracy appeared a rift as profound, if not so bloody, as that ancient one between Guelph and Ghibelline. The Caetani family deserted His Holiness, and all but handed Rome over to the House of Savoy. Victor Emmanuel brought Piedmontese aristocrats to Rome with him. Still other papal families swung to the King; and there were in Rome two aristocracies which were not on speaking terms, even of the most spiteful. The King's aristocrats called themselves "Whites," just to distinguish them beyond any fool's mistaking them from the loyal Papists, whose color, costume, and name have ever been "Black."

The Black aristocracy as a body retired in that year, with its Pope, in wrath and unto itself. In the Palazzo Colonna, the papal chair-throne was turned to the wall where still it remains turned. The Lancellotti bolted the main entrance to their palazzo and opened it again only in 1929, with the signing of the Lateran Treaties. The great Black family Borghese went green with shame upon the marriage of one of their in-laws to Mirafiori, the legitimized son of Victor Emmanuel II—not over bastardy in high blood, which was no novelty in Rome and isn't today—but over this involuntary kinship to the King.

The aged Princess Lancellotti, who saw that bitter time (and who, some Romans feel, is still the grim old keystone of all that is noble in Rome), still lives in it in anger and in scorn; and there are those of the old guard who share her feeling. Also you will find when you come right down to it that any member of any Black family is still pretty proud of the fact, still thoroughly aware of his value in Roman society. But long before the signing of the Lateran Treaties the old quarrel had ceased really to mean much. For all casual purposes, the Black-White distinction had merged into what the Roman socialite calls Gray.

Today, Roman aristocracy (which is Roman society) may be said to revolve around three courts. One is the court of His Majesty. One is the court of His Holiness. And one is the court of His Omnipotence, Benito Mussolini.

Whether the court of His Omnipotence may be called a court at all is food for later thought. Suffice it for the moment to say that it is a court without courtiers; a court in which the bourgeois industrialists or the revolutionary statesmen are with a few exceptions at present only figuratively aristocrats; though they may or may not be aristocrats-in-the making.

As for the court of His Majesty, it is perfectly proper to say that there is a court. There is a *maitre du palais*, there are assorted ladies-in-waiting, there is a court aristocracy, a mélange of great and not-so-great titles. But the Royal Family is a social entity only in the sense that it is the family-before-which-one-is-presented. These days, any Roman socialite, Black and White, or indifferent, is presented as a matter of form. These informal afternoon audiences occur once a month. And a couple of evenings a season, a big, dullish, catchall concert or lecture is arranged, and a lot of people politely attend. But with three of the four daughters and Crown Prince Umberto married, the Royal Family keeps to itself. The only other social event it stages is an occasional informal young people's party for Princess Maria who is nineteen, lovely and unmarried.

But there *is* a Roman court before which the Roman Princes and the Roman patricians are proud to do homage. That is the court which gave this Roman nobility its lifeblood. And it is the court whose sun and center is the throne of Peter the Fisherman.

On the very dais of that throne, chin-deep in hereditary costume and ready reverently and proudly to run any little errand His Holiness may think of, stands one of the two Princes Assistant to the Holy See. They are the well-to-do Prince Orsini and the wealthy Prince Colonna and here they divide the highest honor that may be bestowed upon a princely layman. They never serve before the pontifical throne together; they never so much as dine formally together. For the Orsini and the Colonna were enemies in the days when that meant blood in the Roman streets; the Latins are ritualists to the marrow; and the amenities of enmity must be observed.

These are the two greatest Black families. Prince Orsini and his second wife (by a former marriage in California, the mother of Mrs. Robert McAdoo), not better than well to do, are today put quite in the shade by dignified Prince Colonna and his rich Levantine wife. The latter marriage was frowned on by Rome's Nicer People, but the Colonna are nevertheless the real leaders in Roman society.

On a par, just a little below them, stand the Chigi della Rovere-Albani and the Massimo; and just a little below them are about a dozen princely families, all equally noble. The more recent the family and the fewer the great names it has given to the Church, the less that family counts, in secular society as well as ecclesiastical.

Of course the Church, a living hierarchy, still bestows titles, still has its orders of knights. Nor does it restrict itself to Italy. Plenty of prominent U.S. Catholics are knights of one or more of these orders; quite some few have titles granted by His Holiness himself, and when in the religious heart of Rome, they costume themselves accordingly. To these dignitaries, as indeed to the world in general, the old Black families can be as hospitable and as outwardly courteous as they are inwardly scornful, even of one another.

The Blackest of the Black families keep much to themselves and devote their lives to Church, Children, Charity. The Embassies to the Holy See are their special field of social activity. If you're a little less intensely Black, you give and go to two distinct kinds of party. There are those to which friends, diplomats, even Whites, and even the provincials and the drifters and the riffraff are asked. There are also those parties that are perhaps best described as ecclesiastical: to which only Cardinals and the Deadlier Nightshades among the Blacks are ever invited. Social climax of the Black year is the New Year's audience before the Pope, for which the nobles array themselves in deep black and their children pure white, read before His Holiness a stylized New Year's greeting, and go one by one before his throne to receive his New Year's blessing.

Such solemnities, be it observed, are what particularly make the Romans Romans. But religion and ritual and the hereditary honors don't, after all, take up much of their time. Vastly important in themselves and in the minds of the nobility, they are, nevertheless, chiefly a background for the social life from day to day. And of their life as it is lived, and of the noble Romans as they live it, there are a few things well worth bearing in mind.

One is that, taken en masse, they're broke. Stony broke, and used to it. For generations they have divided and subdivided their palazzi into small and smaller apartments-to-let; and today, not more than a half dozen of the best families so much as own the ancestral palace, the ancestral villa. From time immemorial their marriages have been *mariages de convenance*, but only within the past century have they had to go outside their own country to find profitable matches. In the nineteenth century English wives were stylish. Today (not to mention the Levantine Colonna, the Californian Orsini) the wife of Prince Bassiano, the only happily married Caetani, is a former Miss Chapin of New York. A Dusmet de Smours (background, the Sewickley Olivers;

dowry, steel) is Duchess Lante della Rovere. The gallant half-American Girolamo Rospigliosi, who has been running a liquor company in Manhattan, is married to Marian Snowden of Indianapolis and the fringes of Newport (it was love-for-love when she saw his fascinating rendition of the Black Bottom).

If you marry for convenience in a Catholic and nondivorcing country, the results are inevitable; and about the last thing to grow stale, in any decadent society, is the sexual instinct. It beats double time in Latin hearts. Count out the impossibly superannuated (and Roman noblewomen live to a great age), the supremely religious (not just the *very* religious), the woefully ugly, the happily married (and they are few), and the perverts—and remember that the husband is reasonably likely to be faithful to his mistress, the wife to her lover—and it is fair and true to say that concupiscence is epidemic among the better beds of the town. Another generalization worth remembering is that everybody pretty thoroughly despises everybody else and vastly enjoys saying so. (The men are capable of enmities downright feminine in their dramatic heat.) Social Rome beats any American village for gossip and the love of it; and Roman gossip may be mildly described as 90 per cent malicious, 90 per cent unassignable to any one person, 90 per cent true of some one or other, and more nearly 100 per cent unprintable.

Another thing that can hardly be conveyed is the great age of these families, the vast weight of that age, the vast weariness of that age that is upon the gayest of them. A symptom of that agedness is this: a good many of the old families are not only strapped but pretty well disbanded and on the way to extinction; and if you care to see a fair picture of that aristocracy as a whole, the half-dead are quite as significant to you as the half-living who within a few generations must surely follow them. The Massimo, oldest of Roman families, still inhabit the exquisite palazzo that Peruzzi designed, still have some wealth. But socially they are disappearing fast. And one of the reasons is peculiarly interesting. Back in the nineties all Rome was in mortal dread of the oldest Prince: he was suspected of being a *jettatore*—of having the evil eye. Few Roman aristocrats dare speak his name to this day. One of his sons, driven mad by their fear and loathing (girls he danced with made horns with the hand resting on his shoulder), leapt from a high window of the palazzo, suicide-bound. It did him no such harm because his fall was broken by an unsuspecting policeman, who was severely injured. It all managed to intensify everybody's suspicions about the curse that overdwelt the House of Massimo. The real evil eye, which is Time and Change and which it is quite useless even to fear, is doing its work quite thoroughly, if less melodramatically. You could tell of a dozen and a score of impecunious Princelings scattered abroad from Denver to Copenhagen, ill-married, obscurely laboring, forgotten in Rome. You could list a dozen and a score of splendid names—Borghese, Ruspoli, Altieri, Giustiniani-Bandini, Rospigliosi—all gathering slow impetus along the downward skids. And so it goes. And the best and the luckiest—the pious Odescalchi, Prince Doria, the Colonna—know well that in time they must follow. Meanwhile one of the few families that retains at least a sort of vigor is the Caetani.

The Caetani, for whom, around 1300, Boniface VIII bought $7,000,000 worth of land, gave the Holy Roman Church two Popes, the mothers of two more; they were the proudest and noblest feather in the Crown of Savoy when the run of aristocrats still cared to distinguish between White and Black. Since the death of the old Prince Onorato, who measured six and a half feet and reared sons nearly to match, they're perhaps a little more prompt at meals, and they have probably discarded the huge aromatic log of Bologna sausage which was their father's favorite fare; but their headquarters is still that dour palace in a Roman slum which depressed Vittoria Colonna into buying the Palazzo Orsini and which the American wife of Prince Bassiano once insisted upon leaving. They are still a race of scholars, a race of giants. Leone (six-foot four), Vittoria's allienated husband, left his great Oriental library to the State when he set out for Canada. Gelasio (six-foot two), former Ambassador to Washington, whose free and easy manners have made him the *vrai type américain* about Rome, is a bachelor. An antiquarian as well, he is writing a gigantic history of the family Caetani which reaches the sixteenth century in *libro ottavo.*

Such are the noble Romans. Such are they whose blood is Black enough to be blue. The little life they live can only surprise and disappoint you.

There are parties here and parties there but they are mostly neither here nor there. For the only parties in these days which retain any real style, any odor of oldtime opulence, are those given in Rome's Embassies. Rome, with Ambassadors to the State and Ambassadors to the Holy See (whither the U.S. sends none) is probably more swarmed with diplomats than any other city on earth; and Rome's society depends upon them heavily. The time is past when the best Black families received only themselves and the staff of the Spanish Papal Embassy. Today, everyone goes everywhere—and is critical of everyone. So that it is considerably to the credit of the U.S. that the smooth Ambassador Breckinridge Long and his wife so very popularly hold this, the most socially exacting of our ambassadorial posts.

Black clubmen go to the Circolo degli Scacchi, Whites to the Circolo della Caccia. Blacks, Whites, and Grays alike flock to the Circolo Bernini, which has its quarters in the Palazzo Ferraioli and which is a gambling club. Gambling as a diversion is almost as universally popular as gossip and lechery, and at present backgammon is even more popular than bridge. Rome's two famous hunts, the Roman Foxhounds and the Oriolo Foxhounds, have just been merged. Everybody hunts occasionally, the Prince Odescalchi, who is notoriously pious and is still wealthy, may be numbered among the more serious addicts: but Hunting on the Campagna is no longer quite the symbol and epitome of Roman high life that the American tourist thinks it is. Golf, since the Romans have discovered it, is an infinitely more popular sport; at present, it has put even tennis into the background. The Roman idea of a high old Roman time seldom goes beyond a lot of spaghetti and too much red wine and a flock of guitars. In other words, barring a few local differences, a high old Roman time is a good deal like, say, a high old Long Island time.

In short: ho hum. You don't need half an eye to see that it's a pretty dull life. And the curious thing is that what has been said of the more respectable fold covers as well the activities of the younger set and of the flashier and faster sets, and of the young members of the old families who can't stand the boredom. The gossip may be a little nastier, a little funnier, a little crueler over the backgammon boards at Princess Jane di San Fuastino's than elsewhere, but it's all of a piece. The fun may be a little more whirling in the parlors of Donna Dora Ruspoli (whose third marriage met with no shining ecclesiastical approval) but it's all of a piece, too. The Neapolitan Count Frasso and his wife Dorothy (who is the daughter of the late Bertrand L. Taylor, and who launched Gary Cooper in Venice) sometimes give mammoth gay parties at the Villa Madama; but Cecil B. De Mille wouldn't think they were mammoth or gay, unless he were a Roman aristocrat of the pious stripe. At their most bored and vicious, Rome's noble younglings become what the illustrated journals call Keen Motorists, and burn up those smooth-paved strade that their Duce has laid out along loveliest Italy; and break a few windows; and imitate Louis Armstrong on the cornet; and (perish the thought) drink hard liquor at Rome's few and ill-famed and seldom frequented night clubs.

And yet the wildest of them who has Black blood within him remembers it when his time comes. He's likely to turn up in the family stall at St. Peter's if time has honored him with a family stall. Even the gay-headed Prince Girolamo, who spends his substance far away in Manhattan, looks somewhat seriously forward to the time when devout Prince Giambattista dies, and he stands next in line for the gaudy uniform and the command of the Noble Guard. By such things are these Romans marked and set apart from the loud world about them as the Newport or even the London aristocrat can never be.

The Holy Roman Church, which is their heritage and their faith, plays a faint but constant ground bass to all their living time; and towards the time of death increases, and deafens them to all things else. For instance, the confraternity or guild called the Sacconi Bianchi admits three grades of member: Roman Princes, Roman nobility, and those Roman bourgeois who are lucky enough to have descended maternally from on high. Once a month two members watch all night before the Blessed Sacrament in St. Theodore's, vowing themselves to clean living, clean thinking, inward purity. But that is merely preparatory—the least a man can do who spends his life lightly as a Roman spends it. What this sodality amounts to in the long run is a burying society. When a member dies, the rest bear him in procession,

barefoot all and robed in white, to his grave, in a special cemetery; and there they bury him, with particularly simple rites. So
in due time will be buried the last of the Roman noblemen.
If you want to see new life in Rome, you had best look elsewhere. You had best seek out the immediate and powerful sources
that we have called the court of Mussolini; and best of all, consider Mussolini himself. To the man who is himself the new life in
New Italy, the Roman aristocracy means less than nothing. Rather
contemptuously, when upon occasion he decides to impress a foreign mission with a table load of noble names, he invites good
looking noblewomen to "fill in," tall noblemen to help change the
world's impression of the Italians as a runtish race. But he seldom
bothers to speak to his guests-of-an-evening. And they never in-
vite him to return the call, for they know very well that Il Duce
would never accept. His daugher, the Countess Edda Ciano, is,
of course, as powerful as she cares to be in any society she operates in. When she came back from her voyage to India loaded
with Maharajas' gifts and made what amounted to her Roman dé-
but, envious dowagers vented their spleen by complaining that
the Dictator's daughter seldom greeted them unless they rose
and came to her. They still rise, still come fawning, and still, behind Countess Edda's back, grumble at her brazen cheek. And
the *gerachi*, Mussolini's Bright Young Men (who, the pious hope
persists, can simplify passport troubles and maybe even modify
taxes), are invited everywhere. But if Mussolini himself gives
these noble families any second thought, it probably is in the pet
phrase of the Southern Gentleman: "They know their place."

As stated, Mussolini maintains a court without courtiers. He
rules a hierarchy without benefit of nobility—and does it among
a people whose hierarchic instinct is so powerful that in all its history it has built in hierarchies only; so profound and intense as to
be almost a religion. Despite strong-arming and castor oil—perhaps partly because of them—Mussolini is himself something of
an Italian religion.

And we must also remember that Mussolini has in his control
as powerful a hierarchic machine as the world knows; but its
wheels and its belts are industrialists and bourgeois statesmen.
Excepting a few who have sat up and begged for it (such as Count
Volpi) he has nobilified none of them. Nor is there present need.

But it may well be that the future will demonstrate such a need. Mussolini will not live forever. What manner of man, in the end, will succeed him, not even he can be sure. (But he has admitted that hereditary power has its points.) If the time comes when the Dictator himself—or his successor—cannot hold a people to him single-handed, then the hierarchs who surround and sustain him and who do his business must be dignified in the eyes of the nation by more than mere power of office and mere wealth can give them. And in that case, as one aristocracy declines, a new one is building in this day, of fresh blood and power: which within a few generations may be titled and blooded toward its height—and which within the course of a few more may die the death likewise.

THE
AMERICAN ROADSIDE

The characters in our story are five: this American continent; this American people; the automobile; the Great
American Road, and—the Great American Roadside. To
understand the American roadside you must see it as a vital
and inseparable part of the whole organism, the ultimate
expression of the conspiracy that produced it.

As an American, of course, you know these characters. This
continent, an open palm spread frank before the sky against the
bulk of the world. This curious people. The automobile you know
as well as you know the slouch of the accustomed body at the
wheel and the small stench of gas and hot metal. You know the
sweat and the steady throes of the motor and the copious and
thoughtless silence and the almost lack of hunger and the spreaded
swell and swim of the hard highway toward and beneath and behind and gone and the parted roadside swarming past. This great
road, too; you know that well. How it is scraggled and twisted
along the coast of Maine, high-crowned and weak-shouldered in
honor of long winter. How in Florida the detours are bright with
the sealime of rolled shells. How the stiff wide stream of hard unbroken roadstead spends the mileage between Mexicali and Van-
couver. How the road degrades into a rigorous lattice of country
dirt athwart Kansas through the smell of hot wheat (and this summer a blindness and a strangulation of lifted dust). How like a
blacksnake in the sun it takes the ridges, the green and dim ra-
vines which are the Cumberlands, and lolls loose into the hot

Alabama valleys. How in the spectral heat of the Southwest, and the wide sweeps of sage toward the Northwest, it means spare fuel strapped to the running board . . . Oh yes, you know this road; and you know this roadside. You know this roadside as well as you know the formulas of talk at the gas station, the welcome taste of a Bar B-Q sandwich in mid-afternoon, the oddly excellent feel of a weak-springed bed in a clapboard transient shack, and the early start in the cold bright lonesome air, the dustless and dewy road and the stammering birds, and the day's first hitch-hiker brushing the damp hay out of his shirt.

All such things you know. But it may never have sharply occurred to you, for instance, that the 900,000 miles of hard-fleshed highway that this people has built—not just for transportation but to express something not well defined—is by very considerable odds the greatest road the human race has ever built. It may never have occurred to you that upon this continent and along this road this people casually moves in numbers and by distances which make the ancient and the grave migrations of the Celt and the Goth look like a smooth crossing on the Hoboken Ferry. And it may never have occurred to you that the Great American Roadside, where this people pauses to trade, is incomparably the most hugely extensive market the human race has ever set up to tease and tempt and take money from the human race. For only just now are people beginning to realize that these five characters, as they function in relation to one another, combine in simple fact to mean a new way of life, a new but powerfully established American institution. And that the roadside, the most vivid part of this institution, is a young but great industry which will gross, in this, the fifth year of the great world depression, something like $3,000,000,000.

And even if you're aware of these things as they are, it isn't likely that you know just why they grew so fast, just why they are as they are. Because few Americans are really wise to themselves.

When we say point-blank that this institution, this industry, is founded upon just one thing, the restlessness of the American people, it still won't be clear. Because too many sentimental tourists have written of the joys of going "a-gipsying," have talked too much and too loosely of the American pioneer spirit.

The truth is, it isn't at all easy to say right.

God and the conjunction of confused bloods, history and the bullying of this tough continent to heel, did something to the American people—worked up in their blood a species of restiveness unlike any that any race before has known, a restiveness describable only in negatives. Not to eat, not for love, nor even for money, nor for fear, nor really for adventure, nor truly out of any known necessity is this desire to move upon even the most docile of us. We are restive entirely for the sake of restiveness. Whatever we may think, we move for no better reason than for the plain unvarnished hell of it. And there is no better reason.

So God made the American restive. The American in turn and in due time got into the automobile and found it good. The War exasperated his restiveness and the twenties made him rich and more restive still and he found the automobile not merely good but better and better. It was good because continually it satisfied and at the same time greatly sharpened his hunger for movement: which is very probably the profoundest and most compelling of American racial hungers. The fact is that the automobile became a hypnosis. The automobile became the opium of the American people.

After the autoist had driven round and round for awhile, it became high time that people should catch on to the fact that as he rides there are a thousand and ten thousand little ways you can cash in on him en route. Within the past few years, the time ripened and burst. And along the Great American Road, the Great American Roadside sprang up prodigally as morning mushrooms, and completed a circle which will whirl for pleasure and for profit as long as the American blood and the American car are so happily married.

If you wish to assure yourself, consider Exhibit A: the tourist cabin camp. Like the automobile, it is here to stay.

Much has been written about the auto cabin camp and most of it has been poking fun—at these curious little broods of frame and log and adobe shacks which dot the roadside with their Mother Goose and their Chic Sale architecture, their geranium landscaping, their squeaky beds, and their community showers. Most of the writing has been of the ancient Mencken school.

Only in the unornamented pages of a hotel association's annual report has the truth about them been approached. For only hotelmen, viewing them with alarm, have seen them for what they are, both a sound invention and a new way of life. The geraniums and the architecture are inconsequential; what matters is that they offer pure functionalist shelter and that they work. Just as surely as the great Greyhound bus company grew out of the jitney, an industry is growing out of the tourist cabin. Just because it works. And here is how.

It is six in the afternoon and you are still on the road, worn and weary from three hundred miles of driving. Past you flashes a sign DE LUXE CABINS ONE MILE. Over the next hill you catch the vista of a city, smack in your path, sprawling with all its ten thousand impediments to motion—its unmarked routes, its trolley cars, its stop and go signs, its No Parking markers. Somewhere in the middle of it is a second-class commercial hotel, whose drab lobby and whose cheerless rooms you can see with your eyes closed. Beyond, around the corner, eyes still closed, you see the local Ritz with its doormen and its bellboys stretching away in one unbroken greedy grin. You see the unloading of your car as you stand tired and cross, wondering where you can find the nearest garage. Your wife is in a rage because she has an aversion to appearing in public with her face smudged, her hair disarranged and her dress crumpled. All these things and more you see with your eyes closed in two seconds flat. Then you open them. And around the next bend, set back amid a grove of cool trees you see the little semi-circle of cabins which the sign warned you of. You pull in by a farmhouse—or a filling station, or a garage—which registers instantly as the mother hen to this brood.

If you are a novice the routine is so simple as to take your breath away. The farmer or the filling-station proprietor or either's daughter appears, puts a casual foot upon the running board, and opens the negotiation with a silent nod. You say "How much are your cabins?" He or she says "Dollar a head. Drive in by No. 7." He or she accompanies you, riding with ease of habit on the side of your car. You make your inspection. You do not commit yourself—as you do in a hotel—until you see your room. If you don't like it, you drive on—to the next cabin camp.

HERE BRIEFLY RESTS A RESTLESS TRIBE
The "prim, flimsy Miss Florida," the archetypal tourist cottage, "flourishes in the main stream of evolution of the roadside-lodgings industry." Americans were already beginning to know these places as well as they knew their own automobiles. Photograph by Walker Evans, courtesy of Estate of Walker Evans.

In this one you find a small, clean room, perhaps ten by twelve. Typically, its furniture is a double bed—a sign may have told you it is a Simmons, with Beautyrest mattress—a table, two kitchen chairs, a small mirror, a row of hooks. In one corner a washbasin with cold running water; in another, the half-opened door to a toilet. There is a bit of chintz curtaining over the screened window, through which a breeze is blowing. You think once more of the crowded streets ahead, you nod "O.K." and give the proprietor two dollars. He may, but probably won't, give you a card or a register in which to sign a name. He doesn't care what name you write because in case you seriously misbehave he has your car license number, noted as part of his professional routine. So he pockets the two dollars and walks away. That's all. You swing your car in between your cabin and the next. You unload what luggage you need; you have but a few feet to carry it. Inside you have just what you need for a night's rest, neither more nor less. And you have it with a privacy your hotel could not furnish—for this night this house is your own. And in the morning you will leave without ceremony, resume the motion you left off the day before without delay.

The point the satirist misses when he lampoons American folkways is that most folkways make sense. The American people have created the cabin camp because the hotel failed them in their new objective—motion with the least possible interruption. They have money to spend but not on the marble foyers of their forefathers. Their money is dedicated to motion; the cars in cabin camps are not cheap cars. So they have found the cabin camp good because it gives them just exactly what they want, simply and efficiently. And they made it multiply and they called it all kinds of names from the Wee Hame to Sevenoaks Farm, Mo-Tel to Auto Court.

The history of the cabin camp is lost in the dim antiquity of the twenties. Undoubtedly it grew from another indigenous institution, the automobile camp. The terms are often confused by ignorant landlubbers, but the automobile camp is quite a different animal, of an earlier era in the evolutionary scheme of things, and today hardly more than a vestigial appendage. The automobile camp is an even simpler mechanism than the cabin camp. In its truest sense it is a place to pitch a tent, a lot set aside with rudimentary sanitary facilities and a community kitchen or fireplace. When the great migration was young, automobile campers were regarded as a nuisance. At night you could, in say 1922, see their campfires for miles, a flickering fringe to the trunk roads which led out of the Middle West into California, down into Florida. Half in civic pride, half in self protection, towns along the migratory trails took to roping them off into convenient fields, giving them water to be sure they did not pollute the streams. Then some inspired misfit sowed the seed of a new profession by roping off his own back yard and introducing the profit motive into automobile camping—space free, food and services for gold. Another and another followed. The automobile camp became a cash crop. Then the next step, a henhouse or a rabbit hutch turned into a cabin for someone too lazy to pitch his tent. With the first cabin camp the seed of the last was sown.*

As a business, the individual cabin camp is indigenous and infinitesimal. That is its strength. The chain hotelman can't put the cabin man out of business any more than the mechanized farm can do away with the shack-and-ten-acres. Because each is the product of its own entrepreneur, because each administers without benefit of bookkeeping, and because the industry is quite definitely in the median stage of its evolution, most generalizations—and all specific examples—are misleading. But these observations are safe to make.

The "average" camp has between ten and fifteen cabins, figures its profit by subtracting direct costs from each month's take. Consider the books of the Armitage Cabins, which actually exist but which we shall place, for the sake of lifting the whole matter into the truer air of high generalization, square in the middle of Mr. Sinclair Lewis' mythical state of Winnemac. Mr. Armitage does not think in terms of "percentage occupancy" because capacity is so elastic. It depends of course on how many people he can get in each bed together. But with eleven cabins (theoretical capacity: thirty-one) at the standard rate of $1 per head (farther west he'd charge $2 per cabin), Mr. Armitage took in:

*There are still automobile camps and campers today but they bear the same relation to cabin guests that amateur wireless operators do to radio fans.

	In peak year (*1931*)	Last year
*April	$ 24.50	Closed
May	129.50	20.50
June	179.50	158.50
July	731.00	396.50
August	966.50	586.50
September	561.00	380.00
October	242.25	171.75
November	36.00	Closed
	$2870.25	1713.75

And his take for June, 1934 ($206), was better than for June, 1931.

Mr. Armitage *estimates* that he recovered 75 per cent of these sums. To understand the reason why neither Mr. Armitage nor any other cabin man *knows* just where he is coming out is to understand the whole industry. Mr. Armitage, for instance, knows he employs one man ($14 a week plus board and keep), one maid ($7 a week plus same); he knows his monthly bill for electricity is $20—including cost of pumping water; he knows it costs him twelve cents per couple to launder linen (four pieces at three cents). But Mr. Armitage does not know how to figure his own energy, which is terrific. Nor his wife's, which is pretty good too. Nor how to set up his cabins on his books even if he had any. Because Mr. Armitage went into the cabin business when rabbit raising wasn't what it had been cracked up to be and he cut the hutch into three cabins and opened them himself when his neighbor, who had owned a filling station, wouldn't buy them from him. He knows one new cabin cost him $300, but another came from a henhouse. And what price the rock garden he is so fond of, or the petunia landscaping? He considers them enormously important and they probably are.

There is an even more basic complication. Again typical, Armitage & Co. has two important subsidiaries: a filling station and a restaurant. A cabin camp without a restaurant and a filling station is a flower that has not bloomed. Yet, also typically, Mr. Armi-

*Plotted on a graph, this table would just about perfectly represent the classical every-summer all-state curve in touring. Regional variants will be noted later on.

tage's subsidiaries are not wholly owned. After the Standard Oil
Co. put in his pumps, it took all his time to run them. So he made
a deal with a bright young man (actually a couple of bright young
men because the first—and perhaps brighter—ran off with the
first six months' receipts). And this young man took over the station's operation for 50 per cent of the profits. But Armitage expects $500 from it this year. To launch the restaurant, which his
patrons clamored for, he sold the idea to two sisters who were
discontented managing a boarding house. He built the building—a friend who had inherited a little money helped him out
for an interest. The sisters ran it for a further interest. The sisters
didn't work out. Now it is in charge of a willing young lady who
took a course in restaurant running. She got the sisters' share for
her efforts. Armitage should get $500 from a 50 per cent stake in
her show. In all he may net $3,000 on his whole establishment
this year, on an actual cash outlay, over a six-year period, of between $20,000 and $30,000. He is out of debt except to his back-
ers to whom he still owes a few thousand, but part of his financing
has come from his profits in his own personal sideline: insurance.

The finances of most cabin camps are complicated by similar
situations. An excellent little camp called The Willows, near Lan-
caster, Pennsylvania, adds $2,000 a year from the swimming pool
which was the proprietor's start in the roadside business; and because he has carefully built up a local clientele—"local" means
recurrent parties from Baltimore, Washington, Philadelphia—
grosses as much as $9,000 from the restaurant. You could go on
like that forever. Some camps have vegetable stands; some toy ba-
zaars; not a few, radio dancing; many a local storekeeper runs a
camp as a sideline. You will in fact find every phenomenon of the
roadside when you inquire into cabin financing, but the important fundamentals are the same: their roots are deep in the
homely quality of individual initiative; they provide their promoter first with a living, second with a sense of accomplishment,
of having created something—no race so proud as the cabin camp
keeper's—and lastly, with a little cash at the end of the year—
sometimes for a trip on the road himself to scoff at his competitors, more often to plow back into his property.

No one knows how many such camps there are. The American
Automobile Association estimates over 15,000, and the only thing

you can be sure of is that figure is much too low. For there are a great, great many sorts and degrees of camp, and by the nature of things the A.A.A. is concerned only with the better of them. Besides the tourist cabin camp, which we have just discussed, there are two outgrowths which form each a class distinct unto itself. One is the Tourist Home, the New England and the midland and southern householder with a "Transients Accommodated" sign on the lawn. The signs work: The Tourist Home is one reason why the development of the Tourist Camp east of the Mississippi is relatively retarded.

The other is the super-cabin camp which, in its native habitat, California, attains such stature as to take your breath away. In California you find a camp the size of Venetian Court, at Long Beach, which cost $500,000 to build and which has 200 units. But really the significant thing about the huge, professional $8-a-night California camps (or Motor Courts, or Mo-Tels) is that they flourish nowhere in the U.S. but in that fervid clime. And the same goes for big business in general, for the chains in particular. Back in 1928, in the Middle West, one of the employees of Pierce Petroleum had a Vision—a transcontinental chain of Pierce-controlled roadside hotels. Five such two- and three-story hotels were built (with infirmary, nurse, and Renaissance rest rooms complete) at a cost of $2,000,000, and very attractive they were; and fine flops they have turned out to be, too. To Sinclair, which took them over along with Pierce in 1930, they mean an automatic annual loss of $20,000—which happens to be just the amount their creator laid out in genuine Currier & Ives prints to hang on their Colonial walls.

There's another chain—so far, to be sure, only a paper chain— being forged in Manhattan today. An ex-realtor named Calvin T. Graves, now President of Transcontinental Rest Cabins, Inc., is selling stock, and hopes to put up his first camp, his experiment, near Washington this fall. His camps will be distinguished for modern architecture, for Service and Comfort—and of necessity (since each will cost $50,000 to build) for a relatively high charge. Which any seasoned roadsider will tell you is rather dangerous.

One of these days there may very possibly be such chains strung along the landscape, listed on metropolitan exchanges. And then again there may not. Low overhead is the very essence of the industry and there is little that centralized management could contribute besides capital of dubious value. Besides which, a good swath of traveling America has got the little-camp habit and more and more of America, month by month, is getting it. Altogether, the thing to watch is the common-garden camp, which is even now, if slowly and not perfectly, surely moving out of the median and into the third and probably final stage of its development.

Signs and portents have been the legislation in the past few years and in many states (and often, it appears, at the instigation of alarmed hotels) which has required the tourist camp to live up to certain specified requirements—minimum size, running water, flush toilet, so on and so forth. By no means every camp has complied. By no means all could afford to. But those that have modernized have made things even more embarrassing for the hotels. In fact, it has made something like All the Difference. If further legislating is to be done, not the hotelman but the camp owner should see to it. For already, today, the cabin camp is a luxury to the workman, and every bit good enough for the lower middle class. When it achieves a prettiness satisfying to the delicate sensibilities of the upper middle class it will be all over with the hotels. For the tourist camp is one sound invention that the American roadside has contributed to the American scene. And as an invention it is more satisfying than the hot dog.

Not that the hot dog was, strictly speaking, a roadside invention, but the roadside took the hot dog for its own at a tender age and is responsible in very considerable measure for its growth and present prosperity. The hot dog, of course, was born frankfurter and came into this country late in the last century. Even after a gentleman named Mr. Harry Stevens made the epochal discovery that served in a roll it went well along about the seventh inning of a baseball game, the hot frankfurter might have stayed just another minor oddity had it not been for cartoonist T. A. (Tad) Dorgan. It was Dorgan who christened Mr. Stevens' invention and who, as his great and good friend, plugged it in the cartoons he drew for William Randolph Hearst's papers until the term became a part of the American vocabulary. The ball parks started its adventures westward, the roadside spread it from boundary to boundary.

Best known of all hot dogs (millions are locally made and name-less) are Gobel's. How many Gobel dogs are gobbled down the American maw becomes imaginable when you know that the Go-bel's gross for 1933 was $21,000,000 (the net loss was $242,000). Gobel, the good German, never cared for Mr. Dorgan's epithet, preferred the full word frankfurters or, in moments of intimacy, "franks." To roadside purveyors who agreed to spread refine-ment, he gave signs that employed the Christian name in full.

The hot dog is an American institution if there ever was one, yet it is possible to define the dog belts. Dogs are thick along both coasts, thickest east of the Mississippi. Westward comes the Bar-B-Q sandwich (the roadside name for mere roast meat—*not* real barbecued meat, which is spiced and basted over a trench of smol-dering hickory), holding its lead until it strikes the hot-tamale belt in the Southwest. Over the mountains tamale, Bar-B-Q, and hot dog march together into the dissonance of Southern Califor-nia. But it is down along the Gulf Coast that you will find the na-tive specials, of the snack-and-run sort, at their best—the creole pralines (solid chunks of pecans and brown sugar), the pecan pies, the jambalaya (meat, rice, and tomatoes, deeply spiced), the gumbo (thick soup with okra base, complicated by crab meat, oysters, or chicken), the heavily spiced and locally famous fried-fish sandwich which is peculiar to Bay St. Louis, Mississippi.

Early in the game the roadside took the ice-cream cone to its bosom. *Maestri* of the dairy industry have never interested them-selves in breaking down metropolitan and small-town sales as against the strictly tourist. But once again the roadside has pro-duced its own sub-industry in the so far generically nameless com-merce of distributing frozen sweets stuck to little wooden sticks by passing them out from trucks stationed at traffic-congestion points. Two great genera divide the field: the ice-cream sticks, chocolate-skinned, and the water-ice or sherbet sticks. Last year customers licked 1,000,000,000 sticks clean of ice cream, 300,000,000 of water ice. Prominent among a score of cold-stick companies are the Good Humor Corp. (ice cream) and the Popsicle Corp. (water ice). Good Humors first saw the Sunday evening twilight in Youngstown, Ohio, in 1923. Now some 20,000,000 of them each year are sold, mostly in the vicinity of New York—the whole ice-cream trade is heaviest with urban weekenders, not transients—

from 400 glistening trucklets by 700 glistening young men (a bath and a clean uniform every day). Popsicles, which are distributed through licensees, follow close in the Good Humor wake. Both companies hold their franchises with patent monopolies.

It makes no sense to try to add the roadside feeding to a hard and fast financial total—people guess at $630,000,000. To the All Hots and the Popsicles you would have to add the equally American wheelless roadside dining car, the less esoteric inns and restaurants. And the roadside stand.

Now there are stands and stands. Stands that started on shoe-strings and have become whole shoe stores. Such is the Log Cabin Farms near Armonk, New York, on Route 22. Its history is the history of the whole industry in miniature. It began with the shed that Farmer Frank Webster built in 1916, where first he marketed his rusty cider from a barrel with a tin cup. Next he tried selling hot coffee in his kitchen and soon he put out honey from his own hives. But it was his nephew whose name is Schmaling who really built up the place.

Webster Schmaling was an aviator in the War and when he came back he brought a fresh point of view. When an old friend from the Adirondacks visited him he found out how to build a log cabin and they built one from his own logs. Therein he laid out loaves of bread and plates of butter and cheese and let you make your own sandwiches to go with your cider. The place took its name from the building, rapidly acquired both a character and a clientele. Schmaling used to peddle corn around White Plains and Port Chester at two cents an ear delivered. One day he left a load hitched alongside the cabin. When he came back it was sold out—at two cents an ear on the spot. He never hauled another load: they put up a stand in front of the cabin and sold fresh farm produce in season, and homemade ice cream and cake. The next winter Schmaling fooled around with doughnut recipes and by summer (1920) they had added doughnuts and a soda fountain. Financing: out of profits, typically. And what were the profits? Well, in 1922 Uncle Webster retired to Florida on his share. The log cabin's first financial melon had been split.

Nephew Schmaling built a log kitchen and spent $2,200 on a nickel-slot violin. In no time the machine had brought in $4,000 and Schmaling was hiring twenty-five helpers regularly for the weekend trade. In 1924 he bought the big (2,200 gallons per day) cider mill. But the War had made him airplane crazy, he wanted to fly again and gradually he lost interest in Log Cabin Farms. On that day in March, 1929, when Mitchell saved the market, an old visitor drove up with a new light in his eye. He had heard that the Log Cabin Farms was for sale. August Hussar was a Brooklyn farm-produce jobber who had been playing the market on the side and who was losing faith. He wanted to get out before it was too late, and he'd always wanted a farm. That evening Schmaling mentioned a bottle of rye with which he was going to christen a new plane. Hussar said: "If you'll open that bottle instead of breaking it, I'll buy the farm." Schmaling opened the bottle.

The next morning Hussar had forty-five acres, 800 feet of frontage on Route 22, the cabin and the stands, the house and the barn and the big mill, eight cows, 5,000 White Leghorns, and a great flock of unsold hot dogs. And Schmaling, who now runs the Bedford airport, had $165,000 in cash—the second fortune to come out of the roadside stand.

The next year Hussar added his big $2,500 dining room; he designed it himself and his help built it, with flooring from a seminary in Valhalla and leaded windows from the Florsheim (shoe) estate and cigar and beer and sandwich counters out front. The plant was just about complete. Hussar's taste in the rustic is as sound as his predecessor's—the walls support stuffed animal heads, the chandeliers are cider jugs, and it costs Hussar $300 a year to renew the imitation branches and leaves. The room is kept very dim on purpose, lady motorists like it like that. Nowadays a ten-piece orchestra plays each night and Hussar carries about $10,000 worth of beer and liquor (gin's the favorite) in stock. A lot of people still bring their own but he has less trouble with drunks now than in the old days. The theft of stuffed animals (about a dozen a year) and similar keepsakes is the bother now: that and the ladies' room—"my God they even swipe the tiles off the wall—I'm not kidding." But all in all it's worth it and more. On big nights as many as a thousand guests crowd the dining-dancing place, and counting in the stands and all, Hussar rates very near a million visitors a year, and hopes to take in $175,000 in 1934. Out of it he may net $20,000.

Other histories, other figures. The typical part is the growth, curiously unplanned and apparently inevitable—from an unadorned farmyard, alongside a numbered route, to a posperous local industry. And the succession of owners, one step in the family, one out, all happenchance. Such expansions are not plotted about mahogany tables. Nor are the annual reports bound in calf. Hussar's Log Cabin is a bigger show than Mr. Armitage's Cabin Camp, but his figures are hardly more revealing. He does not break down his income: beer and broilers are one to him. His 1933 expenses he would note something like this:

To 56 employees who live on the place:	
Salary amount	$46,000
Board account	18,000
To poultry farm (feed, repairs, etc.)	15,000
For groceries (bought over and above his own produce)	40,000
For fuel and light	5,000
For "ice cream, candy, and cigars"	10,000
For laundry (he uses no table linen—aprons and coats only)	1,000
For paper napkins	1,000
Miscellaneous	8,650
	$144,650

Against this he took in $160,000. Net: $15,350.

If Mr. Hussar has a specialty it is his doughnuts. But essentially he is an "all-purpose" roadside stander. Throughout the land you are more likely to find standmen concentrating on fresh vegetables, or beer and hot dogs, or duck dinners, or Colonial atmosphere, or whatnot. Their color changes with the color of the soil. The only sound geographical generalization is that theme song of the roadside: "They're dizziest—and busiest—in California." In California, too, flourishes the racket type, the stand that buys its "fresh from the farm" vegetables fresh from the nearest city market, trucks them back into the country, and marks them up smartly for gullible housewives. For in Southern California at least it is almost a tradition for housewives to buy perhaps half their vegetables along the roadsides, and with such a volume the temptation to cheat seems irresistable.

Hot dogs, diners, ice-cream cones, roadside rests, vegetable stands, and all the rest—even $630,000,000 may be too low a figure for their yearly take, a guess small enough to be insulting. But if you use it few men will take issue with you, for few have intelligent figures with which to argue. Best of the latter are the computations of the American Automobile Association. Of the average American on tour, that estimable organization has this to say:

He drives a car that cost him $773 F.O.B. It is inevitably a sedan. For America, which loves the Open Road and which loves To See Things, likes even better the comfort of a closed car.

He takes along, besides himself, 2.5 persons (which makes proper allowance for the half-grown and insatiable child who is so valuable to the roadsider).

He covers 234 miles per day and, assuming that he spends a week getting where he's going and another week coming back, he rolls up a total 3,276 miles.

On his way he spends about $7 per person per day. The $7 breaks down thus:

One dollar forty for transportation costs, which include gasoline, garaging, and accessories bought en route. One dollar forty of it goes for lodging. One dollar forty-seven cents goes to restaurants and to eating places of all types. One dollar seventy-five cents of it his wife takes good care of: this goes in exchange for linens, lotions, goggles, kodak films, postcards, beads, baskets, pottery, blankets, antiques, balsam cushions, and so on ad lib., ad infinitum. Forty-two cents more goes into candy, ice cream, hot dogs, and similar roe. And fifty-six cents of it goes to theatres and to places of amusement. How all this breaks down further between the drugstores and the retail stores in the towns as distinguished from roadside trading posts, no man can say. But any man who has taken the average American's trip knows, better than figures could tell him, this all-important fact: that more and more powerfully, the habit is upon us to refuel and eat and sleep and amuse ourselves not in the towns as towns—they slow us up—but along the open roadside which is a new kind of town in itself, and in the little towns that have all but turned themselves into roadsides.

And just in case the breakdown seems insignificant, minuscule, remember that the man in the $773 sedan multiplies to the extent of some 8,000,000 such cars bearing around the country some 28,000,000 spending human beings, and that in a year their money adds up to:

Transportation	$600,000,000
Lodgings	600,000,000
Retail Goods	750,000,000
Food	630,000,000
Amusement	240,000,000
Confections	180,000,000

Remember, too, that nobody knows how heavily the short-drive and the weekend trades and the roadside trade that comes with the drive-to-Maine-to-spend-the-summer swell this total. And remember also that this conservative total $3,000,000,000 is more widely and steadily and variously distributed throughout the whole country than any other $3,000,000,000 you could name. Which gives significance to the fact that this figure is up 20 per cent since last year.*

But widely distributed as this trade is, the tides that float it can be charted. To begin with, always seeking paths of low resistance, they flow first along trunk routes—the Broadway of America, the Meridian trails, the nameless conglomeration that is universally known as Rowt One, and the rest. Along these great migratory trails, this people moves in the following habitual waves: every winter they swarm southward from the Middle West and the Lake States toward the Gulf, and mail home a somewhat gruesomely carved and ornamented Florida coconut. Every spring and summer the South swarms toward the westward fingers of the Great Lakes and buys from Wisconsin Indians the Indian souvenirs made in Japan and Rahway. Every summer a great hinterland wave converges on unwelcoming Manhattan and another washes clean through the peak of New England and another swales across Kansas and bravely tries to fall in love at first sight

---

*Although sharply hit by repeal, even American touring in Canada is up.

of the disappointingly blunted, scarcely perceptible line which they know means the great Rockies ahead. Winter and summer alike the restless waves flex and reflex among the palms and the lush stage props of California: in winter, the native sons themselves get into their cars and swim over the roadstead making love to their state in a touristic-narcissistic orgy which reaches its peak about the middle of February. And every summer, by the thousands upon thousands, come the out-of-staters, to get an eyeful of all they've seen before or heard tell of. They expect outlandishness—and they get it.

For two years a Chicago Fair has caused a concentric swirl of cars by the million. And if you don't believe in the power of hearsay, consider this story: last winter a certain Texaco official, Stuart Hawley, who does a good deal of driving around, decided that it would be fun to see if, singlehanded and out of whole cloth, he could start a migration into the beautiful and neglected Northwest. So, at an Illinois gas station, he would observe: "Back East they're all talking about Montana." And in a Connecticut gas station he would observe: "Down South they're all talking about Washington and Oregon. It's great country all right." And the result is that the first waves of discovery have begun to lap the northland shores and 250,000 cars are expected.

The Northwest is news as a freshly discovered tourist mecca. But the painted deserts of the Southwest are a decade-old fixture. So also is that intensely tourist-conscious state, Virginia; and Colorado, which spends $250,000 a year publicizing itself. Yet remember that the least tourist conscious of all is the island of Manhattan through whose Holland Tunnel and across whose ferries and bridges come 9,125,000 each year, to be ignored by the inhabitants, absorbed by that city. In the winter the invasion is more apt to come from the West, in the summer the South takes over. Of chief interest to Midlanders are the Ozarks. The anthropologist would concern himself with this habitat of the most primitive of American Whites, but to the tourist trade the Ozarks are more likely to mean Caves.

The cave is something very special in the roadside life. Not quite fish and not quite fowl, it combines the art of nature and the art of the entrepreneur. Yet it is pure roadside, for it is an institution built by and for the roadside. And few of the uninitiated real-

ize its extraordinary growth as a commercial venture in the last
few years. A good cave may gross $150,000 a year.

The raw material for this money-making contraption is an underground opening whose limestone walls have been intricately
fretted by aeons of falling ground water, carbonic-acid charged. It
is more valuable if it twists and turns mysteriously, if it boasts a
still pool (always called an "underground lake") or a running
stream (forever the "River Styx"), if it is replete with arches, clus-
tered stalactites, narrow winding passages. Such underground
openings are not uncommon throughout the limestone mountains
of the eastern seaboard and you may chart the cave belt as winding through the states of Pennsylvania, Virginia, Kentucky, Tennessee, and Missouri. There are literally hundreds of caves here-
about, half-explored, unexploited.

The finding of such a cave is, for commercial purposes, merely
the first step. And the least expensive one. For all roadside at-
tractions the cave takes the greatest capital to exploit. Investigate
and you will find shafts sunk to reach them (some have elevators).
You will find $100,000 "lodges" built over the entrances—to
house rest rooms, lunch counters, and, above all, souvenir stands.
Uniformed attendants will lead you along gravel and concrete
paths, carefully cleared. All good caves are electrically lighted,
often with ingenious indirect effects. Each point of possible interest is named, the bent being for whimsey and romance.

When you have seen these things you will have followed the
march begun by such humbler caves as Floyd Collins' and Tom
Sawyer's—though the latter, perhaps the longest-commercialized
of caves, clears a steady $10,000 a year, in the teeth of its gaudier
young rivals. You will have seen the Luray (Virginia) and the
Mammoth (Kentucky) Caves. The Carlsbad (New Mexico) and
the Howe (New York) Caverns—to name but four. And of the
four, the Howe Caverns will serve you for a case history of cave
promoting.

Lester Howe discovered them in 1842 but there wasn't much
touring in those days and in 1927, when a Syracuse steam-heating
engineer named John Mosner and a Syracuse lawyer named Virgil
Clymer went out to look over the lay of the land, they had been
closed to the public for forty years. A cement company had
blocked off the entrance, but the gentlemen got options on the

land that overlay them and sold stock among their friends. Here the blazed trail of roadside financing crossed the boulevard of U.S. industry and the roll includes such titles as President of the Audit Bureau of Circulations (P. L. Thompson—also of Western Electric), former head of Cluett, Peabody (Walter H. Cluett), the President of Batten, Barton, Durstine & Osborn (William H. Johns), and also one shoestring king (Richard Ward). It took these gentlemen two years and they sank just short of a half million in putting their caverns in shape—concrete shaft, boat on precious lake, and all. On May 27, 1929, the opening day, 2,200 people paid $1.50 each and sank 156 feet by elevator into what any cave entrepreneur would describe as fairyland. They walked through two and a half miles of phantasmic beauty named, among other things, the River Styx, Juliet's Balcony, the Alcove of Angels, Dante's Inferno (lighted in red), the Temple of Titan, the Home of the Fairies, the Pipe Organ, the Lagoon of Venus, the Winding Way, the Sleeping Fountain of Somnus, and the Silent Chamber. And then they rose to the surface—"marvelling anew," says the Howe folder, "over the profoundness of it all." And pleased enough to find that an attendant had wired little plates to their rear bumpers, plates which would advertise Howe Caverns the country over; no charge.

There were 86,000 visitors in the Caverns' first year—gross take: over $130,000 on an investment of $500,000. Howe Caverns, Inc. has back the $80,000 it had to borrow when its shaft struck shale, has earned reserves of $66,000 for depreciation and a surplus of $24,000; and it has paid $54,000 in dividends. Last year for the first time, with but 58,000 in attendance, it went into the red; but so far this year, thanks considerably to advertising campaigns conducted by Batten, Barton, Durstine & Osborn, attendance is 30 per cent ahead of 1933.

Caves are merely the most clearly realized, the most neatly exploited, of those minor lodestones that finally draw the traveler to a halt and his silver from his pocket. The lodestones, as you may have gathered, are somewhere near infinite in number and variety and strength: they run all the way from a dyspeptic bear with an insatiable appetite for Coca-Cola to the great World's Fair at Chicago. And they swing all the way back through such items as the World's Biggest Sweet Peas in Orlando, Florida (fifteen feet tall, floodlighted at night), and the grave of General Lew Wallace at Crawfordsville (Athens of Indiana), and near Lexington *Man O' War*, the grizzling mild sovereign of his race. You could go on like that forever. The American autoist does, reacting delicately to the wonders of this land out of the midst of his easy coma, in ways so revealing of his inmost mind that someone must one day do a trilogy in his honor, in full homage to his roadside. The work won't date, we can assure you. Not, at any rate, before the spirit that most deeply moves this people is tamed out of their blood.

T.V.A.:
WORK IN THE VALLEY

The mountains and blue lapsing hills are encysted with time-wrought wealth: coal and iron by the thousands of millions and limestone and fat clays by the billions of tons, and bauxite and copper and zinc and manganese and barytes and mica and olivine and kyanite and silky talc and, in all, not less than forty of the minerals most useful to mankind. All these await, for the most part, cheap power and the new processes that cheap power will make feasible. And the silver rivers yellowing and widening with weight of clay, which bind this valley into unity deeper than man can fence his states; a linkage and veinage of moving waters ill-kempt for navigation, capable of apoplectic flood, but muscled with a munificence of power that man has scarcely touched.

Steep land planted to corn, runneled and ruined with rain; flat land planted to cotton, worn and warped like a wrecked heel. A new season spreading its smoke on the air and its health on the earth. Cities that you would describe as provincial; towns you would describe as rube; farms so pitiable you would be sure to laugh at them. In fact if tall talk has led you to believe that by now TVA must already have changed the face of its valley, you are much mistaken. It is the same with the valley's two million people.

Yet they are all very well aware that TVA is at work. As for their several attitudes, they're precisely what you might expect. Every man is most interested in himself. A Knoxville businessman who was born and raised upstate feels TVA may talk a good deal but that anything TVA can do to raise the standard of living is all to the good. A La Follette undertaker to whom has fallen the job of removing several hundreds of the coffins, at $20 a shot, from the Norris Reservoir area, holds that TVA is doing a fine work. A Knoxville marble man is not so sure about the wisdom and efficiency of his government. Here is TVA babbling all manner of bright talk about putting the valley on its feet: here on the other hand are Morgenthau and Ickes asserting that of the millions to go into new public buildings, not a dollar shall be "wasted" in making "mausoleums" of them—calmly slitting the throat, in fact, in the name of economy, of one of the leading industries in a valley the government is spending still other millions to bring to life. The Mayor of Tupelo, on the other hand, is all smiles, and they are all genuine smiles, for his was the first of all towns to crouch at the brink of TVA's cheap power, and drink. A share cropper a few miles above Wheeler Dam, on still another hand, is anything but smiles: TVA has bought the land he farms right out from under him; he gets no money; what is he to do?

And so on. Speaking more generally: Republican families in the northeastern mountains are all but convinced that Democrats are capable of honest intentions. In such dealings as they have had, they have found TVA no sucker and no bleeder; eager with suggestion; carefully never officious in following it up. They are favorable; and still a little skeptical; they will wait and see. The people of the southwest are grateful to Mr. Roosevelt as for rain from heaven: for the first time since reconstruction, the government is paying them attention: this time, they are convinced, the attention is benevolent. The only real trouble: they are so eager for help that they forget to help themselves. They have repeatedly asked TVA to help them organize and to speak at demonstrations against the utilities—a thing which of course TVA has had firmly to refuse. Just here, in fact, you approach the core of one of TVA's major problems.

TVA knows that it is, among other things, a passel of smart Yankees descended to improve a tetchy people; knows also the limits of its power; knows also that the more independently a man helps himself, the better off he is. For which wise reasons, TVA is most extraordinarily shy of stepping over the line. It must, very delicately, put ideas into the valley heads; then sit tight and wait for the valley to come and ask. What TVA also knows but may not

realize seriously enough—such realization may be impossible—
is that generations of poverty and habit breed a quite indescribable inertia; that hopeful and faintly skeptical apathy and an almost childlike dependence are in general very possibly the live-
liest attitudes that can be hoped for without very considerable
guidance from above. And granted even that, are your troubles
over? When all is said and done, the real crux of the problem is
simpler and more cruel: ideas are practiced by and upon human
beings, who fulfill them only more or less workably, never perfectly. The better the idea, the more inevitable the compromise.

So much, in a broad-spoken way, for the valley and its people.
As for the people who are responsible for carrying out the enormously ambitious and complex job that is TVA, there are, in all,
some 12,000 of them. You may see them swarming like mites on
the rising bulk of Norris Dam, of Wheeler Dam; buying and
clearing and damming the steep land long miles above those
dams and burning all brush so that even the soft May landscape
sours with autumnal smoke; boring into the earth and stone
where Pickwick Landing Dam will rise; swathing soft slopes of
land with terraces; training up seedlings by the million, the next
forest generation; at watch in the huge white hall where Wilson
Dam broods power; at work in the phosphate lands and in the
monstrous nitrate-phosphate plant at the Shoals; at work in scores
and hundreds of offices—at Muscle Shoals (the official headquarters) in officers' Wartime quarters revised for business: at work in
Chattanooga in the wild omelet of limestone which is the Old
Post Office; in ramshackle Temporary Building F in Washington,
where none can smoke and a Director up on business can hang
his hat; in Knoxville, the field headquarters, in East Tennessee.
Above all in smoky Knoxville, where 1,100 errand boys and typ-
ists and accountants and statisticians and architects and geologists
and geographers and pressmen and lawyers and executives and
coordinators and directors, crammed into five office buildings,
tend their Authoritative muttons.

For the best beginning, get up about seven (for Knoxville business starts at eight) and, after breakfast, walk up sooty Gay Street
and turn down smudgy Union and on past Market Square straight
on to the New Sprankle Building, a block this side of the Masonic

THE VALLEY LAND
Although some of the land in the Tennessee River valley was still arable
and excellent, all was "subject to the spreading murder of erosion,
which unhindered could make all the South one desert." Photograph
by Charles Krutch, courtesy of TVA.

CURING THE LAND
"On steep land the CCC builds check dams, covers the barrens with
brush mats. On land less steep farmers lay open terraces (the four
parallel bands) which hem the hillside fast." Then the land would be
ready for fertilizers and crops. Photographs by Charles Krutch,
courtesy of TVA.

Temple. Go upstairs and through the brisk bare corridors into
one of the brisk bare offices and there, if you are lucky, you will
find yourself face to face with the very men who run this show.
They are three: two of them soberly dressed, sixtyish, one
rather sportily dressed, in his middle thirties. The man with the
broad hands, the heavy, delicately cut aquiline head, is Dr.
Arthur E. Morgan, onetime hydraulic engineer, famed President
of Antioch College, and Chairman of the Board of Directors of
the Tennessee Valley Authority. The man with the drawled, hu-
morist's mouth and the stringy body of a farmer is Dr. Harcourt
Morgan, onetime President of the University of Tennessee and a
member of the Board of Directors; and if you would have him as
he is you must temper that picture with light washes of cultivation and of city living. The quick-handed, quick-faced man is David Eli Lilienthal, who is one of the more brilliant of the Frankfurters who populate New Deal offices, who has seen service on
the Wisconsin utilities front, and who is the third of the directors
of TVA. When, in July, 1933, these three men first met in the valley and set up their tent, they were three men alone, and their
first task was to understand how their whole job hung together.

TVA is a corporation created by the Tennessee Valley Authority Act, which was Roosevelt's development on Senator Norris's
hard-fought Shoals theme. It was granted by Congress an initial
$50,000,000 (appropriations total $75,000,000 to date, of which
some $70,000,000 is spent). Primarily, TVA is in the valley for the
purpose of developing the Tennessee River system for navigation
and flood control. That means, first of all, building dams. When
you build a dam, however, a great many things happen at once.

In the first place, you back up water and you generate power.
More power, a lot more perhaps, than you'll need to operate the
locks, which are a part of your development-of-navigation program. It would be criminal waste not to make use of this surplus power. Therefore you sell it—to farmers, municipalities,
industries.

Also when you build a dam, especially if it is in steep, loose-
landed country, you must look to your reservoirs; you must bring
erosion under control. The control of erosion breaks into two
parts: reforestation and just plain erosion control. For the latter,
if you are to grow healthy and tenacious cover crops, you need

fertilizers; particularly you need phosphate fertilizers. With phosphate beds in the heart of the valley, with a plant to hand at Muscle Shoals, you make them and use them.

But you don't own all the land that drains into the river; farmers own most of it. Aside from your basic (and legalized) interest in the welfare of the farmer as a member of society, there is an entirely hardboiled reason why you should consider him seriously: potentially, he is a voracious power customer. He needs money to pay for his power; he also needs to be persuaded—as he best can be by an improved standard of living—that he wants and, indeed, needs it.

Good soil, planted right and kept good, will help enormously. Hence your expansion of the erosion-control program to include terracing, fertilizer, and planting demonstrations. But he can farm the land and more besides. Suppose, for instance, he learns to use and to market the natural resources that surround him. And suppose he can find part-time work in factories. Here, from several paths at once, you converge on industry.

The farmer needs extra money, extra work; TVA needs two kinds of customers: farmers and new industries. There is much to be said, to the advantage of everyone concerned, for a balancing of industry and agriculture. To certain types of industry—notably the electrochemical, the electrometallurgical—cheap power is of prime importance; it so happens that your valley is rich not merely in cheap power but in the very resources essential to those particular industries.

It therefore behooves you to study carefully those resources, to heel yourself, in fact, with every sort of information that may be of value to industrialists interested in setting up shop in the region. And to know your land and its people and all that is actual and potential in them, from stem to gudgeon: and so to determine each detail of their present that it shall build without waste or conflict into the future which is likewise your responsibility.

Here, then, assembled according to their more salient and simple interrelations, you have the several parts of a social-industrial-agrarious creature—or rather, the mirage of the whole creature it is your business to create. When you go about creating it you find out this in short order: TVA is authorized to build dams, to operate them, to sell power, to develop good fertilizers.

Beyond that, TVA has no power whatever. TVA is authorized only to guide. It can be useful as a guide by having ready to hand information so valuable and so thorough and patently wise and far-sighted that industrialists and farmers can but use it as the best of all possible advice—and by working eternally in cooperation with county and state and federal agencies.

Here, if you like, is a difficult hole. Wouldn't it be far more convenient and to the point if, to be brief, TVA *owned* the valley and the people in it? The answer is, that it might indeed be far more convenient and to the point. There are many names for it these days, and Socialism will do. The facts, again, are different. The way good work is done by a democratic government in the fourth decade of the twentieth century is the way TVA is doing it.

To return to the directors themselves, their duties are of two kinds. To determine in conclave all matters whatever of policy and project and procedure, and individually each to boss specific chapters they have divided thus:

A. E. Morgan supervises everything to do with the dams; all regional planning and housing; the educational and training program (barring agriculture); all engineering; everything to do with raw material for fertilizer; all social and economic organization and planning; and forestry. He shares with Harcourt Morgan all matters pertaining to industry besides the duties of administration and of the coordination of a unified program.

Harcourt Morgan has charge of everything to do with agriculture, including both the entire fertilizer program (barring raw materials) and the planning of rural life and the relation of local industries to agriculture.

David Lilienthal looks after the distribution of power; the operation of the electrical generating plant at Muscle Shoals; the purchase, construction, and operation of transmission lines; power accounting; and, in fact, the whole electrical division, whose headquarters are at Chattanooga. He is also in charge of the legal department and of everything to do with land buying.

These men make their decisions never singly, always mutually. They are perhaps most notably distinguishable thus: Lilienthal for uncommon legal sophistication, for boldness, for impatience of compromise. Harcourt Morgan for temperate skepticism and for his absolute knowledge of valley people, valley folkways, valley politics. A. E. Morgan for his ability as an organizer and above all for the breadth and immediacy of his conception of the job as a job that begins and proceeds and ends in terms of human beings. What this means in the way of results is that each man in turn balances and rectifies into single focus the two sharply differing points of view that belong to his profoundly individualistic colleagues.

Just how the task was skeletonized into articulate action and just how the skeleton was fleshed with human beings we must pass over briefly. But you should be aware of that scrupulous and utterly nonpolitical care with which the whole country was sifted for keymen and their assistants; of the care likewise with which 100,000 applicants were screened and screened again for the few thousand workmen who would best do the work and who would best absorb TVA's training. Let us now train our lenses upon those workmen themselves and upon the work they are doing.

First of all TVA's jobs—the stone dropped in the pool—is to build dams. TVA is at present well over a third done with $34,000,000 Norris Dam and just under half done with $38,000,000 Wheeler Dam and just getting going on a new $22,000,000 dam at Pickwick Landing near Shiloh field. It plans within the next decade to build three more dams, the Hiwassee and the French Broad (both storage) and the Aurora (run-of-river), whose costs are estimated at respectively $13,000,000, $30,000,000 and $42,000,000. That's not all—complete development of the Tennessee River would (and in time may well) involve the building of twenty to thirty dams—not all, but more than enough for the moment. Let us consider only those that are on the immediate fire. Here is what they will mean for navigation, for flood control, for power development. *Navigation:* the Pickwick Dam will back water to the toe of Wilson Dam; Wilson Lake lies back fifteen miles to the foot of Wheeler Dam; Wheeler Lake will stand eighty-six miles back to Guntersville, Alabama. All told TVA's first three dams will provide 358 unbroken year-round miles of channel whose minimum depth will be seven feet, from Paducah at the mouth to Guntersville. In the long run the river will be navigable plumb to Knoxville. *Flood control:* the average annual flood damage for the basin comes well over $1,000,000, a good three-quarters of it upstream from Wilson Dam, and most of that at Chattanooga.

Norris, blocking one of the principal tributaries, will cut this damage at very least in half. The Hiwassee and French Broad dams should bring the toll almost to nil. In the long-range terms TVA thinks and works in, it isn't beside the point to observe that out of flood salvage alone Norris Dam will pay for itself within seventy years. *Power*: storage dams build up power at distances and steady its production to a year-round level: they must be operated as part of a system. Norris Dam during most of the year will be storing water and generating no power. During the low summer months its two 50,000-kilowatt generators will be pressed into service, and the water released will level up production at Wheeler, at Wilson, at Pickwick, and at all subsequent run-river dams TVA may build.

Let us first consider at some length Norris Dam and Norris Town and all that relates to Norris. For here is TVA's first big job and here, in action and in accomplishment, is TVA in microcosm.

Norris Dam is being plugged into a 400-foot gorge on the Clinch River, twenty miles northwest of Knoxville and 232 miles as power flies—when the transmission line is built from Wilson Dam. If statistics have power to charm, here are a few: its over-all length will be 1,872 feet; it will be 210 feet thick at the thickest of the base; it will stand 266 feet tall from the lowest part of the foundation to the twenty-foot roadway that will cross the top. It will back water up the tattered valleys of the rivers Clinch and Powell some forty-seven miles, creating a reservoir with an overall capacity of 3,650,000 acre-feet, a 775-mile shore line—one of the largest reservoirs on earth. The dam itself will be one of the six or eight largest ever built. Together with the powerhouse that will buzz upon its down stream toe, it will comprise 1,030,000 cubic yards of concrete.

All this is being built in limestone, honeycombed country, and the first and arduous job was to check against reservoir leakage and the stability of the site itself. The foundation was clay—seamed and not necessarily trustworthy dolomite. You find out what to do about that as you plug a watermelon: by making and examining core drillings. At long last informed and satisfied, the builders washed all seams under pressure and, under pressure, forced cement grout into the drill holes. A continuous grout curtain thirty to fifty feet deep underhangs the entire dam and from each grout hole a steel bar stands up, to anchor the dam. It was only then that such work could get under way. Meanwhile, work is in progress upstream.

Upstream, TVA is buying some 150,000 acres of land. Of this, 45,000 acres will be under water at flood time; the rest TVA is buying in the interests of policing its reservoir and of controlling soil erosion. The job of buying this land—over 80 per cent of it is bought to date—from farmers and of helping them move elsewhere and of removing the graves of their forefathers involves what people who have no interest in human beings like to call human interest.

Heeled with detailed instructions, two men visit each tract to be bought and make independent appraisals, which are passed along to TVA's Board of Appraisal and Review. The farmer gets his offer by mail; two weeks later a land buyer shows up, a man innocent of authority to jack the offer a dollar up or down. It very effectively reduces bargaining to a minimum; and valley farmers are tall bargainers. Not that there haven't been objections. For one thing the average man considers the government a complaisant and easy mark; for another, hill farmers measure their land the old-fashioned way—by the dimensions of the land itself, no matter how steep and uneven—and not as the dead level of a map squares it off. Quite a number of them called in independent appraisers, who informed them of the new way of surveying and who, in general, remarked that TVA offers were entirely fair offers. Thus it would seem that TVA has earned some valuable local respect as a close but scrupulous bargainer. In relatively very few cases has the argument run so far as a condemnation process. The only men with a really strong kick are the farmers Longmire and Hawkins, who happened to own the farms at the dam site. TVA claims it was farmland so far as these farmers were concerned; the offer is $30 an acre, which of course—for valley farms are smallish—doesn't pile up to very much. Longmire and Hawkins claim it's dam site by God and worth every cent of $3,000 an acre. TVA is half resigned to losing the case, but not to any such tune.

Since one of TVA's ultimate hopes is that every valley farmer shall farm land that should be farmed, you might expect an experiment in that direction here, where the families of a whole minor valley must perforce be uprooted. But a lot of water must flow under the bridge before such things can come to pass. Meanwhile TVA must avoid the very appearance of bossing. TVA therefore scours the countryside for available farms as good as or better than those to be flooded, at equivalent prices, and makes panels of them, directories, for the convenience of those who want the help. Quite some few, but no thundering majority, have availed themselves of it. But few of these movers left the hills for the lowlands, better land or no better land—and none of the towns or "settlements" in the reservoir area bothered to survive the flood as communities.

One old man made a solemn vow, and news. His forefathers had brought fire into the valley 150 years before; it had never been allowed to go out; he would by God not budge an inch unless TVA took it safely with him. On further questioning the old man granted that maybe once or twice when he'd been gone a couple of weeks it *had* needed right smart cheering up when he got back; yes, it might have went out in the meantime. Once he was gone a whole summer. Yes, it stood to reason it might have. (TVA moved it all the same.)

Besides the living, there are ninety-eight cemeteries in that area, over 6,000 graves. Most of them, people wanted moved. Those who prefer some sort of service can get an undertaker; TVA pays him $20 a grave. Otherwise TVA does the job. There are all kinds. Nameless graves and unsurvived; and those who preferred to leave their people lay. And there was also the woman who stood very silent, not crying, in the rain, in rain-sagged calico, and watched the walnut coffin raised and fitted into its new board box: and who lifted her wet skirt to take her tears only when the box was crayoned with "TVA" . . . and the directing numeral. . . . And meanwhile archaeologists are making hay over TVA's Indian findings.

Meanwhile, moreover, 1,000 men are busy clearing the land and 6,000 CCC boys are at work on erosion control. The CCC boys are the physical end of the activities of the Division of Forestry; of all that we'll speak later. As for the clearance, you have to lick clean the eighty feet that will be exposed as the lake level fluctuates, but below that only loose or dead stuff and such standing timber as will protrude above water level are taken off. The

timber comes in handy downstream in the training shops, the cof-
ferdams, and the forms. Whither, to the workmen, let us now
return.

The average workman on Norris Dam—and you may take him
as the average TVA workman—is thirty-two years old. The
chances are two to one he's from a town or city—by all odds most
likely from a small town and a farm background. The chance that
he has ever done such work before is next to nil. He has completed one year of high school; the chances are two to one he's
married; if so, he has between two and three dependents; the
chances are two to one, also, that he's taking one or more of the
free training courses. After his five-and-one-half-hour shift he
boards a truck and rides the four miles to Norris where he loafs,
works in his garden, studies, eats, plays games, or sleeps, according to his disposition and the time of day. When he sleeps, it may
be in one of the big pine bunkhouses; it may be with his wife in
one of the model houses. When he eats it may be at home; it may
be in the large, clean, pine cafeteria, where some 2,000 rather
coarse and quite good meals are served each day. Near the cafeteria there is a big combination post office, bank, commissary,
and recreation hall—pine, of course—and the chances are eighteen to one that the worker is banking his savings and they are
ninety to one that, as a member of the Workers' Council and of
the community, he has soberly voted against the sale of beer—all
that's allowed in Tennessee—on the premises. Evenings, in the
recreation hall, there may be a dance, or a basketball game, or a
movie, or a lecture. The families of all wage levels turn out and
mix with genuinely friendly but never (on the part of the workmen) entirely absent self-consciousness. Sundays, everyone who
feels like it goes to church. TVA, remember, follows very carefully
the policy of forcing nothing on nobody. TVA decided not to force
God. Partly a mistake, that was. Murmurs arose in the valley
of Godless Socialism up at Norris. So TVA called a quick vote
among the townspeople and almost unanimously they asked for a
preacher, nonsectarian. They rather like the man who took the
call but they are not perfectly satisfied: unfortunately he has a
slightly foreign accent.

Norris children go to the new brick schoolhouse, which is the first of the permanent public buildings. Needless to say (though TVA keeps carefully quiet on the point) they get better schooling than they would find in most other places in the valley.

Norris adults go to school, too. Among the workmen themselves, take note, you find everything from illiterates to degree holders. The degree holders and their wives, and the wives of engineers and superintendents, are voluntary teachers. The studies run from the three primary R's through literature, current events, and the natural and social sciences. Most popular course among the men: natural science. Among the women: domestic science. A library is getting successfully into swing with more than 500 readers in and out every day. The librarians aren't wildly theoretical about it; the books range from just above the pure pulp level through *The Robber Barons* and an encyclopedia of religion, the main idea being, after all, to get people to read. Various volumes of the *Britannica* are chronically out: most thumbed of all the books, though, is a *Dictionary of Automotive Mechanics*. This spring, traveling libraries are being sent upstream to the clearing crews.

TVA is taking a lot of care to fit its training to the variety of the mass and the desires of the individual. In the trades shop, which is also the general repair shop for Norris, there are four main divisions: Woodworking, general metal, automotive, electrical. The wood comes downstream from the clearance gangs; men in training dry and dimension it, learn general carpentry from it, build furniture for TVA offices and for their homes, learn even woodcarving if they want to. They also learn how to put up farm buildings.

A popular course is auto mechanics; the men learn it from indisposed TVA trucks and cars. By popular request, there is also a course in ground aviation. Still others learn blacksmithing, welding, general machine-shop practice, plumbing, wrought-iron work. In the electrical department they learn, besides the technical tricks of the trade, a good deal about the efficient use of electricity; a good bit more about smalltime industries that can be run with cheap power—they absorb, in fact, a great deal that is important in TVA's future. In this same shop they also learn blueprint reading and there is a course in foremanship. A good

many of these men who come from west Tennessee will be moved
to the Pickwick site when work gets under way there. A good
many of these who began as unskilled laborers will be skilled
workmen. A good many who began as skilled workmen will be
foremen. The same combination of economy and training goes on out-
doors. A poultry plant demonstrates the operation of a small
poultry enterprise as a rural occupation—and furnishes eggs to
the cafeteria. A communal farm garden furnishes vegetables. On
the general farm, in direct line with the agricultural program
they're going light on corn; they're plugging hay as an erosion
checker and as food for a small dairy herd. The dairy itself (some
of the cafeteria's milk and butter: twenty-five ineffable Jerseys
from out Nashville way) is still another day-by-day demonstration
and training ground: TVA is very anxious, in the interests of soil
conservation and farm prosperity, to make the eastern valley
cattle-conscious. Other phases of farm training: the right crop to
the right soil, stock breeding, principles of marketing, use of
farm agencies, etc.

For the town itself. A temporary construction camp would
have cost TVA over $1,000,000; the cost of this permanent test-
tube town, including all improvements—land, buildings, streets,
water supply, sewage disposal, electric service—was $3,500,000,
of which about one-third went into the camp, out on the edge of
town, which houses the single workers. This too was built to last.
The eight bunkhouses, TVA figures, will come in handy for industrial purposes once the dam is finished.

The town is a painstaking and by no means negligible experiment in town planning and in low-cost housing. It is so laid out as
to expand, in due course, to a maximum 10,000 population—laid
out in general on the English garden-city plan: concentrically, a
broad, permanent, outlying swath of woods and potential park
country; a broad, permanent belt of garden lands (one-half acre
to four acres per family); and, in the middle, the houses themselves. With exception of some low-gabled ceilings, some brutally
unyielding cement-and-tile floors, and (garden-city theory or
none) the inconvenient distance between home and garden, the
results are almost completely admirable. And they are also, as

seems to be irrevocably typical of every American attempt at that sort of thing a little bit depressing, a little bit suburban, a little bit dull . . .

The houses are divided into three general groups (there are several esthetic variations within each group) and all of them, in style, are developments on architectural themes indigenous to the valley. Group 1: one hundred and fifty-one brick and frame houses. Of which the average house, including its share in the town utilities, costs $6,180 and rents at an average $30.88. Group 2: eighty cinderblock houses. Cinder blocks—cheap, insulative, termite-proof, and by no means unpleasing to the eye—are TVA's happiest housing discovery. A four-room, one-story, cinder-block cottage costs $1,890 to build, rents for $14.50 a month. Group 3: sixty cinder-block, frame, or stone houses, each of four rooms, each with fireplace and bath, and sometimes, a rear porch. An average house in this group costs $2,074 to build and rents for $22. There are also two-family houses, five small apartment houses—and one experimental steel house. Rents in Norris run as low as $12 a month (half a two-family house) to as high as $45. Chairman A. E. Morgan, by the way, lives in Norris, in one of the white brick houses.

By the fall of 1936, at the latest, Norris will be emptied of all TVA employees except those relative few who will have charge of maintaining the finished dam and the lower end of the reservoir. What will become of the town then is something TVA makes no pretense of knowing precisely. The combination community center and business block is under construction now; and TVA has people in training in trades enough to run a town—and more than enough people to do it—if enough of them should decide to stay. But of course the thing necessary to make the town a self-sustaining and self-respecting community is an industry, or two, or three. TVA's new ceramic laboratory is just going into operation there and a number of TVA's employees are learning the trade in their spare time. Suffice it here to say that fine china potentialities seem to be among TVA's better bets and that Norris may very possibly become a china town. In any event, TVA's investment is covered: several companies have already made bids for the town; whether it becomes kennel to electrometallurgy, electrochemistry, ceramics, or what have you, remains for time and chance to designate.

All the same, TVA isn't repeating itself at Wheeler site, and doesn't plan to at Pickwick. It may be that Norris was over-planned as many a first child is over brought up. Or it may be simply in line with TVA's general policy of waiting for the test tubes to work out thoroughly before swashing the vats full. Whichever it may be (and possibly it is both), the six bunkhouses and the recreation hall and the cafeteria at Wheeler and the fifteen permanent houses (for the future maintenance crew) add up to something that, but for the lack of followers, is much more like an ordinary camp. The training program is less elaborate, too. Roughly there are three branches: prentice work on the actual job, courses given by foremen and engineers in the neighboring towns, and lectures and study courses in the recreation hall, arranged and asked for by the Workers' Council. You can get some idea of the earnest intention of these men out of this: without any official noseleading, they ask for such courses as the social and economic history of the U.S.

A couple of matters swing into relevance here as they don't up at Norris. The Wheeler country is also the Muscle Shoals country and the Scottsboro country, and in those parts you run smack into a couple of new problems. These problems walk on two legs and breathe the best air they can get, and the name of one is share cropper and the name of the other is nigger.

The Negro. With white men by the hundreds out of jobs, TVA very quietly, but very firmly in line with its policy, began hiring Negroes by tens and twenties until their employment percentage tallied with the population percentage in those parts: about 20 per cent. Having hired them it proceeded to pay them the same wages and gave them housing precisely as good as that of the whites and training perhaps better. (Reason for good training: there are swarms of first-rate Negroes out of work; a Ph.D., for instance, heads the Negro training staff.) Meanwhile such TVA men as know the country at first hand were set for anything up to and including a lynching. Nothing happened, and they figured out why. TVA, and the Negroes too, had sense enough to stick absolutely to Jim-Crowism, which isn't necessarily edifying but which feels better, at any moment, than bright coal oil and buckshot. Moreover, TVA's workmen had no longer to fear that their jobs would be washed from under them by cheap Negro labor; TVA wasn't taking that advantage, so commonly taken, either of its Negroes or of them. TVA ran foul of some objection on the part of leading citizens of local towns when it began training them toward a higher possible standard of living—but it reminded them (a) that neither intermarriage nor insurrection was being preached and (b) that the Negro was undeniably a member of the community and might better be a decent than an indecent one, and went on about its business.

The Share Cropper. He may be either white or black. The share cropper who builds Wheeler Dam gets free and good training toward a better life; the share cropper upstream who clears the reservoir gets more of the same and he and his neighbors get all the firewood they want to haul away, gratis. But you can't practice a proper rotation of crops if your job, as a tenant, is to wring the very gizzard of land you don't own with cotton and cotton and more of it. You're in an even worse hole if your plot is above the Wheeler site and TVA has to buy it from under you. Your landlord gets the money, all you get is moving orders. TVA does all it can, and has found new places for a good many tenants. But the share cropper and the Negro are two profoundly painful problems that TVA, by no fault or oversight of its own, has no constitutional power either to solve or to get far under the skin of. Out of 230,000 farmers there are 95,000 tenants in the valley. Not enough, perhaps, to balk TVA's program; but enough to lift them beyond mere sentimental discussion.

Wheeler Dam itself is quite a job. Salient features are these: on the north side of the river, a navigation lock sixty feet wide by 360 long, with a fifty-foot lift. Between this and the north bank, space is provided for a still bigger lock—110 by 600 feet. The dam itself will be 6,340 feet long. Not counting the lock, it meant the excavation of 550,000 cubic yards of rock; 650,000 cubic yards of concrete and 5,700 tons of reinforcing steel will go into it. The stone cradles are now hewn and will hold eight 32,000-kw generators. The dam will back a 140-square-mile lake eighty-six miles upstream to just beyond Guntersville, Alabama. TVA began work in November, 1933, scooped through ten feet of bum stone to a solid foundation, and is about half done with the job.

So far, there are not more than 400 men at Pickwick Landing, a few miles upstream from Shiloh. They are still in process of going over the ground. As always in building a dam the preliminaries will be arduous and lengthy, what with access roads and a camp to build, and the foundation to be checked. At Pickwick, moreover, there is a terrible overburden—forty feet of earth—before you hit solid rock. Pickwick will be the longest of TVA's dams—7,710 feet—and will stand 103 feet tall from top to toe. The navigation lock will have a sixty-one-foot lift, the highest single lift in the world. The whole job will take about 750,000 barrels of cement, will probably be completed within two and one-half years from now.

Of course TVA's engineering work is nothing but a hard-wrought means to sundry ends. In the meantime those ends must be brought into specific focus and must be planned toward. If by chance you are a little weary of hearing of planning, hearken to this semiclassical example of the lack of it. If, as is very likely and soon, TVA dams the French Broad River, a new $1,000,000 highway bridge just above the site will be flooded under. The bight of the story is that the location of the dam was O.K.'d by the federal government in 1929; the location of the bridge was O.K.'d by the federal government a couple of years later. You may conceive, then, that the task of planning the future usage of 28,000,000 acres is a difficult task, of some relevance to hard sense.

The job may be broken into three broad phases: land-use planning, agricultural planning, industrial planning. And the basis of these—or, as A. E. Morgan says, "the basis of human economy"—is land-use planning.

This work is in charge of Earle S. Draper (best known as the man who laid out Kingsport, Tennessee) and a staff of a hundred men busy in the fields of architecture, town planning, highway planning, and regional planning. Now under way, for example, is a comprehensive study of all phases of transportation—water, rail, highway, and air—which must of course spill beyond the brim of the valley to include such traffic hubs as Atlanta, Birmingham, Memphis, Cincinnati. The purpose: to work out an integrated system that will best serve all valley requirements both freight and passenger, making the most economical use of every type of transportation.

As for a piece of demonstration, there is TVA's Freeway, which like the town of Norris was built out of the Land Planning laboratory, and which runs from Coal Creek across the Norris Dam site around Norris Town and southward to join the Cincinnati-Knoxville highway. What it amounts to is a modified Westchester Parkway, the modifications being that there are no underpasses and that in some cases abutting owners are granted direct access. It is banked to high speed; it is laid out with an uncommonly good eye for unfurling the best available scenery (which, including the tumbled velvet of the distant Smokies, is pretty good scenery); and it embodies the following principles, which are well ahead of any other highway practice in the South. The right-of-way is never less than 150 feet wide. Intersections are kept at a minimum and are specially planned for maximum visibility and safety. Abutting landowners have access only at points chosen from the standpoint of safety to Freeway traffic. The entire width of right-of-way is healed over by a system of grading that molds all cuts and fills into the landscape, and by judicious planting of shrubs and trees. Adjoining farmers are allowed to farm the land to within ten or fifteen feet of the pavement—in return for an agreement not to allow billboards and similar truck in their fields beyond the right-of-way. The Freeway has quite some reputation in the valley: the 8,000 rubberneckers per week (the fair-weather average) who go out to give Norris the once-over seem to write home about it more than about anything else. That TVA, forced to build either a five-mile railway arm or a heavy-duty highway, should have elaborated the necessity into this twenty miles of experiment and demonstration is as typical of its methods as was the building of Norris in lieu of a construction camp. (The five miles that replaced the railroad, by the way, cost only $250,000. The railway line would have cost $500,000.) Of Norris, the Land Planning and Housing Division's heaviest field-study and demonstration job to date, we have already spoken at some length.

The Division's other job is the collection of facts about land and the organization of those facts into clear shape for reading. Which is, after all, simply a good definition for a map. TVA is spending a lot of time and a lot of money developing a first-rate topographic map. It is no longer the simple and relatively cheap procedure it was two decades ago. Once the main network of levels and horizontal controls is made into a foundation map, you take a plane two miles into the air and make a system of vertical photographs. You can photograph thousands of square miles of country in a week—granted a high ceiling and a steady light—but the matching of a week's photographs and their reduction to a common scale and their final regimentation into mosaic is quite another matter; it takes six to eight months. But is well worth the trouble and the cost. An air map contains far more information than ground surveys alone can give you. Take A. E. Morgan's word for it: "A question arises as to the possibility of a waterpower development. Six months of surveys formerly would be necessary. With this basic data a better conclusion can be reached in a week."

Just what farmland is so steep, so eroded, that it should be put into forest? Or taken out of plow crops and put into pasture? In the purchase of forest lands what tracts of good land shall be saved for farming? Where, once again, shall roads run? And how will they relate to rivers and railways and reservoirs? The answers to all such questions are being prepared, acre by acre. Nor can it stop with the skin of the land. A corps of geologists is at work exploring and appraising mineral resources. If a dam is built here, will valuable mineral deposits be drowned out of use? In relation to these resources, and to the land, and to transportation facilities, where should factories appear? Of the facts that alone can give the answers there must be compiled a dictionary more exhaustive perhaps than any such dictionary has ever been. The Land Planning Division is compiling this dictionary; but it will be required and indispensable reading for the men carrying forward every phase of TVA's work.

One kind of valley land you can lift like a tooth from the rest, and that is the land which is in forest or ought to be. TVA's Forestry Division has these five jobs. First: permanent adminstration of all TVA forest lands, of all farm and grazing lands and forest workers' houses in the area, the development of fisheries, wild fowl, and game; the build-up of the forests from a timber-growing point of view. Second: erosion control and reforestation work—most of it on nonagricultural lands—throughout the valley. Third: the development of nurseries and a corresponding study of plantations already made and of the new and best possibilities. Fourth:

planning for the use of nonagricultural lands within the sphere of TVA influence.

Finally, the Forestry Division has its relations with other agencies such as the U.S. Forest Service, the seven state forest services, the state game commissions, the U.S. Bureau of Fisheries, the U.S. Biological Survey. In this field of public relations the position of the TVA Division is of special importance and interest. Briefly, the situation is this:

Of the 28,000,000 acres of land surface in the valley, the best figures available so far show approximately 17,000,000 acres of forest land. Of this, 6,000,000 acres are small and scattered farm woodlands; about 1,000,000 acres are in those parts of national forests within the valley; about 500,000 more are included in the Great Smoky Mountains National Park. This leaves 9,500,000 acres unallocated. Of this the Forestry Division has figured some 6,000,000 acres as most suitable for national-forest purchase. TVA requested the Secretary of Agriculture to see about buying it up: the National Forest Reservation Commission has granted the official right—and the funds—to buy up half these acres and the U.S. Forest Service is now doing the buying. (Just a sample, you see, of TVA's "cooperation with existing agencies.") The other 3,000,000 acres are being hashed over; TVA expects some definite action on them before long.

This leaves 3,500,000 acres still unallocated. The Forestry Division hopes the seven state forest departments will buy up most of it. If not all, then probably the Division itself will step in. It is definitely not to be allowed to lie around at loose ends.

From all this you can see, with half an eye, the obvious. TVA doesn't look forward to any large-scale permanent forest operations in the valley, whether by small landowners or by timber companies. And in very fact, according to Division-head Edward C. M. Richards, "The Division does expect that the management of the farm woodlands will continue under private ownership and regulation. But all indications in the valley point in the direction of the necessity for the public ownership and operation of the large timber tracts if adequate development on a permanent sustained yield basis of the forests, and thus the permanent protection of the watersheds, the navigation, the power dams, and flood control in the Tennessee Valley are to be assured."

As for the physical end of the labor, you should remember that there are not more than fifty men, all told, in the Division. The "architects" of the job, if you like. The "contractors" and laborers (the latter need no quotes) are the twenty CCC Camps, the 6,000 CCC boys who are doing the most pressing and immediately necessary chapter of the work. Work is concentrated just now within the 1,856,000 acres that comprise the entire watershed above Norris Dam; fifteen of the camps are in that region. They attacked first the lower half-million acres, where erosion is most active and most critical, will soon climb toward and into Virginia. They use these four types of check dam: burlap bags part filled with soil and sprinkled with grass seed are laid in the washes and the shallow troughs. Brush dams stop gullies too deep for bags. Deeper gullies take log-and-plank dams up to five feet high. And, toward the lower end of big-time gullies, or wherever the drainage will be permanent, rock and mortar dams are built up to eight feet high. Besides which, all steep and galled land is staked and wired over with brush matting sown with grass seed. Best week's work for one camp: over 200 rock dams; better than one a week per man. CCC accomplishment up to January 1, 1935:

27,826	rock dams
28,331	log dams
2,866	brush dams
23,578	Bag dams
5,446,491	yards of brush matting
6,000	acres of timber-stand improvement
45,000	yards of diversion ditches
200	miles of truck trails
130	vehicle bridges

All that is mere preliminaries. Check dams and brush matting slow the runoff and baste down the soil until a cover of grass or vines or shrubs or, most permanently of all, trees, weft it forever into place. They are trying every kind of cover—Bermuda grass behind the dams, bush clover (lespedeza) where sheet erosion is most virulent, even honeysuckle, which every Tennessean despises: it will grow not merely all over your land but in your ears at the slightest encouragement. And, by the millions, trees: not merely the famously efficient black locust (5,000,000 of these) but trees of much greater timber value—the black walnut, the tulip poplar, a whole assortment of oaks and pines, the blight-resistant Asiatic chestnut. For the development of these, the Division has established two nurseries (one at Muscle Shoals, one at Clinton in East Tennessee: combined capacity, 60,000,000 seedlings) and has planted in each some 3,000,000 young trees. Near Norris, too, it has started a tree-crop nursery and test orchard where it will demonstrate what can be done with improved crop trees, and will dispense grafting wood and planting stock. The Division expects an expansion, soon, of the CCC and, accordingly, of its own activities.

If the U.S. really learns to take care of its land, and really cares to preserve it for the future, it will be just about the first civilization that has done so, and the time is spoiled rotten for beginning. Not to mention great swaths of the continent at large that we have manhandled, consider merely the general South. These past four generations, we have wrung the very blood from the land and shipped its health to market and seaward by the sewers and left it exhausted and misplanted for the rain to do the rest. Left to its own devices and the rain's, that whole land could be desert before another century had passed.

Or just take the Tennessee Valley. By quality and by geography, it breaks very roughly into three parts. By quality it is a third good, a third middling, a third godawful, nearly all in danger. Geographically: the east and north are steep, planted much to corn when planted at all, sickly most of it, rooked with gullies. The west and south are gentler sloping, wearied with a surfeit of cotton, slowly more sterile year by year, year by year quite surely sloughing its skin. In three or four of the middle counties there is land as rich as any on this continent, and the wounds of rain heal swiftly level as the harmed flesh of a healthy child, for this land overlies phosphate beds. But elsewhere in the valley you would hardly set a camera down and fail to get some record of the great mange of the land.

So the jobs ahead of TVA are these: to save and to restore the land. To learn and to practice its best uses. To teach and guide and perhaps ultimately to distribute the farmers accordingly. If you think this could be nicely handled by Home Folks Unassisted, take the word of Mr. William M. Lanedess of the Agricultural Division: it can't. As county agent for Shelby County, Lanedess used to spend a day apiece at one farm after another, checking up on erosion and telling what to do about it. He figures that if he had kept on with that job alone, day by day, he would have been back for a second visit to his first farm at the end of fifteen years.

On slopes up to fifteen degrees, the first job is terracing. Terracing is a simple enough matter: you lay open, across the axis of a hill, a broad and shallow trough, with the lip of earth on the downhill side. How wide apart these troughs are laid depends, of course, on the slope and the soil. At the far ends you clean out permanent gullies, and check them with dams. It is no invention of TVA's; in fact TVA found a terracing program started in Alabama, an overworked county agent trying to run it. TVA called in all state agricultural representatives and together they drew up a procedure whereby TVA and the agencies work hand in glove, with funds chiefly under contract with the land-grant colleges of the states. The county commission or the terracing cooperative or the "club" of farmers and agents (the setup answers to several names) contracts for equipment at around $4,500 per unit, leases it from the manufacturer, liquidates the lease by charging $2.50 an hour for terracing, about half of which goes toward liquidation. When they started, just one company—Caterpillar Tractor—had the tractor-and-special-plough equipment they needed. Several others put it out now; farmers have watched four in the same field putting on a demonstration. Terracing doesn't cost much, and the secret of its cheapness is Diesel power. Its cost is a fifth the running cost of the old gas tractor, farmers figure; and they figure too that thirty mules would do the same work at the same speed, more expensively. Twenty thousand farmers are involved. Of the ninety-nine farm counties in the valley, the Authority is concentrating its first attention on the seventy-five nearest the rivers, and that goes not merely for the terracing but for the whole agricultural program.

But terracing, even on feasibly gentle slopes, isn't the whole story, turn to the east; to the valley east and north of Chattanooga.

Of its 14,000,000 acres, 8,000,000 are in farms. Of this 8,000,000 more than a third is pasture, more than a third in small patches of woods, the rest—well under a third—is in crops. Of the crop land, about half is planted to corn. Plenty of that corn is planted on land steep as a cow's face—the steepest registers an all but incredible 88 per cent. Off every acre of that corn land, corn and steep soil being what they are, you lose thirty and forty tons of topsoil every year. As for the pasture land, that too is steadily weakening: the pasturage like a poultice withdraws the phosphorus and the lime from the soil; there is less for next year's plants to draw on; as the sods weaken the carrying season steadily shortens and the feeding period steadily lengthens out; first the legumes go, then the grass, then the land wastes swiftly open—a bare and spreading sore.

The wards of the key that will open this deadlock are two. One is in the roots of legumes, and the other is down at Muscle Shoals, at Nitrate Plant No. 2.

If good crops are to grow indefinitely, the soil needs plant food. Of lime, which sweetens the soil and the flesh of its produce, the valley reeks. Of potash, nearly all soil except numb sand has enough. Of nitrogen, you can get plenty by planting legumes— clover, peas, beans, alfalfa, vetches—which enlist nitrogen out of the free air and nail it into the land. But the phosphorus that you need to raise those legumes—or any other crop—is not so easy a story. All we need say here is that in shipping its grains and its meats to market and in committing its sewage to oblivion, civilization very steadily imposes an enormous and perhaps ultimately suicidal tax upon the land. And though in time we may learn to respect our sewage—attempts to extract phosphorus from it have been technically but not emotionally successful— and may learn also to wangle phosphorus out of sea water, the chief source still is the vast graveyard of those prehistoric beasts whose bones are thawed long since into the earth but whose burden of phosphorus has been processed by time into phosphate beds such as those to be found in Florida, in a few of the western states, and in middle Tennessee.

The sequiturs, intensely in brief, are these: TVA is farming a number of the mid-state deposits, not by large-scale methods, wastefully, but by truck and shovel, sparingly: "phosphate farmers" must guarantee to put their land back into shape for cultivation after the mining, and are shown how. The phosphates are shipped to Nitrate Plant No. 2, at the Shoals. Where, by the end of last summer, TVA had completed a $65,000 experiment with a pocket-size blast furnace which was to develop data for the design of a small commercial-size unit. The designs for this in turn are now nearing completion.

Ordinary superphosphate runs 16 to 20 per cent plant food (P_2O_5). It is possible—but at too high a cost—to produce concentrates up to 52 per cent. The superphosphate TVA is producing analyzes at about 45 per cent, and the problems to be solved are two: the technical improvements that will bring down the cost to take advantage of an ultimate 25 per cent saving in cost of delivery; and the education of the farmer in the use of this new high-powered fertilizer. So far, TVA has produced some 7,000 tons. It is being distributed to Agricultural Experiment Stations, to demonstration farms, and for use in erosion control. Trading problems rear no ugly head as yet: distribution will be the same for a long time to come, and production will be geared accordingly. Notably, the fertilizer will go to some 2,000 demonstration farms—now being selected—all over the valley: and they will be not merely large-scale laboratories, but large-scale and highly variegated schoolrooms where the whole of farm practice will be studied and taught.

To sum up: TVA is very definitely committed to the extensive development of grazing lands and of livestock raising. In the east to hold steep soil in check; in the west to board the seesaw opposite the fat King Cotton; in all the valley to improve the land and to alter for the better the life of the farmer. TVA is also definitely committed to the attempt to break the one-crop system. TVA is also hopefully but less definitely committed to the effort to distribute the valley farmers upon land they can farm. Much of which is a long, long way off and TVA knows it well. The share cropper is still one problem; the natural inertia of many a farmer, the backwardness of many another, are two more. Already TVA realistically knows that its moving-to-better-land must be done step by step: a man must have learned to farm mediocre land before you saddle him with excellence. So far, what the Agricultural Division has done in the way of action and demonstration is of necessity merely the fringe of a huge fabric ahead. If you want to see where it all leads to, you had best glance that way again six months and a year and ten from now. And if you are inclined already to pass judgment or to line up conjectures the only answer is don't.

But no matter how effectively the land may be saved and well brought up and wisely planted, and no matter how neatly the farm population may be tailored along this land, that is only half the story as TVA sees it. The other half is to give the farmers— especially those scores of thousands who for all improvement to come will never again farm on a commercial scale—work, and extra money, alongside his farming: work on his own, in cooperatives, in factories.

To bring this about the Industrial Division looks toward two distinct kinds of industry, small and large. So far as the men on the small-industries staff are concerned nothing is too trifling for serious attention and for trial. Their job is sensibly and profitably to fill out all the cracks between the factory to come and to act in some cases as proving ground for the large-industries section. Typical of their tinkerings, findings, experiments:

One broad intention of the agriculturalists is to plant the valley much more extensively to grasses, to hays, to legumes; to build up dairying, to develop grazing lands and herds upon them and fresh meat for a rural population which sells a calf for $4 and buys him back, in pieces, at $36, and which accordingly has resigned itself to fat back and to malnutrition. That brings up a number of jobs for the industrialists.

Item. To design and to estimate costs (for local manufacturers) on mowing machines light enough and cheap enough to fit the small and tilted valley farm. *Item.* To design and to install cooperative feed mills at country crossroads. *Item.* To organize cooperative cold-storage stations. *Item.* The development of a two-man industry, so that, for example, two farmers, using cotton muslin, local mica dust, pitch made from cottonseed oil, could in two days' work a month turn out enough dirt cheap tarpaulin to dry the legume hays of three counties.

Now, en route to the large-industries end of the picture, let us shift gears and mention the Tennessee Valley Associated Cooperatives, because very probably, in the long run, it will be the agency that will push the smaller findings of the Division into action. The TVAC was created in March, 1934, to handle FERA's $300,000 allocation as it might see fit among local groups. So far it has spent some $75,000, has created about a dozen cooperatives, which thus far involve over 2,000 families, most of them in communities where as high as 70 per cent of the population was on relief. These cooperatives of the first year had mostly to do with canning and exchanging farm produce—in the chief interest of developing a decently varied winter diet as against the typical belly bastinado of turnip greens and salt pork. TVAC will expand its canning activities this summer. It is also getting under way with other lines of attack—crafts and the utilization of mineral resources and of forest products. The respective gists of these three programs: *Minerals*: farmers can mine many of them with truck and shovel, selling, for the time being, to TVA process researching, and cleaning up an average $150 cash each per year, which is good money in that vicinity. *Forest Products*: the scattered patches of forest are of great aggregate commercial value, provided they are worked on a small scale. TVAC is establishing small "barnyard factories" where farmers, in their off time, can make useful wood articles. TVAC finances the undertaking and helps with the marketing. *Crafts*: the mountain women have a definite talent for handicrafts. TVAC looks toward leveling the costs of raw materials, developing adequate selling agencies. Already several private companies, including one of the big midwestern mail-order houses, have suggested desirable specialties and have made bids in advance.

The large-industries end of the Division has to qualify itself for an entirely different function and that is as a catalytic agent. Since TVA owns neither the industrialists who may set up shop in the valley nor the new materials they may use nor the land they may locate on nor anything that is actually or potentially theirs (except floods of cheap power), its business is to arrange a program that combines (a) the best interests of the valley and its people and (b) the best interests of the industrialists themselves. It must in fact become so definitive and so authoritative a clearinghouse of information and advice that no prospective industrialists can afford to ignore its help or to run counter to it.

TVA hopes to have for sale the cheapest power in the country. Though most heavy industries count the cost of power as a relatively small part of their total value, it so happens that in two fields—the electrochemical and the electrometallurgical—that relative cost is well above 10 per cent. The valley is peculiarly richly qualified in the raw materials that can furnish these industries. There is an abundance of rural labor, some of it already trained, more training on the way. Already an extremely impressive array of uncommonly impressive gentlemen have descended upon TVA by mail or in person to make inquiries, and the prospects look good to these gentlemen.

In view of such general facts (substantially and specifically supported in his own mind), Mr. Lilienthal has made bold to state: "It is my firm conviction that the Tennessee Valley region is to be the scene of an expansion of industry which in the course of the coming decade will change the economic life of the South."

Not all the above can stand on its own slightly feathery feet. To single out a few things one by one and bring them closer to earth: the platoons of interested parties mentioned above are, naturally enough, not to be called by name or by company. Besides a lack of fondness for betrayal of business confidence, TVA makes consistently serious efforts to let accomplished facts do their own talking. As with many another confident hope on TVA's part for the future, you must resign yourself to a suspended faith in the substance of their word: the skeletal facts are still either in process of hardening, or confidential, or both.

As for the abundance of rural labor, that leads to the heart of a discussion of decentralization schemes. The idea of decentralization is no figment new or peculiar to TVA, but an idea that during the past two decades has been steadily more seriously studied and entertained by economists of various hues and by industrialists as well. The chief forces that caused the concentration of industry during the past century—the necessity for coal, the necessity for settling along the thin arteries of the railroads, the lack of transportation that forced workers to live under the backside of their work—are now reversed. And there are added reasons why some industrial developments may profitably in the future diffuse and subdivide. A few are these: lower operating costs; more efficient distribution; more efficient management; greater flexibility of small or branch organizations; the relationships between bad health (thanks to bad living conditions) and efficiency; the growing realization of the menace to society of large numbers of workers being thrown from their jobs upon no such means of support as a farm reliably gives. To which TVA can add the fact that its valley, developed for the most part since the decline from peak of the centralization forces, is uncommonly amenable to the farm-factory balance; that in fact the locations of many of its raw materials all but predestine decentralization; and that power will be sold at a uniform rate throughout the valley.

Looking toward all of which, the Industrial Division is conducting an exhaustive county-by-county survey of the whole valley. Heretofore, thanks to politics or local pride or whatnot, that sort of data has customarily been so concealed or glossed over that it is more dangerous than useless to the man who would map any industrial possibilities from it—and this is obviously just as true of the U.S. at large as of the valley. Here in fact is a gap that has never before been filled. Whereas you can get plenty of impartial information on the agricultural end of things, as an industrialist you must find out—or expensively try to—the truth for yourself. No bureau exists to give you those benefits of that impartial engineering point of view which is, precisely, what TVA is busy bringing into focus. All of these findings are to be at the disposal of relevant gentlemen who inquire.

As for the possibilities, go down into the valley with creation in your eye if you want specifications. If, meanwhile, you care for appetizers, recall in the first place the mineral wealth of the valley, in the second the fact that the really extensive use of much of this awaits only the cheap power that will make industrially possible new electrochemical and electrometallurgical processes. And then see toward what new lodes on the industrial compass these materials assemble: *coal*, plus cheap power plus the constituents of air, equals the 4,000 compounds of organic chemistry. *Iron*, plus cheap power plus *manganese*, *chromite*, still rarer alloy minerals, equals the cheap production of numerous ferroalloys. *Bauxite*, plus cheap power, equals cheap supplies of aluminum, alumina cement. *Zinc*, plus cheap power, equals an extensive electrolytic zinc industry. *Limestones* of maximum purity and in huge abundance: cement. Brick and tile *clays* in like abundance, and variety, including the *kaolins*: porcelains, highest grade chinas. *Barytes*: paint. *Mica*: insulation. *Kyanite, olivine*: refractories, linings for extreme-heat furnaces, spark plugs. To name but a few.

The expansion of one example must do. It is in the field of ceramics and particularly involves kaolin. Almost nowhere in the U.S., thanks at bottom to high power rates, is electric firing of ceramic wares carried on. Notably ill-developed has been the use of kaolin, which is the chief ingredient of porcelains and the finest chinas, which is rare on all this continent, and of which there are rich deposits in the eastern valley. Under present methods of firing, seconds cut the profit to and through the bone. Moreover impurities cannot be removed economically from the lower grades of kaolin. In TVA's new ceramic laboratory at Norris, however, with some of the foremost ceramic engineers of the country, Mr. R. E. Gould is at work developing (a) cheap processes for purifying low-grade clays and (b) new high-heat, cheap-power firing equipment which will reduce seconds to next to nil—at no or virtually no extra cost. All this work is being undertaken from the point of view of practical, commercial methods. Mr. Gould, who has spent the past five years at the Giesche Porcelain Works at Katowice in Poland, where commercial electric-firing methods are a long shot ahead of anything tried in the U.S., will simply go on from where he left off there, checking his refinements with commercial-scale tests. And despite the ditherings a few months back of a number of ceramic companies the fact remains that TVA's findings will be available to private industry— that TVA will by no means go into the business. Even at this laboratory stage of the game, the chances look at least good that this country will manufacture its own high-grade chinas; and that out of the whole ceramic field a really large and important industry will be developed in the valley, which is very richly equipped with all the raw materials.

But in TVA's industrial program as elsewhere, watching, waiting, and no premature judgment are the only keys to common sense.

And that, gentlemen, in broad and charcoal strokes, is just about the whole of the canvas to date. Not quite the whole, to be sure. We should observe in passing that the two key states, Alabama and Tennessee, have during this past winter laid legislative tracks along which TVA can run into its new country—tracks laid and greased especially to facilitate the execution of the balkiest and only hard-fought part of TVA's job—the job of selling cheap power to people who want it. And having noted this, we should pause for a moment before the part of the canvas that depicts the Electric Home and Farm Authority promoting and financing the sale of low-cost electrical gadgets; before the towns of Tupelo and Athens, which, as customers of TVA, are buying more than twice as much power as before for less than half what they paid before. And before the farmers of Alcorn County and the citizens of Corinth who, combined in one association—which may well be model to the whole future of rural electrification—are buying power at one low and level price, and through membership fees and revenues are acquiring, from TVA, their transmission equipment. And before the farmers of Lauderdale County, TVA customers who are nicely giving the lie to the journalist who, last fall, snapshot every poverty-stricken privy he could find and laughed at the possibility of such farmers having power-buying power. And before those fourteen municipalities of Northern Alabama for whose use TVA contracted, with Alabama Power Co., to buy transmission equipment. And before the Birmingham court where certain preferred stockholders of A.P.C. protested that sale and the constitutionality of the whole TVA. And before Judge W. I. Grubb, who ventured no definitive answer to the loud question of constitutionality but whose opinion—quite definite enough—was that TVA is running an illegal business. And who likewise forbade the fourteen towns to accept PWA loans with which to build their own transmission systems. And before the heavy potential customers Knoxville and Chattanooga, which are respectively building and, having voted, preparing to build, their own transmission systems. And in Washington, before Senator Norris and Representative Rankin (of Mississippi), co-sponsors of the original TVA Act, who last March were hammering through protection against further delay by litigation.

And before the three directors. They were inclined, perhaps strangely, to name Judge Grubb's decision "A TVA victory"; nevertheless, a few weeks afterward, they came in a unanimous flying wedge north and into a huddle with the President. Since that time they have been confident of a favorable settlement of that question which rests for the time being in the beard of Chief Justice Hughes—and confident too that legislation can mend what the bench may conceivably damage.

And if still you think their road is steep into dubious frontier and their whole endeavor a gamble, remember that roads which lead to high places commonly have that character; and that, for an instance, the establishment of this government was in its time a gamble. And: that if some gambles have turned out worse than that, some others may turn out better.

SARATOGA

leven solid months of every year the small strange city of
Saratoga Springs or Saratoga, or The Springs, or The Spa, is
as dead a home of 13,700 people as you can locate.

One solid month of every year, thanks to the existence of
a race course and thanks to a season, it is such a city of
45,000 as you will not find the like of anywhere else on earth.

The Saratoga race course is neither the greatest, speaking in a
money way, nor even the fanciest of American courses. Miami's
Hialeah and Los Angeles's Santa Anita run neck and neck for the
title fanciest; and magnificent Belmont on Long Island is assessed
at $4,200,000 as against Saratoga's $1,015,000.

The same thing goes for the Saratoga season. But it has a special intensity that you will not find elsewhere. For one thing it has
been an annual habit since 1863 and marked the genesis of U.S.
horse racing. For another it grants none of that leisure for the
gentle build-up and the dying fall which is the typical rhythm of
more typical seasons but is brutally shear-lopped fore and aft.
Still another reason, and perhaps the most important of all, lies
in its location. Other great tracks and their turfmen are parasitic
to sizable cities. But when you come to a small town thirty miles
north of Albany in the foothills of the Adirondacks for thirty days'
racing, you come to sit down and stay the time out, night and day.

The sort of people who come there whose names you would
know and who are Turf and Field clubbers (they most likely have
boxes at the track as they would have permanent pews if they
were pillars of churches) are such people as Mrs. Payne Whitney
and Mrs. R. T. Wilson. A generation ago Mrs. Whitney's father-
in-law William C. and Mrs. Wilson's late husband Richard, with
some friends, bought the track from one Gottfried Walbaum and

established it powerfully and permanently in the sporting and social worlds. And along with these ladies you will find Colonel E. R. Bradley and George Loft and John Sanford and the Billy Hitts and Samuel D. Riddle and the brothers Morton and Charley Schwartz and F. Ambrose Clark, who have all been in regular attendance for the past twenty-five years. Others no less illustrious are Jock Whitney who last summer flew over from Hollywood to be on hand for the Whitney Memorial and who has probably the finest stables at the spa; and his slim and hatless wife who is out watching the workouts at six every morning. And Mrs. Margaret Emerson, and her son Alfred Gwynne Vanderbilt who as a child used to play on the club lawns during the races and who now, a pleasant and droopy twenty-two-year-old with the appearance of a diffident yearling, operates one of the most formidable of all U.S. stables, and who pilots his own plane down from Sagamore Lodge in the Adirondacks. And Cornelius Vanderbilt Whitney, who flies down from Tupper Lake. And Herbert Bayard Swope, Chairman of the State Racing Commission; and George H. Bull, head of the Saratoga Association for the Improvement of the Breed of Horses (the most high-minded definition of racing), which organization runs the whole horse end of the Saratoga show.

Then there are Thomas Hitchcock and F. Skiddy von Stade and the W. Plunket Stewarts and John D. Hertz and Pierre Lorillard, Sr. and Jr. And the sportsman-politician William Ziegler who for years paid Edward Ashton $7,500 for the month's use of his million-dollar turkey farm. And Albert C. Bostwick and the Walter M. Jeffords and Mrs. Oliver Iselin, who fell hard for horsing about a half dozen years ago and who is now an owner, and Mrs. Isabel Dodge Sloane, the owner of Cavalcade, who paid last year's top rent ($5,000) for a town house. And Marshall Field and William du Pont Jr. and Mrs. T. H. Somerville and the Charles H. Thieriots and William Woodward and Mrs. William C. Wright and Willis Sharpe Kilmer—to name just a few of the better known.

By way of completing the crazy quilt, add now a powerful Tammany contingent and at present of course a powerful LaGuardia contingent (for sports and politics as well as sports and society are of interlocked bloods, and down in Albany last summer, for instance, legislators daily made every effort to shut up shop "in time for the third race" and every effort to adjourn the special session in time for the last half of the season). Add gentlemen of the persuasion of Little Augie and of Charlie (Lucky) Luciano (Capone's numbers man) and of Dutch Schultz, whose hide-out is visible from Saratoga's highest point; and some of Manhattan's georgetted and hennaed madams (for the humbler brothers of the racing fraternity contribute generously to prostitution) with high color and with mouths like Mexican stirrups; and scores of gentlemen with the traditional beefsteak pans and with diamond-horseshoe stickpins and noses that are blooming in Bacardi. And old, hard, and crafty John Cavanagh, the war lord of the betting ring, the arrival of whose namesake, the train called the Cavanagh Special, symbolizes the opening of the season; and Cavanagh's hard, smart, rigorously controlled clan of bookies who handle—it's any man's guess—$300,000 or $700,000 in bets in an afternoon, of whom more later; and carload upon carload of mute inglorious Rothsteins—the sort who take part-time jobs or no jobs at all the better to attend to their true vocation—the whole of the chancier end of Broadway that can possibly make the grade; and, though they are more typical of the smaller and cheesier U.S. courses, a straggling nevertheless of hopeless small-time owners (of two horses, or of one plug) who have managed somehow to make it and who smooch around town desperately persuading the gullible to take a piece of the horse (by which course, late or soon, just about every native Saratogan—and they're not so damned gullible either—gets reamed) and who are likely either to ride their steed out of town at season's end or to sell him for busfare.

Finally the staffs, both household and stable, of the big-timers who own or who rent Saratoga's monstrous thirty-and-forty room "cottages" and of the owners of horses and of local stables—the very best trainers and the very best jockeys on this side of the earth; trainers like Mrs. Sloane's R. A. Smith and C. V. Whitney's T. J. Healey and jocks like Bradley's Don Meade and Mrs. Payne Whitney's Sylvio Coucci and C. V. Whitney's Sonny Workman. And half a thousand and more of the sweetest-moving and deepest-hearted and most royal horses in America. And the swarms of "help" that move up from the South and the swarms likewise of "entertainers." And the weekenders who, swelling this crowd by thousands and thousands more, really restore it in wild full measure to the lordliest appearance it ever had in the 1900's or the twenties. Such are the creatures who like a swarm of locusts alight upon the town and who, throughout the progression of thirty days and nights, as filings upon a magnetized paper, array and derange themselves in the all but indescribable patterns that together make up America's strangest season.

Far as living is concerned, they shake into position as a furnace shakes down: the dust at the bottom and the clinkers on top. Thus: Class A owns its own cottage, may even keep a caretaker there throughout the year, and need or need not own local stables. Class B rents its cottage—often the same one year after year— preferably near the track or along Broadway, or a farm nearby, or a "cottage" (large suite) in the south wing of the United States Hotel. Class C rents the smaller cottages and the mere houses along the less sanctified streets. Class C-Prime takes the better quarters offered by the Grand Union or the United States hotels. Class D fills up some more of these two great hotels and the half dozen second stringers and in brief the whole of Saratoga's twenty-four hotels (2,500 rooms). Class E moves in on the dozen or so year-round boardinghouses and the fifty or so year-round rooming houses; Class F and Class G-6 and so on down are catch as catch can and they always can: for Saratoga is the very apotheosis of the transient town and the difficulty would be to find a house within the city limits that didn't have something to offer. Of the hotels, six are of a hundred rooms or more and eight make a point of offering kosher food. There are some pleasant, conventional, relatively "modern" hotels. But most of them saw at least Diamond Jim Brady in his prime, and rival his facade and regalia. The true old aristocrats are the 650-room United States, and the 600-room Grand Union which, biting its lip, claims this slight edge: it didn't used to admit Jews under their right names.*

There are big parties in the cottages, there are long games and long drinks and desperate-phone-calls-to-New York-for-more-money in the rooms of the hotels, but by and large the place

---

* Back in the old carriage days a gentleman of prominence, named Moses Thompson plodded the dusty miles to Saratoga, wet his nib to register for a suite in the Grand Union. He got no further than the second s in Moses when the book was snatched from under him by a horrified clerk.

people live, in Saratoga, means only the place they come back to to sleep it off and to fortify themselves, with brandies or with bromos, for the next grind. For there is, twenty-four hours of the day, a plenty to do.

Ordinarily the hotter night clubs, along Congress Street, sign off somewhere between six and nine, but there are those who leave early—there are even those who go to bed beforehand—to go a mile out Union Avenue to catch the morning workouts. If you're out early enough you'll see the greatest of racing colors (not on the shriveled jockeys merely but upon blankets and buckets and even hitching posts) begin to assert themselves in the cool ambiguous light; and in the long, whitewashed stables the thoroughbreds and their mascots coming serenely awake; and in the long, low, whitewashed complements of these stables which are dormitories, the trainers finishing dressing and finishing the heavy southern breakfasts—muskmelon, fried chicken or steak, creamed potatoes, hot bread, homemade preserves, and sardonic coffee. And out on the tracks before the voided stands and the great dim swash of dewy, coleus-embossed grass, the loveliest running, as pure unadorned running, that you'll ever see; and the scattering of owners and of the bookies' and the turf sheets' clock men, quiet over their thumbed watches.

Most of the workouts are done with by the time the dew is dry; and all horses must be off the tracks by ten. Between workouts and track time is the fag end of the day at Saratoga, the time of day when the sportier thousands of the mob catch a draggle of sleep and when some of the socialites and a sifting of the regulars decide to give the baths a try. Yet even at this time of day things are going on: down at the Recreation Field there are ball games and tennis and horseshoes; and all along elm-fledged Broadway, bookies are already laying and the less curable addicts are already playing the afternoon's races. You will see the bookie in his least formal moods at Saratoga; and he's worth seeing, for he is in a sense the very axis not merely of the whole horsy crowd but of racing itself.

Owning and racing horses is an absorbing but not a particularly lucrative life's work. You can make money at it, to be sure: about as dependably as a poet lives off his poetry. The thing that keeps the so-called sport of kings alive at all, when you dispense with the pious eyewash, is gambling—or, if you like, betting. Speaking very broadly, there are two ways you can bet on a horse: by hand, and by (pari-mutuel) machine. In New York state, you still bet by hand. In other words, you still bet with a bookie. Bookies and betting managed to stay very much alive in the dark age between 1908 and 1934, when they were restored to semi-legality and the right to operate openly. But we take them up only with their definite public reappearance last year. A hundred or so bookies started in Saratoga's restored and enlarged betting shed; about seventy of them survived to see the end of that season. They are totally under the thumb of the same profoundly shrewd, sixty-nine-year-old Irish John Cavanagh who had run them in the great days before 1908 and who had managed to keep some sort of order during the lawless interim. In general let it be said of them that they stand up to their betting stools out of a rich and various stew of slum and bootblack boyhood, poolroom, gymnasium, and stableboy youth, smart-moneyed and toutish young manhood, and, ultimately, the combined backing and skill and solid standing it takes to set them up in business. Have no illusions about the skill they need. Bookmaking even more than most gambling is a compact of sport, narrow trade, art, and higher mathematics, and it is not merely a one-man but at least an eight-man job. A bookie has this setup: a block man (usually the bookie himself, he handles the slate, manipulates the odds), a money taker, a sheet writer (who records the bet), a cashier. These occupy the stools in the shed. Besides these, he has outside men or runners, who move around in the paddock or whereever the tips are at whitest heat, check on competitors, and keep the book in line with other books. And one or two "representatives," who handle the bulk of the clubhouse bets. (Not only club members rate the house and the enclosure and the seats square at the finish, but anyone also who pays the double admission fee. The betting ring is always outside this privileged enclosure—and inconveniently far from it at Saratoga—and most experienced regulars watch the odds on the club blackboard, shop for better prices, and do their betting through the representatives.) As for clockers, we saw them at work in the early morning; they work for several men at once. The wages of a bookie's staff men run around $15 a day. This plus admission fees for them, plus his

high-priced supplies (Mr. Cavanagh modestly calls himself a "sta-
tioner"), plus his daily "contribution" (to Mr. Cavanagh and thence
to the association) brings expenses to something like $300 or $400
a day. The rest, to each bookie, is pure gravy—when he gets it.
No substantial bookie comes to a day's racing heeled (in an ar-
mored car) with less than $10,000; but he can be cleaned of that
in no time at all; and often enough is. But on a good day, there's
no telling how much he may take. Memorial Day at Belmont this
spring was a really happy day: five out of seven favorites, including the great Cavalcade, lost. Pip-squeak bookies who were ex-
cited and unprofessional enough to name their winnings spoke of
$3,500 and such for the day, and as for the taciturn big-timers,
turf writers next day were estimating their average profit at
$15,000. Even so not all bettors walked home. One man had
the caginess or the foolhardiness to play $200 at 10 to 1 on Sea
Cradle, collected $2,000, and flawed an otherwise perfect day for
Tim Mara.

Racially, the Irish predominate among bookies; there's a fair
number of Jews and Germans, and a keen scattering of Italians.
Customarily, a bookie has a side business of some sort in Manhattan (more often than not it's just a front), keeps his real name or
his number out of the phone book, has wide half- and underworld
and sports and stage and political connections, winters in Florida, and dresses a lot more conservatively than you probably expect him to—only shirts and ties, as a rule, give him away. If you
want a few samples closer to, *Long Tom Shaw* is probably No. 1
in the States. He is six feet three tall, fully built, gray, quiet in
his naming of the odds, and notable throughout his world for his
swift and paperless mathematics. Other bookies check on his
prices through field glasses. He is the son of a New Orleans con-
fectioner who owned trotters, and he used to be a bicycle racer.
His Manhattan office is listed as real estate. *Tim Mara* is a large,
curly-headed, thick-fleshed Irishman with the wide, relaxed,
dimpled, big-mouthed, and keen type of Irish face. Timothy
James Mara's life is too colorfully involved to bear writing on a
thumbnail. He was born forty-eight years ago in Greenwich Village; sold papers, Madison Square programs, candy in a Third
Avenue theatre; was a Ziegfeld usher; sold lawbooks. Became a
bookie in 1910. Of late years has been in and out of bookmaking.

Some of his avocations: customers' man in Wall Street for Al Smith's pal Mike Meehan (1927–30); coal business (Mara Fuel Co., still listed); liquor business (Kenny-Mara Importers Co., 1933, still listed; a Scotch labeled Timara); owner of New York Giants (football; he has never played the game). He has been often in court, most spectacularly in a row over what Gene Tunney owned him for build-ups, political lubrication. Has two sons: John, president of the Giants, and Wellington Timothy, who is at Fordham. He is a fight promoter (Schmeling-Baer, the second Ross-Canzoneri); plays rotten golf; has never driven a car since, twenty years ago, he was in a bad accident; has a place at Lake Luzerne, near Saratoga. He is variously known about the tracks as (a) just a big good-natured guy and (b) the ultimate truculent mug. But everyone agrees that as a mental mathematician he's second only to Shaw and, as a bookie, among the most eminently successful.

Roy Orfutt, a tall, loose-hung owner of Kansas City real estate, is the only bookie who makes a book on the *fourth* horse. He was once a horse trainer, used to own horses, has the reputation of being a wizard handicapper. He lays big bets and you can see him, cool and calm, watching a race on which he has bet $30,000. It is said of him, as it has been said of others, that he has in his veins not blood but ice water. Anyhow, he winters in California. The other equally important eastern bookies are Peter Blong (whose prices are the ones posted on the clubhouse blackboard), Ben Davis, Bob Kennedy, Frank Moore, Bob Shannon, Max (Kid Rags) Kalik, a dangerous-looking, beady young Italian named Johnny Ferrone, and Maurice (The Dancer) Hyams. The Dancer is a sort of Saratoga specialty. All the bookmakers are in holiday humor in that town (nowhere else do they take their stand in the morning street, or hash over the afternoon during the early evening); but The Dancer is ready for betting in the evening as well—on next day's races. He used to be in show business, a hoofer. He could have been a comic as well. He affects the big, sloping, sweaty suits, the wild collars, the wide gestures of the professional funnyman; has a line of sales phrases that draws all within radius of his loud hoarse voice; has a comeback for anything you throw his way; has been known to gallop the whole length of the homestretch, rooting for the horse he wants to win.

He names extremely attractive (and extremely cagey) prices. Favorite sport of the regulars, of an early evening, is to loll down Broadway and watch The Dancer put on a show.

The bookies do business morning and evening then, and some business days ahead, and still more business comes in over the wires from Jersey City (which handles Manhattan), from Detroit, from Baltimore (which is all the way illegal). But they handle the shank of their business—of the sort anyhow that you as a layman will see and take part in—at trackside between races. Betting warms up around the third race, cools off generally with the sixth or seventh. In the course of a middling lively afternoon half a million might change hands. It's very seldom indeed, by the way, that a bookie welshes: but a credit bettor does often enough, and the bookie has no legal redress. (Pre-1934 betting was all on credit; a great deal of clubhouse and "regulars'" betting is still on credit.) At season's end one reasonably successful bookmaker signed off to this effect: "I've got $3,000 in cash, and $100,000 in paper"; and one leading bookmaker, in business since 1913, has suffered $4,000,000 in bad debts during the outlawed period. They take a certain load of bad debts for granted.

Well, the bookies and the ball games break up around noon and the sleepers-off wake up, grab lunch or breakfast and a couple of drinks, and move on out to sit down before the real reason why they came to Saratoga at all: the ponies.

Saratoga was the first American course, and in this greatest of racing states it is the last of the great old courses. Once its brothers were Sheepshead Bay, Brighton Beach, Gravesend: and all these have succumbed to the cold, expanding wave of Greater New York stonework. Saratoga is the last of the old great courses, and every great American horse has boiled into its homestretch: Victorian, Questionnaire, Equipoise, Cavalcade, Twenty Grand, Whichone, Boojum, and Man O' War, who there lost his only race (the Sanford Memorial) in twenty-one starts. No single race is staged there than can quite match the Kentucky Derby for plain glamour, but at Saratoga there's perhaps the most notable *succession* of races you'll ever see. Their names are names people reflex to all over two continents: the Saratoga Handicap, the Travers, the Whitney Memorial, the Sanford Memorial, the Wilson Stakes, the Grand Union Hotel and the United States

Hotel Stakes, the Merchants and Citizens Handicap, the Alabama, the Flash, the Saratoga Special, for two-year-olds, the only American race that hands *all* money to the winner.

On the last day comes the Hopeful, which in two-year-old interest is second only to the Belmont Futurity, and the Saratoga Steeplechase Handicap, which climaxes the month for gentlemen riders, and the Saratoga Cup. Saratoga is maybe specially notable as the greatest of proving grounds for two-year-olds, the great developer of the great horses: it is in the $40,000 Hopeful Stakes that the two-year-old is first asked, each year, to go six and a half furlongs (four-fifths of a mile). Many owners hold their most promising two-year-olds out of the spring meetings in favor of a Saratoga debut. You not only uncover champions at the spa; you see great upsets too. They can happen any time and any place, of course, as when, at Belmont last May, Cavalcade lost his rider near the start. But you'll seldom see anything to match that muddy Saratoga day in 1930 when Jim Dandy, a 100-to-1 shot, beat both Gallant Fox and Whichone.

When they look at it merely as a business investment, Marshall Field, Thomas Hitchcock, Widener, the Whitneys, and the other stockholders in the Saratoga Association for the Improvement of the Breed of Horses have, beyond any reasonable doubt (they don't quote their losses, though), cause for headaches aplenty. Nevertheless depression struck racing late and racing recovered early, as the following figures (gross receipts—concessions, bookies' contributions as well as gate—not for Saratoga merely but for all New York tracks) will indicate:

	Racing days	*Receipts*
1929	171	$2,919,800
1930	178	2,789,000
1931	171	2,257,700
1932	170	1,536,600
1933	154	1,340,000
1934	178	2,843,700

One sound reason why racing was hit so late is simple enough: there's a heavy gambling attendance, and gamblers', or smart, money has fewer fingers in the collapsing economic pie than your, or not-so-smart, money has. The reason receipts bounced so gaily from the 1933 figure, lowest since the War, to 1934's, is even simpler. It is merely that the passage of the Crawford-Breitenbach Bill (so-called; Joseph Auerbach, counsel to the Jockey Club, drafted it), which is as full of loopholes and as deftly woven as any fish net, though it doesn't declare betting legal, makes open betting at the track, cash in hand, possible. Plenty of the regulars still bet on credit, but it makes a difference to plenty more and an infinite difference to the confidence and interest of the semilayman and the layman. Another clause in the bill, which explains its passage nicely enough, gives the state 15 per cent of the gate; the federal government gets 10 per cent. Thus last year the state received $285,000, of which—to get back to town— Saratoga contributed $52,360. This is Saratoga's own 1933–34 story:

	Racing days	Receipts	Paid admissions	Purses
1933	27	$314,400	150,100	$111,000
1934	30	509,400	191,200	200,900

The association has still gaudier intentions upon the season just opening; and one of the solidest ways of expressing such intentions is to fatten the purses and the "guarantees" and to announce plenty of "added money." The meanings of these terms will become clear in the course of seeing how a purse is made up and what it costs the association out of pocket.

At Saratoga, thirty-six "stakes" are run; a great many more "overnight races," so-called because you enter your horse before noon today and he races tomorrow afternoon. Now about the stakes.

If, last fall, you had entered a horse for a certain race this August—and you could have entered him no later—you would have paid, say, a $50 subscription fee (the fees throughout differ with the races). If your horse was still entered this spring, you would have paid another $100. And if, this August, he starts, you pay another $300. Thus the association is able to estimate in advance a minimum income; from which it is possible to work out a *guaranteed* (i.e., minimum) purse. The association puts into the stakes added money; and this is the only sum for which the association itself is directly responsible. It comes out of its own pocket: re-

ceipts, et cetera, may or may not cover it. The Travers, for instance, is guaranteed this season for $20,000, of which the associ-
ation pays $9,000; the rest they have got or are sure they will get
from subscriptions. For all the thirty-six races the association actually pays, this year, $73,000 out of its pocket: that is, in added
money. The small overnight races cost the association a lot more. There
are about five of these a day and each of them pays between $900
and $1,200; and they will cost the association some $160,000 this
month. For this season the association has announced increases
of $25,000 in stakes. Of thirty-six stakes twenty will be added
money and only fifteen merely guaranteed—the Saratoga Special
is neither—as against respectively nine and twenty-six last season. The Alabama, for three-year-old fillies, will be worth $10,000
and will cost the association $5,000; the Saratoga Handicap will
be worth $11,000 and will cost the association some $7,500.
Everything possible, in short words, to draw the horses and the
crowds. Last year Narragansett wheedled away for its debut a few
good horses, a thousand or so spectators. It was not enough to
hurt, but not the sort of thing to let take hold.

For about three hours each day, then, Saratoga's whole hetero-
geneous clientele is coalesced and most intensely concentrated
around one single point: the swiftness of the movement of horses.
It is a concentration whose essential quality is best caught in the
noise a few thousand people make when first they all become
aware the horses are off. It is neither an enthusiastic nor a quite
human noise: it sounds rather uncannily like a wave displaying
itself along a stony beach. You catch that essence a second time
when the field gets its stride, loose as lather, swimming along the
white barrier on the backstretch . . . And then at length the last
horse in the last race, whom nobody but his mother ever looks at,
brings the day's most beautiful and most serious business to a
faintly ignominious close and, with the twilight and the evening
and the depth of a night ahead, thirty thousand people, more or
less, are disunified and scattered at large upon the resources of
the town and of the surrounding countryside.

There's never exactly a letdown from then on. Everyone has
plenty to talk about, money to riffle (or losses to gripe over), and

places, of all sorts and kinds, to go. The first place is right across from the clubhouse entrance and it is the home of Sam Rosoff the New York subway man. It looks rather like an orphan asylum, but that's typical of Saratoga homes. Rosoff is already on his porch, hollering to his friends, and if you're one of them you stop off and have a drink. If you're not you float along with everyone else on the same wave of casual excitement, up into town where, first thing, everyone has a drink and then nearly everyone has another and a good many have a third. Now Broadway is abloom, full-blown, with prostitutes. And now every bar, and now every degree of restaurant and every hot-dog stand is standing them up; and by now those who can afford it are on their way to the fancy clubs out in the country. What you do after your supper or hot dog depends partly on who, socially and occupationally, you are, and partly on your money and your day's luck. There are weekly professional boxing shows at Convention Hall and, seven miles east, at Luther's White Sulphur Springs Hotel on Saratoga Lake, where both Dempsey and Tunney have trained and where Dempsey owns a cottage; and there are amateur bouts (jocks, stableboys, townies, etc.) once a week at the Racetrack Recreation Center. Three years ago there was dog racing at Ballston Spa, six miles south, and the poorer end of the crowd flocked to it. So every entrepreneur, purveyor, and procurer in Saratoga raised a frightful howl, and the track was closed under legal pressure. Or there are always the bookies under the trees, with today to hash over and tomorrow to hash out, and The Dancer putting on his act.

Every night except Saturday and Sunday of the two middle weeks the place to spend the time between dinner and night work is at the yearling auction. All the horsier of the socialites turn up complete in soup-and-fish to match their wits against the smartest judges of horseflesh in America. Looking around the ringside you'd get snow-blind with starched facades, Kleig-eyed for the diamonds—you couldn't do half so well at the opera. This is beyond any dispute the No. 1 horse market in the country. Here (for 1933) are figures: in Saratoga alone; the sale of 388 yearlings brought $429,000. In all the rest of the U.S. the sale of 389 yearlings brought $90,000. The average yearling in that year went for $1,105 at Saratoga, in Kentucky for $259, in Maryland for $157, in Virginia for $151: and the relativities run pretty much the same, good year in and bad out.

The show is staged by Mr. E. J. Tranter for the Fasig-Tipton Co., whose real name is Mr. E. J. Tranter. Tranter's father was such a good cricket player than when he died the flag on Liverpool's Municipal Building dropped to half-mast; and Tranter, handling as he does some 90 per cent of all U.S. thoroughbreds sold at auction, doesn't do so badly by himself. The best U.S. stables hang on to their best for the Saratoga sales: regularly represented are Phil T. Chinn, W. R. Coe, Marshall Field, Willis Sharpe Kilmer, Colonel E. R. Bradley, and a dozen others.

The bidding is exciting but quiet, as smart bidding always is, and the pleasant thing about the yearling sales is that for all your judgment you can never be sure what you're getting; and that prices prove less than nothing. In 1928 Man O' War's son Broadway Limited went to W. T. Waggoner for $65,000. Broadway Limited never finished better than fourth, and his career ended among the saddest and cheapest of platers as he was trying to win a $900 purse at Lincoln Fields at Crete in Illinois in 1930: he died trying to win it. Man O' War, who won $249,465 for S. D. Riddle before he was retired to stud in 1921, who has sent more than 360 to the races, who has brought as high as $5,000 for one service, and around whom an entire stable has been built up, went to Mr. Riddle as a yearling, at Saratoga, for $5,000. Cavalcade went for $1,200, Head Play for $550, Hustle On sold to W. R. Coe for $70,000 and never started. Peak price in Saratoga's history was the $75,000 C. V. B. Cushman paid for New Brooms. If you're still unconvinced that prices and your judgment mean nothing, this proposition will interest you: one of the season's races is the Saratoga Sales Stakes, run by last year's yearling purchases. Colonel E. R. Bradley will lay you even money you can't name a single horse at the sales who will win that race or any race on any track the following year.

Every August Saratogan is a gambler at heart and often by profession. Yearling bidding, the favorite midevening sport, is a gamble; and as the crowd moves on to its night spots it is settling down less to routine night-clubbery than to a serious evening's gaming. Every night club is a casino. The smart clubs are out a way in the country—the Arrowhead, Piping Rock, Riley's—and you can go there for low as $5 a head for dinner and cocktails and they'll send a carriage for you to boot. If for any reason they don't want you they take their dislike out on your check—and you don't go back. Until last year the still snortier Brook Club, which used to be run by the well-known bookie Max (Kid Rags) Kalik, refused entrance to all those not dressed and to all those not listed in the human studbook; but at last it broke down too. It also burned up. Well, once you get to these places, you meet a man with a stack of dollar bills a foot thick and a century prominent on top, who calls for your play, and you meet Broadway, nearly as large as life and a lot more natural. Entertainers of the caliber of Helen Morgan when she was in her prime, and the Yacht Club Boys, and Harry Richman. Saratoga runs less to the hot than to the potted-palm styles of music and entertainment: Ben Bernie and Whiteman, who are both nuts over racing; Vincent Lopez (who played second base for the Lopez-All-Stars, a morning team built around Mara and the speed skater Joe Moore, and who nearly ended his keyboard career with a slide into second); Abe Lyman, Henri Busse, Emil Coleman; that sort. The great favorites are Lopez and Bernie. Bandmasters and their boys take Saratoga jobs as a holiday, what with the racing and all; though their hours, Lord knows, are no shorter than elsewhere.

The routine dancing and drinking, however, is mere celery-and-olives: the serious work of the evening is of course around the faro banks and the bird cages (one kind of crap device; highest odds against you of any sucker game; the ladies love it; you can buy it in New York at Abercrombie's) and the wheels (for the sophisticates) and the crap tables (for the vulgar). There are times and places when figures or even estimates are worse than worthless, and this is one of them: how much money floats that tide is any man's guess. But besides the chronically rich you must remember that a good number of people have made a cleaning that afternoon, and that becalmed money burns in a gambler's very heart. In other words the big race money gets back into full circulation. Almost any tout, by the by, is optimistic enough to bring a tux to town; and at these clubs you see some pleasantly inappropriate mugs looking over their whitewashed fences. But money at the smart clubs is likely to find its temporary levels along between two and four, and both ends of the crowd move out in search of hotter and louder entertainment. The cheaper folk in the smaller clubs such as Klub Kentucky, Felix, Wagon Wheel, Dutch Mill (now Asia Gardens), and the Little Club, which dot the town and neighborhood (and which are likely to change or not to open year by year), are at large in search of the same. Everyone finds it in Saratoga's imported Harlem, on Congress Street.

The least moneyed people of all have been warming it up since around midnight and by now it fully affords the crowding and the brain-blinding racket you need, at this ebb of your vitality, to keep you happy the rest of the night. The main clubs here are Jack's Hi-de-Ho, the Harlem Club, the Green Cave, and they all have their milk-chocolate floor shows, but no black bands of any particular note. Last summer by the way the Little Club went the whole town one better: offered Jack Mason's Playboy Revue, an all-boy show with sixteen female impersonators.

Down the dark of the street in the hindward shadow of the Grand Union, life becomes more drab. Thanks to our easy twentieth-century upper-middle-class promiscuity, you may well be under the vague impression that prostitution went on the skids along with plug-helmeted policemen and young gentlemen who made a conspicuous profession of sowing their wild oats. It didn't. It is worthy of mention here only because it is rarely more noticeable in the U.S. than at Saratoga in season. The girls come in all shades and from many places—dark-fleshed out of the deep South following the colored "help"; girls from the railroad streets of Troy and some of the political darlings of Albany; some of the great New Orleans breed of mulatto professionals; quite a number of follow-uppers from Manhattan. They come singly and take rooms, they come by teams and fill houses, their contracts are made along the Broadway dusk, and their business goes on all night. A big newish house (white girls) a way out of town chastely proclaims itself with the sign TRANSIENTS.

And then along about five, the night spots thin out and the rest of their work is only for those who die with great difficulty; and out beneath the trees in the long low whitewashed buildings the odor of coffee stains the air and you hear the thud of a hoof and the strange and princely language of a horse.

And there comes one last night also when, as the ultimate parties blare and fritter toward their red-eyed end, you hear throughout the streets of Saratoga the heavy and the deliberate steady rumble, as of an army in orderly retreat, of the departing horse lorries.

And every next morning the streets are as strangely empty as a new-made corpse of breath; the windows of the big hotels are blinded with Bon Ami; already the cottages are being boarded up and the furnishings shrouded in the smart clubs; a top-heavy obsolescent bus mulls down empty Broadway bearing toward the mineral drinks and the baths its quota of sad-eyed hypochondriac Jews; and swift and broad upon the lush elms and the kaleidoscopic slate shingles and the wild gables and the apoplectically swirled colonnades and the bare porches and the egregiously extensive and pitiable slums of this little curious city there settles, delayed a little but by no means dispelled by Saratoga's other season, the season of waters, the chill and the very temper and the very cold of death.

THE U.S.
COMMERCIAL ORCHID

Y ou should know right at the start that there are no less than 15,000 species of orchid, of which a good many of the more restrained types, such as the moccasin flower, and the lady's-slipper, thrive familiarly in our own temperate woodlands. From now on when we say orchid we mean orchid as you understand it: the big, flagrant, tropical job whose normal career runs from hothouse to Milady's collar bone to the garbage can, rustling up, in transit, considerable satisfaction to Milady, considerable expense to her decorator, and considerable profit to the fellow who raised the orchid.

Today, in the U.S., 800,000 to 1,000,000 of these commercial orchids are sold in a year at retail prices ranging from seventy-five cents (off season, for cheap skates) to $8 and $10 and even $12 (in season, for non-pareils) per single blossom and in quantities varying from a very few hundred per mid-summer day to a great many daily thousands around Christmas and Easter. The florist who retails the orchid, in spite of the fancy price he puts on it, doesn't stand to make much off it; the man who grows and wholesales it, in spite of the fancy costs he poured into it and in spite of the strong irregularities of the season, does. There are about forty such growers in the U.S., and most of them don't amount to much. A scattering of them have the Pacific Coast trade more or less to themselves; a half dozen or so more, located in Westchester and New Jersey, ship flowers into Greater New York. Of these eastern orchidists the most notable are shrewd Mr. Sam Gilbert, who represents the Richmond Floral Co. of Staten Island, and Lager & Hurrell of Summit, New Jersey. But by and large these growers concentrate on developing and selling individual plants, and ship on the cut flowers as a sideline. There is just one company that really counts in a large way in the commercial-orchid field, and that is Thomas Young Nurseries, Inc., of Wall Street and also Twenty-eighth Street in New York, of Bound Brook in New Jersey, of Cleveland, and of Chicago. Thomas Young Nurseries: whose 160,000 mature plants in two flocks of hothouses produce no less than 70 and as high as 80 per cent of the U.S. orchids sold in season—and a strong 50 to 60 per cent of all U.S. commercial orchids; whose monopoly is nicely protected on the one hand by the high price of good orchid plants, on another by seedling problems, and on still another by a strict government quarantine* against imported orchids as bearers of insect pests. So you can see that all in all, in any story of the U.S. commercial orchid, this one company is pretty much the whole show.

The story in brief is simple. In 1929 big business got hold of a good commodity, which was nevertheless untouched by any save the most tentative and erratic business methods, and took just those large if obvious advantages of it that any gentleman who knew his business would be bound to take. For one thing, the orchid had known only localized distribution; big business gave it national distribution. For another, the orchid had never known promotion; big business promoted merry hell out of it. For the rest, this success story can thank a combination of competent management with those talents peculiarly native to the orchid itself. If, to begin with, you want some picture of the orchid "business" prior to 1929, old Thomas Young himself will furnish a fair one.

In 1922 the Cornell plant physiologist Lewis Knudson discovered that orchid seed will germinate much more dependably in solutions of agar-agar than in anything else; and thus solved the toughest single problem of the orchid hybridist. One of these, the Bound Brook, New Jersey, fancier Thomas Young, took such proliferous advantage of the find that by 1927 he was orchid poor. Thousands upon thousands of unexpected new plants forced him

---

*Framed in 1919, the quarantine forbids any grower to import more than 400 plants in a year; the orchids face government fumigation; most of them die along with their pests in the process. This quarantine appears to discourage growers: of 14,000 plants authorized for import in 1934, only 9,000 were actually brought in.

to a choice. Either he must enormously expand his greenhousing facilities, and go into business in a large way if only to defray that expense, or he must sell out. Now for a long time Young had done some business in gardenias and had carried on a sporadic and fortuitous trade in cut orchids, but he was no sort of businessman at all—never even kept any books, and had always raised the orchid pretty much for the orchid's sake. Also, he was now sixty-five years old, and tired. He chose to sell out, named the naively low price of $800,000, and sat down and waited.

People came, florists and wholesalers, and yearned around, and went away: big money wasn't highly concentrated in the florist trade. Two of the nibblers are worthy of mention, one because of an act of mercy, and the other because, if he had taken hold, this might be quite a different story. The shrewd and ritzy Manhattan florist Max Schling, good friend to Young, wanted to buy and couldn't, and told Thomas Young his $800,000 price was loony low. The spectacular Morton Goldfarb (M. Goldfarb—My Florist, Inc., the Philadelphia Gimbel's, Macy's, Bamberger's, Abraham & Straus), who is reputed to have grossed $2,000,000 in flowers in 1934, wanted to buy, too, and also couldn't, and is still sore he didn't have the money. My God, if he'd had that outfit by now he'd have flower shops on the corners of every major city in the country, like United Cigar; and he'd sell nothing but orchids, gardenias, and roses, at set prices; he'd mass produce; and he'd be cleaning up.

But time went on, and there were no takers. In the next couple of years Young had to double his hothouse space, rent his own wholesale store (first of its kind in the orchid trade) in New York, and in fact was on the verge of being forced into big business if only by default. He felt awful.

And then with opening of the febrile and outlandish year 1929, a very different kind of fish swam past, struck, and swallowed Young's bait right to the armpit. And Young drops out of our story, free of his burden. Free of most that had comprised his life, for that matter.

Wall Street's Charles D. Barney & Co., through its new "new business" man, Carl Beckert, and through the promoter Arthur Bunker, got wind of Thomas Young's plight and investigated: and before long it was a deal. Barney's Reybarn Investments, through Barney's Selected Industries, Inc., bought out Young for $2,750,000 cash, rewarded idea-man Bunker with 25,000 of its 150,000 common shares and the temporary presidency of the new company, shook out the rest of the stock in the laps of Barney partners, named its officers, filed away newborn Thomas Young Nurseries, Inc., in its fat portfolio, and sat down to await statements on something novel in history: the handling of orchids as a big business.

The results at the end of 1929, which were reported in the first issue of *Fortune*, were pretty indeed: net earnings of $800,000 on a $2,750,000 investment. Earnings in the years since have of course diminished considerably—have even, two years, blushed red. But they have diminished by no means so much as you'd have every reason to expect of earnings on one of the most eminently useless commodities in existence during six of the most eminently lean years of an era. Gardenias have, to be sure, done their part—10 per cent gross and doubtless a lot less net; but the gardenia market has been stuffed so full it has busted. (Few years ago the flower wholesaled at $14 to $18 a dozen; now the best are $1.50 to $6.) Scarcely assisted the orchid has, in fact, done very well indeed by its impresarios: so well that today, though all the Young properties, green goods included, are assessed at only $2,800,000 you couldn't buy Thomas Young Nurseries, Inc., for $30,000,000. Here, for the past six years (each ending May 31), are gross sales and net profits or losses as listed:

	Gross Sales	Profit
1930	$ 718,630	$333,890
1931	593,040	105,850
1932	348,650	(80,010) loss
1933	266,490	(56,070) loss
1934	384,290	32,240
1935	387,540	24,790
	$2,698,640	$360,690

Indeed, thanks to the breadth of Young's depreciation policy, the story is really happier than that. On an average, during each of the past six years, $67,500 has been written off to equipment depreciation, a total so far of $405,000 or 49 per cent amortization of Young's $903,000 plant. Seven or eight years at that average, which Young's intends to continue, will reduce the book value of the plant to $1 and returns from then on will be almost pure gravy.

Thomas Young Nurseries, Inc., breaks down into three corporations: the New York, the New Jersey, the Cleveland. The New York company, the small and rather dingy wholesale store on Twenty-eighth Street, is operated by Vice President H. E. Kenyon (under Beckert's surveillance) and is owned 100 per cent by the Jersey company (thirty greenhouses, 300,000 square feet of glass, 25,000 gardenia plants, 130,000 mature orchid plants, 175,000 orchid seedlings). The Jersey company also owns 76 per cent of the Cleveland company (ten greenhouses, 40,000 square feet of glass, 30,000 mature plants, no seedlings), which still again in turn rents and runs another wholesale store, likewise small and dingy, in behind the world's biggest hotel, the Stevens, in Chicago. And of course all these companies are owned by Reybarn Investments, which again is owned by Barney & Co. Twenty-four per cent of the Cleveland company is owned by its President, Parmely Webb (son of Myron T.) Herrick, who made news in Paris eight years ago when he lent a suit to a weekend guest of his father's, Charles A. Lindbergh.

As a heavy Cleveland socialite, Herrick was a particularly fortunate appointment for that branch of the business. But then too, setting up a plant in Cleveland and opening a store in Chicago were both thoroughly smart moves in the first place. Subtle but definite climatic differences between Ohio and Jersey are such that one plant can often ably complement the other by season as well as geography. It's mostly a geographical advantage, though. Bound Brook serves the thick, surrounding herd of seaboard cities; Cleveland is generally free to serve Chicago and the great breadth of hinterland. When Barney's went into the business, remember, the orchid was almost purely a short-haul, indeed a metropolitan, commodity. Within a year Barney's had extended the shipping radius to 1,000 miles and now, thanks no less to distributive machinery than to heavy promotion, Young's gets orders steadily from small cities and small towns which never entered the conjecture of the old-time orchidists. A fourth of Young's orchids today fill provincial orders. Within the first year after it

opened, the Chicago store was doing almost as well as the one in
New York; of late it has done rather better.

Boss of the hole outfit since 1932 is Carl Beckert, President
and Treasurer of the New York company, President at Bound
Brook, Vice President at Cleveland, and a pleasant and intelligent commercial type who quite precisely looks his part: an olym-
piad at Yale and a couple of decades of upper-middle-class business activity. None of the Barney partners meddle in much,
being chiefly interested in Beckert's annual statements. Beckert
himself has no need to overstrain: Cleveland and Chicago, which
are carbon copies of the eastern outfit, are in capable hands, and
so, for that matter, are Bound Brook and the New York store, and
so is the important job of promotion.

Be well advised, before we proceed along the Thomas Young
assembly line at Bound Brook, that you are seeing the merest
sketch of what is there for the trained horticulturist to see. For
the orchid has unbearably complicated reproductive habits and
through all the stages of its life must be watched over with a care-
fulness whose specific lore would fill volumes and which in the
long run thaws off the deep end into pure intuition.

A modest one-story affair with beaverboard walls and linoleum
floors serves to house the brunt of the purely business end of the
whole company: the rest is a shining, hypnotic realm of glass by
the acre and of coal and water and moss and moist cinders and
quietude and tender care. Beckert's office allows itself a few
touches of executive dignity—a gleaming desk, a bookcase full of
treatises on financial management, advertising, orchid culture.
For a layman, Beckert has learned quite a bit about orchids, but
he puts on no authoritative facade. He comes out from New York,
not perfectly regularly, early of a morning, runs through things
with Mr. Babey (pronounced Bobby), and often as not leaves for
town by noon, for an engagement. Mr. Babey, who looks scarcely
thirty, is in actual charge not only of the office force and of the
packers and shippers, but of the hothouse staff (most of which
worked under Young) and even of Godfrey Erickson. Erickson,
however, is given plenty of latitude, and that is well: for this silent, curiously gentle, all but mystical Swedish ex-sailor, who has
no interest in Young's beyond the flowers as flowers, is possibly

the most valuable man in the whole outfit. He has spent twenty of his forty-five years in these greenhouses and he knows, as none of the management makes any claim to, just about all any one man can know about raising orchids.

The two biggest greenhouses (65 by 200 feet) and six of the standard size (35 by 250 feet) are devoted to 25,000 gardenia plants; the rest of the thirty to orchids. The orchid houses may strike you as surprisingly cool for tropical plants; the average temperature is 62 degrees to 66 degrees Fahrenheit. When a crop needs forcing the temperature may be raised as high as 90 degrees. The houses are steam-heated. Air conditioning was once considered, but it was discovered it would cost $27,000 to condition one twenty-five-by-forty-foot greenhouse, and the idea was dropped like a hot potato. Young's uses aluminum paint in its greenhouses for cleanliness as well as erosion resistance, and repaints every year. Cleanliness is of immense importance, and every square foot of earthen floor is turned and freshly cindered once a year to keep down weeds and fungi. Orchid plants used to hang in baskets, but the roots dried out too quickly, and now ordinary pots do the job. There is no standard way of benching the pots; the matter rests with the individual grower. Erickson is for stadium-wise tiers rather than level benches, arranges his plants in one vast geometric alignment, and centers immense importance on such abstruse minutiae as the distance a given plant should occupy, at a certain age, between the roof and the floor; a matter of mere inches. A strange man, Erickson, and an able one. Able to say that his orchids "tell" him "what they need" and to make that, somehow, not fatuous but almost credible.

All of the Young orchids, except for a few thousand lady's-slippers, are of the great division of epiphytes (devourers of air) and average two flowers per plant per year and are generally productive for around twenty years. The nurseries are specially distinguished as having the world's largest and best collection of whites. No orchid is pure white, but the whiter the better: they're particularly popular for weddings, and bleaching is a common practice among some growers. Keeping, of course, only the commercially useful plants, Young's has also more varieties of orchid than any other grower, and is the largest if not indeed the only grower interested in crops rather than in the development of individual plants. Most popular orchids are members of a showy family called *Cattleya*: each hybrid differs, and blooms at a different time of year so that—if you want it—a continuous supply is obtainable. In 1935, 318,000 of the flowers Young's sold were cattleyas. For its crop in general, the company must depend on two sources, the mature plant itself, and the one to three bulbs into which it subdivides each year—bulbs which themselves are blowing off flowers a year later. Raising from the plant and bulb is, as orchids go, fairly simple; merely a matter of taking all sorts of care. Here, very briefly sketched, is the extremely important job of hybridizing, of raising seedlings—a job which at Bound Brook is handled by three men.

The raw materials are simple enough: coal, pots, water, osmundi for orchid plants to grow in, agar-agar to nourish the orchid seeds themselves. Coal, pots, and a lot of water are necessary to any greenhouse. Osmundi, the stuff any orchid plant, seedling or not, grows in, is a springy, nitrogenous sort of moss which looks like matted horsehair, smells a little like a zoo house, grows like a lot of footstools in Florida bogs. Young's buys about 7,000 sacks of it (2,000 for Cleveland) a year at about $1 a sack.

Even less expensive is the agar-agar. Bound Brook uses only about five pounds of it a year, at $3 a pound, in its 1,600 test tubes. Agar is a tawny, powdery derivative (translucent gray in solution) of Oriental seaweeds which has long been important as a culture medium in bacteriology. Since 1922 it has been a godsend to orchid hybridizers. For the orchid seed, unlike that of any other plant, does not wear enough food to nurse life into it, and orchid men in the past had fed it peat moss, fungi, pure manure, burlap, turkish toweling, and virtually everything else short of a bit of old lace, without any predictable success.

The new generation begins with the flower; and with the genital subtleties of the orchid Charles Darwin managed to fill a thick book. Discretion is the better part of valor and we had best say little more here than this: nature contrived every flower, as you must know, as nothing more nor less than an invitation to the rape; and the orchid takes advantages of that privilege spectacular and complex far beyond the point of mere abuse. A bee, lured among those lordly floral leaves, hikes his thighs around many unusual corners, departs woolly with pollen, and, falling for another labyrinthine love trap, leaves that yellow dust against the sexual organs of another orchid. Shortly the flower droops shut against any later invasion; down the stem a plant womb swells in the course of nine to fourteen months to the size of a child's fist and, gently exploding, delivers posterity upon the mercy of the air and of nature. In the nursery, of course, the plants are fertilized not by random bees but by careful, selective hand and, long before ripeness, the womb is sealed in a waxen sack. And the seed, five hundred thousand to a million of them, looking like fine wheat flour, are taken to the laboratory, which looks hardly more elaborate than the kitchen of a modern farmhouse. And there begins a job years long.

With platinum-pointed, flame-sterilized needles the seeds are sown, 200 to a test tube, in a solution of agar which hardens and shrinks, holding the roots of the seedlings firmly in place. Plugged with cotton, and entered in the studbook, the tubes go to a small hothouse where they are kept under high temperatures for a year or more. If fungus gets in (and nobody knows how it does or whence it comes) it will kill practically the whole batch; otherwise, the losses in this most critical stage seldom run above 2 or 3 per cent. Out of each unharmed tube, however, only the fifty or so hardiest are selected. At this stage the seedlings, infinitesimally exploded into three or four leaves, are only about a quarter of an inch high. At the ends of long steel needles they are lifted from their stiff jelly bed and put, fifty together, into community pots packed tight with fine-chopped osmundi. At the end of a year of hogging nitrogen, the thirty hardiest are taken out and planted five to a pot. The weaklings are thrown away. At the end of another year each plant gets its own pot: and again only the sturdiest are kept. By this time the original 200 seeds have produced possibly twenty-five or thirty plants, of which fungus has killed far fewer than Young's rigid selection.

Once the plants assume individual status, it takes them another four years to flower, six to put out a full crop. And trouble doesn't end there. For orchids are hybrids from wayback; and they are as subject to Mendelian law as any fruitfly or human being. In short, for all the care you've put into the matchmaking, you can never be perfectly sure what will come of it. Some otherwise healthy plants refuse to bloom at all. Others flower minus the baroque lip which is the esthetic point and purpose of the orchid. Others run all to lip. Others are hideously miscolored. Moreover they're as likely to bloom in summer as in winter, and the attempt to force or curb the plants into step with the season accounts for a 5 to 6 per cent crop loss and is seldom, as yet, a howling success at best. The sexless, the deformed, and the bruise-colored, then, reward the grower's years of care with total loss, and the same is pretty much the story when the good ones flower off season. However, once the plant has put forth its flower, all chance ends: it will dependably duplicate that flower for the rest of its natural life. And in the long run this work with seedlings, which is virtually the whole fascination to the fancier and which for the commercial orchidist corresponds to lab work in any industry, is eminently worth the candle for the sake of the occasional windfalls which could occur along no other channel. Such a windfall is the bestselling *Cattleya*, Athena, a cross made by Young himself and so named by Beckert because he hoped the word would be easily pronounced by Greek florists, of whom there are many. Last year was the tenth birthday of the Athena seedlings, the first Athena crop; and Young's now has 2,400 Athena plants, a big productive regiment. The special goal now is a dark purple cattleya which will bloom in season. They've got a good cross already between a couple named Fabia and Brilliant but it blooms in August at the season's very nadir. About 20 per cent of Young's orchids sold today come from seedling-born plants; the rest from plants bred out of bulbs.

After such a trip you may begin to gather something of the why of the ultimate high retail cost of the orchid. The Young nurseries bring to flower 450,000 orchids, more or less, a year. Three-fourths of the mature plants [are] at Bound Brook. Bound Brook costs run over $300,000 a year. Counting off a probably generous 10 per cent of that to gardenia culture, the cost of raising the average single cut orchid can therefore be figured, if quite roughly, at around eighty cents.

For a number of good reasons, moreover, you'd probably best stay out of the business. To say nothing further of the quarantine, the plants cost money. Finest hybrids that bloom in wearing season can't be had for less than $200 each; some have been sold for as much as $5,000; and a few years ago Lager & Hurrell reported getting upward of $10,000 for a plant bearing a pure white flower. So, you can see, it would cost quite a handsome penny indeed to buy, say, just 20,000 mature plants. It may occur to you then to build yourself a crop out of seeds. It has already occurred to a number of small growers, and they are having a tough time of it indeed. Not merely is seedling culture a hard, delicate job; you have to increase your equipment like a snowball as time goes on (a handful of seed can populate 7,500 pots) and your overhead snowballs for years before you've flowers for sale. Young's, with many plants both mature and young, and plenty of capital, can afford to discard the expensively curable sick and the exhausted (has done away with 45,000 mature plants since mid-'32) and to take supremely good care of its stock. Less well equipped firms take a beating. They can't expand in step with the expansion of their seedling army and, reducing care costs such as re-potting to a minimum, they get a low yield of orchids that are inferior at that.

A lot of care is taken in cutting and packing orchids. They are never plucked till they're in full bloom for unlike other flowers they fail to develop further if taken from the plant in bud. Once cut they are quickly popped into individual, water-filled tubes, racked in trays, taken to the sorting room, sorted by kind, size, and color, and placed in a refrigerator for the several hours of "hardening" thanks to which an orchid, given a reasonable amount of care from then on, will last a week to a fortnight without wilting and can be transported anywhere in the country. Carefully arranged in boxes braced against crushing, the floral leaves closely watched against folding under, which cracks and blackens, the orchids are sewed into place with cloth tape. The boxes are filled with macerated waxed paper which absorbes no moisture, and tightly sealed. In warm weather the case is closed in another, much heavier: in cold, within two, swathed in many layers of paper. For long journeys each flower takes along its own tight-stoppered flask and the boxes are labeled Handle With Care in flashy red italics. On any long haul they are shipped by express; last Christmas the Twentieth Century tacked on a special car for the sole benefit of Young orchids. Back in 1929–1930 there was even some smart talk about airplane shipment. It hasn't come to much for two good reasons: packaged orchids are bulky, and such rapid transit is uncalled for. The orchid at this stage, in spite of general impressions to the contrary, is a hardy flower. Young's packs its orchids in the evening. At four in the morning a truckman comes around. He has a key to the shipping room and another to the New York store, and he generally reaches the store about seven. If a special call comes during the morning another lot is rushed off by train, reaches the store about eleven. In town, Vice President H. E. Kenyon and his three assistants never know how many they'll get that day.

Young's New York wholesale store is a good plain job, three steps down from West Twenty-eighth Street's sidewalk near Sixth Avenue, in the heart of the wholesale florist district. Only note of swank about this little box which orchidizes the whole eastern seaboard are a few handsome color plates on the walls. Four smooth-topped benches run the length of the main room; a room behind is occupied by a big refrigerator similar to those used in meat stores; downstairs is a hide-out for flowers kept for favored customers. Young's ships in 300 to 500 orchids a day during the slack season, 3,000 to 5,000 during the rush. The season follows precisely the contours of the in-town social season, thickening all through the fall and rotting away from the bosoms of June brides, with a peak at Christmas time, smaller peaks (which Young's is working hard to develop) for Valentine's and Mother's days, and Mount Everest at Eastertide: within Holy Week U.S. orchidists get rid of 30,000 to 50,000 of the flowers.

By a little after seven of a morning, business begins to thicken up all along the street; Young's orchids are laid out the length of the benches and blue-faced quick little men are sidling and soon crowding alongside. Kenyon quotes a price to the first men who come into the store; they slope out down the street; he waits to see if they come back right away. If they do, he's all set; if they don't, he comes down on his price. The grapevine is in full swing: and prices may vary a lot from one hour to the next. The florists call *Cypripedia* Cyps ("sips" in New York, "sipes" in Chicago), *Cattleya* Catts, but generally don't bother with the technical names, just so the orchid looks salable, i.e., showy. If they want a special type they ask for it by description, Brasso with purple lip and such. Most of them buy only three to five flowers but some, like Schling or Morton Goldfarb, may buy hundreds and, in a big rush, thousands at a shot; and shippers usually buy a lot. Sometimes the haggling gets violent; Goldfarb is at times a star showman, throwing his hat around, breaking pencils, cuffing blossoms behind their ears, and shouting "Christ what lousy orchids!" The trading is as subtle and as merciless as any you'll locate in any market west of Bagdad, but it shakes down plain enough averages. To give you the summertime spirit of the thing, we quote the weekly *Florists Exchange and Horticultural Trade World*: "Orchids continue to drag; no one receives any great quantity but in spite of it, not a few have gone to waste. Good, clean, fresh blooms are commonly offered at fifty cents and seventy-five cents and small or stale samples, quite presentable, as low as twenty-five cents; no one even mentioned a dollar this morning." (A lot of "small or stale samples" are picked up by pushcart men, sold in Harlem.) As a rule, even in summer, Young's refuses any offer lower than seventy-five cents for fine hybrids, and rarer types run high as $1 and even $1.50. In season the low rises to $1 or $1.50, the general high from $4 to $6, and the extra-specials have rated as high as $10. Prices now are up from what they were in 1932 and 1933 but retailers still remember the Easter of 1930 when three orchids sewed together brought $45 and $50.

By ten any average morning, winter or summer, the day's business is virtually completed: from eleven or so on, the store is quiet as an attic, and smells like a recently used mortician's chapel.

By price, demeanor, and reputation the orchid is obviously tops in its field in what is politely describable as aristocrat appeal. Yet the most that the old-style orchidists had ever done about promoting it was to list off names and prices in the florists' trade sheets.

It wouldn't have been like the Young management to let such an opportunity slip by. The Young management didn't and doesn't: today Young's spends about $40,000 a year on promotion. Of that about 60 per cent goes for trade advertising, about 30 per cent for retail advertising. Since 1933 the latter job has been capably handled by a publicity organization known as June Hamilton Rhodes, Inc.

Rhodes, Inc., isn't at all the sort of organization that likes to call itself an "agent"; it is an "assistant." It has quiet tie-ups with producers of lace, velvet, jewelry, orchids, and such luxury commodities, and the service is of two sorts, both free of charge: furnishing raw materials for pictures or the pictures themselves to newspapers and style magazines; and writing, for these same organs, news releases. Rhodes has a round thousand outlets, of which the most important are those magazines whose livelihood is derived from amusing, flattering, and frightening the literate females of the land and giving them advisory service on what to buy. Rhodes is a particular master of indirect advertising: nothing so vulgar as brands, prices, company names, ever roughs up the tranquility of its copy; nor does copy ever accompany a picture. The picture alone the prose alone, is held to be quite, quite enough. So whenever you see in the fashion magazines appealing photographs of sweet young things from a hall bedroom who have about them that inescapable aura of refinement which undernourishment can lend the most ill-born demeanor, and who are molded slick as damp sea cow in velvets and chastely strung with costly jewelry, you will usually observe that they are garnished off to boot with a corsage of orchids, you will know who is responsible, and you may or may not be persuaded that it is after all rather a bloody shame that any woman must ever be deprived of copious supplies of any one of the triumvirate. The literature, which is of the same cut as the art, is perhaps best comparable to the voice of a female radio announcer: chilly contralto didacticism. Besides which, stylish, energetic Mrs. Rhodes herself, or more often her personable assistant Miss Fox, who handles the Young account, turns up in the flesh at fashion shows, wearing orchids and giving chats about them designed to overcome those scraps of prejudice against the flower which still, here and there, linger on. Of late, too, there have been tie-ups between orchids and other class commodities such as Fisher Bodies, Lux Soap, Pepperell Sheets, and Packard Motors. Even the trade ads have the Rhodes touch though they're written not by Rhodes but by the Franklin Press in Philadelphia, which gets out the exceedingly handsome color plates—first ever used in orchid advertising—on whose hind side the copy is printed. Ordinarily the advertising, in the *Florists Exchange and Horticultural Trade World* for instance, is pretty forthright and plain-jane. Young's, in its trade copy, does stoop so low as to mention itself, but the general sentiments expressed are still and definitely on the flowery side, considering the surroundings. The slogan, "Never be without an orchid," has been found specially effective.

No man even half awake to the social, economic, and political realities of our time could for an instant doubt, after a glance at such methods, that Young's promotive expenditures are worth their salt and to spare. Young's does, to be sure, pay a price for the elegant reticence of its promotion: every other orchid grower in the country has steadily neglected to spend a red cent on advertising. Young's, by keeping its own name off the Rhodes copy, takes the whole trade for a free buggy ride. But Young's can afford it. The whole business has its effect, and not merely on the public but on the florists, who have no soft ideas about orchids; in Young's wholesale store they've even been known to sit on them.

It's a funny thing about the florists. They make money off orchids, to be sure, but that is by no means the only reason why they carry them. Confessed one, in a recent survey: "Any florist in the fashionable districts must carry orchids or have people conclude he is not a first-class florist." Which is one of the lines Young's plugs hardest in its trade advertising.

Carrying the orchid no more for profit than for prestige, the florist does his own valuable bits of promotion. A fat lot is added to the purchase price by the fact that satin-covered boxes, many of them in bizarre shapes, and ribbons of velvet and silk and incidental backgrounds of other flowers are used to exaggerate the sacred stature of the orchid as a gift. You can get it in heart-shaped boxes for Valentine's Day, for instance; and if you care enough about your dear deceased to want to express your grief in expenditure, you can buy a coffin cover woven of orchids.

Even so, retail prices aren't what they used to be, even with the smartest of the florists. They used to run high as $15 and more per single bloom. Today, this is the story of Max Schling, one of the smartest: of any thousand orchids in season, seven may bring $10 to $12; twelve as high as $8; twenty-five will go for $5 and $6; the rest at around $3.50. And in summer you can buy an orchid for seventy-five cents and can't pay more than $4 without insisting. But again even so, the principle remains strongly as you'd expect it to be. To quote another florist: "Society people want orchids because not everyone can have them due to their price. In this shop men won't buy the $6 and $7 orchids but choose the $10 and $12 blooms instead. In other words, it is necessary to keep the price of orchids up in the luxury range to continue their popularity with these people."

When Barney & Co. took over the Young Nurseries, Young had 129,000 mature and 25,000 immature plants and it had for years been possible, thanks chiefly to the agar discovery, to mass produce orchids. It still is. And instead of mass producing, remember, Young's has thrown away 45,000 mature plants in three and a half years. You can credit depression, and good care, for this only in part. Orchid production has been ironed out to its present delicate balance by one chief and obvious consideration: for the people the orchid appeals to. What we have quoted one florist as saying, plenty of others will admit, and the admission tallies with a conclusion arrived at early in Barney's orchid career in a J. Walter Thompson survey of the New York market: that people like orchids because of their high price. And, though one glance at an orchid, another at any dozen orchid wearers, and a third at orchid promotion, will convince you that there's more to it than that, nevertheless high price is inevitably and indispensably involved in the orchid. Manufactured at a rough cost of eight cents per blossom and produced in great masses, it could profitably sell for a lot less than it does: and who would be the buyers? Morton Goldfarb would tell you, plenty and plenty of people who can't touch it now. But how can anyone be sure? No one can. The one reasonably predictable fact is that if the orchid became anywhere near as cheap and abundant as the rose, few of its purchasers would be those several sorts and degrees of ladies and gentlemen who at present so satisfactorily enjoy the privilege of supporting it.

Which of itself explains why Young's reduced its orchid stock and why production and demand are so neatly geared to the present near-million a year. And why also none of the forty U.S. orchidists ever make any really vicious gestures toward underselling each other.

SMOKE

hose who, lifted on the vantage of the stratosphere, have seen the planet a little in perspective, might tell you how the clean earth resembles a thinly planted garden of toadstools, of which each is a city's lifted smoke, the breath of a collective beast, the breath of our time: foul, sterile, baneful to the things we cherish (to light and well-being and silks and satins and polished metal and carved stone), and engendered by our civilization everywhere, like a curse that some obscure and nameless god might have laid upon us when we emerged from an age of barons and wandering knights and tenures and handicrafts into the urgency of the industrial revolution. We live by what we make, but of practically every great material thing we make, smoke is somewhere at some time the concomitant, the universal debit, the perfect liability from which, except in few and egregious cases, no good thing has ever yet been derived.

And of this monster of our sleeplessness much is known—and yet little. Volumes have been written about it; some valid, dry, and technical; others that pile incredible statistics one on top of the other to create a body of half-truths that must be taken seriously simple because no sufficient knowledge exists to refute them. Even a sufficient definition is difficult to arrive at. Smoke is everything that comes out of a chimney, the visible and invisible waste of the process of combustion. In its narrow and most visible sense it consists of unburned particles of carbon or tar sustained in the gases of incomplete burning, increasing as the efficiency of the combustion declines; and this is *black* smoke and the least defensible from any point of view. But in a wider sense those same gases (carbon dioxide, carbon monoxide, sulphur dioxide and trioxide, nitrogen, and some free oxygen) sustain other particles such as ash to create smokes of putrid gray-brown-yellow shades, each specific to some particular furnace; and also in this broad sense these gases may simply carry invisible compounds of arsenic, ammonia, or (most common of all) sulphur, the latter combining with moisture and oxygen in the air to form traces of the destructive sulphuric acid. So that plenty of belching chimneys are emitting not smoke (carbon) but clouds of ash; and plenty of apparently smokeless stacks are spilling tons of noxious gas into the air. Thus three kinds of materials comprise the bulk of smoke: carbonaceous (carbon, soot, and tar), ash (mineral matter), and sulphurous gases. All to the certain but unappraised peril of beautiful things.

Let us abide by the simplest definition of smoke, as everything that comes out of a chimney. And as if we were creatures of Oz, let us enter this dual world of science on the one hand; of, on the other, semi-science—shadows and penumbrae, suspicions, insidious, half-verified chemical reactions and deductions. It has been *suspected* that, above our industrial cities, relaxing upon them like a slow and ceaseless fall of snow, there floats a cloud of dust, some unknown part of which is smoke, and whose density may be anywhere from 1,000,000 to 3,000,000 particles per cubic foot, as compared with a country-air content of about 200,000; more fantastically, that, were the annual smokefall upon our cities gathered into a single pile, it would create a sloping mountain some 1,500 feet high; or, spread equably upon an average city, would bury the streets twenty-one feet deep and so in two decades lay down all but the highest skyscrapers for archaeologists of another age.

It has been *suspected* that, in the sulphurous nimbus of the great railway terminal beside it, the Cathedral of Cologne is swiftly rotting; that Notre Dame and the Sainte-Chapelle have been more withered by the fumes of Paris during the past fifty years than by the weather action of all previous centuries. In London, where the curse took root more than a hundred years ago in the brash childhood of the industrial revolution, the great stone masses of the Houses of Parliament have been so vexed by the acid of the air that thirty-five tons of corrupted stone have been stripped from them by hand. Into the acidulated and porous mortar between the foundation stones of the Pittsburgh jail an iron rod was driven two feet by hand. And if such be the effect upon stone and mortar, what of life itself? It has been *suspected* that the conspicuously high death rate of pneumonia and influenza (104 per 100,000 in the U.S.) is at least partially due to polluted air. Smoke has been *suspected* of complicity in sinusitis, conjunctivitis, anemia, rickets, and cancer of the lungs. For what the facts may be worth: in twelve typical smoky cities the death rate exceeds that in twelve less smoky communities by 31 per cent. In 1929, in Illinois, ninety three city residents out of 100,000 died of pneumonia; in the country and villages, only sixty-three; in Chicago, ninety-nine. In 1926, the year of the coal tie-ups in England, death from respiratory diseases in many English towns sank to its all-time low.*

Thus the black beast, confused and confusing, its statistics almost as elusive as its own disembodied form. What happens to it once it stands out of the chimney depends chiefly on wind and on the density and size of the particles. These average about one to two microns, a micron having a diameter of .000039 inch. In calm or slow weather, and upon cities trapped in mountains, the particles settle concentrically around their chimney according to weight and aggregation. A slow wind lays and a fog binds them upon the town. But even a ten-mile wind can carry the finer particles hundreds of miles. According to one pair of scholars ninetenths of the smoke stays indefinitely in suspension. What does settle is the heaviest and dirtiest, and most cities produce smoke a great deal faster than any normal wind can carry it off. In New York the WPA Health Department Survey has estimated that 300,000 tons of soot, tar, cinders, and fly ash are discharged into the city's atmosphere in a year. And again in New York the U.S. Weather Bureau, having taken observations in Central Park for the past six years, estimates the annual average weight of solid material per cubic mile of air has varied during that period from 1.3 to 1.8 tons.

The smoke survey expert Osborn Monnett has called St. Louis the smokiest city in the U.S. But no one really knows. The U.S. Public Health Service investigated fourteen cities in 1931–33

*These and some of the preceding suspicions are from *Stop That Smoke* by Henry Obermeyer.

and found that the air pollution was heaviest in St. Louis, Pittsburgh, Chicago, Boston, and Baltimore, not necessarily in that order. These had an air-pollution index of 137, the average for all the cities being set at 100; whereas Buffalo, Cleveland, New Orleans, New York, and Philadelphia had an index of 97; and Detroit, Los Angeles, San Francisco, and Washington only 56. Limited in money and men, the Service set up only one station in each city, it is itself, therefore, wary of deductions and comparisons. For winter, it found that in every ten cubic meters of average air in these cities (which is about a day's breathing for one man) there are 3.3 milligrams of unignited carbon, plus 1.8 milligrams of ash, spread among some 8,000,000,000 particles of dust (of which tire rubber, asphalt, stone, horse dung, and glass are other ingredients), plus some 2,000,000,000,000 "condensation nuclei," which are simply minute particles upon which water vapor has condensed. The Service found that the pollution peak for all the cities comes in the winter (December or January); that the degree of pollution varies with temperature and time of day and inversely with wind velocity; that winter air is twice as polluted as summer, markedly with carbon and sulphur; that the cleansing effects of rain are surprisingly small; and that wind, wind direction, and topography are vastly influential. The quality and the quantity of the dust vary spectacularly everywhere. These are among the more reliable facts about smoke.

Twenty-five years ago black smoke was all anyone paid any attention to, and railroads and industry, proportionately to their conspicuousness, were recognized as the chief offenders. Today the focus has shifted to include serious consideration of the less obvious contents of smoke, and it is definitely known that by no means all of this nuisance is industrial. On the contrary, the industrialist usually burns economical fires, whereas it is estimated that the householder and the small one-lung-factory owner, who burn the cheapest possible fuel in ramshackle furnaces, utilize only a half or even a fourth of its latent heat. Black flues and red ink share the rest. The modern family hearth in the basement is what causes the air-pollution curve to rise in winter. It has been *more* than suspected that 85 per cent of the smoke over Salt Lake City is domestic. Back in 1918–19 the big industrial plants of that city provided about 46 per cent of its total smoke, railroads about

20 per cent, and residences only about 19 per cent; but during the ensuing decade some 90 per cent of the industrial nuisance was corrected, while the household nuisance became worse. Twenty per cent of Chicago's smoke in 1933 was domestic, 43 per cent came from apartment houses and big heating plants and only 25 per cent from strictly industrial plants. The outrageous rise in the proportion of domestically created smoke has occurred in spite of the fact that during the period oil furnaces for the home became more or less perfected.

In indirect taxes on merchant and householder, smoke is as greedy as the New Deal. On one smoggy day in Pittsburgh, the loss to retail merchants was estimated by retail authorities at $40,000. One Scranton retail store reported in 1934 that it was protecting the clothes racked on display with slip covers, of which 1,000 were laundered each month. Of two Scranton stores, one in and one outside the smoky district, the difference in operating costs due to smoke and dust was about $8,000 a year. Minneapolis estimated its smoke-pollution damage in 1931 at $4,500,000. Chicago thinks its bill for atmospheric pollution is about $30,000,000 a year. St. Louis estimates its excess laundry bill at $1,200,000; dry cleaning, $1,200,000; painting, $1,100,000; renewing of sheet-metal work, $1,500,000; cleaning and renewing wallpaper, $1,300,000; curtains $75,000; the extra cost of artificial light, $250,000. It is suspected in St. Louis that the loss on merchandise to 7,000 stores is $2,800,000; the extra cost of cleaning and decorating 6,000 stores, $1,800,000; the cost of extra precautions against smoke and soot in 1,500 stores, $750,000; the cost of extra artificial lighting in stores, $1,000,000; the total *extra* cost to St. Louis citizens, $19,000,000 a year.

What, then, is to be done, or can anything be done, or if anything can be done is there any hope of persuading citizens to do it? The answers to these questions are diverse, but they all go back to three simple, abbreviated facts: (1) theoretically all carbonaceous (black) smoke is unnecessary, is indeed a sign that fuel is being wasted by inefficient combustion; (2) about 95 per cent of the solid content of smoke of any kind can be removed by smoke reducers, of which the chief one that the reader need be aware of is the famed Cottrell electrical precipitator; (3) of the remaining byproduct gases, some can be removed by a "scrubbing" process or by washing the coal before firing, which removes not only 25 to 50 per cent of the sulphur but some of the ash as well. Nevertheless, in the present state of the technology, most of these gases must inevitably go up the stack.

To these basic and more or less theoretical points there are exceptions. Incomplete combustion is a requisite of some processes of ironworking, for instance, and hence black smoke in the steel country need not surprise you. Similarly, power plants, which are usually equipped with the most efficient combustion chambers and firing devices, occasionally feed fuel in wasteful, smoke-producing quantities in order to meet some unforeseen emergency such as a thunderstorm. Thus in the present state of industry, smoke practice must always deviate from smoke theory. But so far as the elimination of black smoke is concerned, much progress is being made by reason of the fact that any industrialist who can tolerate the sight of it belching from his chimney must be involved in one of two special situations. He may be a bonehead. Or he may simply be unable to incur the sometimes considerable expense entailed in a several-sided readjustment between his fuel and his firing equipment. Black smoke, whether issuing from bituminous coal (which creates it easily) or from anthracite (which creates it with great difficulty) is a sure sign that heat is being wasted. And heat costs money.

But while the industrialist is therefore quite open to argument concerning smoke control in his combustion chamber, he is likely to be much less interested in spending money for smoke reduction in his flue. The several devices for eliminating suspended matter in the flue have an economic appeal only in cases where a specialized waste includes valuable material. The simplest of these devices is the settling chamber, in which the velocity of the gases is slowed long enough for the largest particles to drop out of the smoke stream. There are, besides, dustboxes, centrifugal separators, filters of steel wool, "scrubbers," which spray jets of water across the stream, and so forth; and many of them are highly efficient for such waste products as ash. But they will never become universal until city ordinances require them; which is probably a long way of saying never.

The most advanced of all the smoke eliminators, especially for the catching of very fine ash, is the Cottrell electrical precipitator, which consists of a series of metal plates hung in the smoke stream with wires stretched between them. The wires discharge a continuous direct current of negative polarity, which ionizes the particles in the gas stream, which are thereupon attracted to the positively polarized plates and accumulate as waste. The Cottrell system is widely used for recovering valuable byproducts from the smokes of certain manufactures. The U.S. Assay Office, Manhattan, recovers about 300 ounces of gold ($10,500) to the ton of smoke, chiefly from its refinery. To cheat the curse of the industrial age, Anaconda geared a Cottrell precipitator to its mammoth stack near Butte, Montana, as long ago as 1914. During the War one cement plant made more money from Cottrell recovery of potash in smoke than from selling cement. But the Cottrell precipitator is expensive to install ($10,000 to $500,000); and in common with some other smoke reducers it gathers the waste so thoroughly that the user has a hard time disposing of it. Some research is being conducted to remove this barrier to smoke removal. The Research Corp., of New York, for instance, has endowed an investigation into the possible uses of ash from powdered bituminous coal, the disposal of which from a smoke reducer costs about $1 a ton. Results indicate a possible use in mixing the ash with certain types of cement.

Barring the elimination of byproduct gases, then, the *technical* problems of smoke abatement are solved. Technically, smoke is reducible almost to nil. Unfortunately there are other problems. Sum them up in one rubber stamp: human nature. Thereunder, place the initial difficulty of rousing a community to action; the further difficulty of keeping up interest; the further, of wangling a full staff and half enough cash for the job. In the entire U.S. there are not such. Place there the virtual impossibility of keeping track of residential smoke and of rectifying residential firing equipment, fuel, and firing methods: all of which are liable to be lousy. And place there the habit plenty of politicians have of diluting civic bureaus with nincompoops.

Antismoke ordinances do, however, exist. They took strong growth in the nineties in such expanding inland cities, logically, enough, as Chicago, Pittsburgh, Cleveland, St. Louis, Cincinnati. The two vast clouds that the Wartime and the post-War booms lifted above the coal cities of the eastern seaboard and of the bituminous belt, drew them into line by dozens and in all sizes, and today about 150 cities of 30,000 inhabitants or more have smoke ordinances.

The results achieved by some of these municipal bodies are beneath neglect; by some others, fairly remarkable. St. Louis coal runs high in sulphur (up to 5 per cent) and St. Louis is now the only city to require the use of washed coal, from which about a third of the sulphur will be removed. In Hudson County, New Jersey, the control is notable in that it concerns itself with an entire industrial area rather than with a municipality. The county authorities cooperate unofficially with the municipality of New York; they have ingeniously put the railroads, the waterfront, and industry on what appears to be almost a competing basis and have reduced black smoke (including railroads') by 85 per cent.

But the limits of municipal regulation of this sort are somewhat narrow. The average ordinance confines itself to forbidding the eruption of a certain degree of black smoke for more than a certain number of minutes per hour. No adequate measurement for ash or gases has been devised. No municipality has seen fit to require the installation of smoke reducers. None has so far dared in earnest to trouble the happy wastefulness of the householder.

And even the most effective smoke commissions of the East must look westward with envy upon those cities of the Pacific Coast where oil and gas are the dominant fuels and the trade winds are strong, and with special envy upon Dallas, which is fueled by natural gas and which is one of the most nearly smokeless cities on the continent. Enviously, but not hopefully. Electrification, and the use of gas and oil and hydraulic power, are increasing. But no realist sees any more likelihood in the ultimate elimination of coal on the eastern seaboard than in the cooling of the sun.

But America is still young in woe; the true, sad veterans of the smoke war are the English. And the story of that war can perhaps best tell of its ending where it began, in London. Steadily throughout a century London has been fighting smoke; today it is fighting it more resourcefully than every before. And today, that somber and stone scab fumes like a tenement fire in the rain of the morning after—one of the hugest and smokiest cities of the earth. Moreover, there is a certain appropriateness in that; and the appropriateness is smoke. For smoke since the beginning of brain has been a metaphysical substance. It is indeed and literally the breath of our nature and of our need in the shaping of our time, and it is not strange that no strength of our ingenuity can avail entirely to lift it from us.

HAVANA CRUISE

orce of habit awakened elderly Mr. and Mrs. B. early and they were strolling the long decks hand in hand a half-hour before the dining saloon opened at eight. Two heavy women in new house dresses helped each other up the stairs, their lungs laboring. They were Mrs. C. and her feeble sister. They and the B.'s nodded and smiled and said what a lovely morning it was and moved on in opposite directions. Mr. B. replaced his alpaca cap and told his gentle, pretty wife how fine the sea air was and what an appetite it gave a fellow. The sun stood bright on the clean, already warm decks, the blue water enlarged quietly without whitening, and sang along the flanks of the ship like seltzer.

Miss Cox appeared with her aunt Miss Box, a frugal and sweet-smiling spinster. Miss Box wore a simple print and a shining black straw garlanded with cloth flowers; Miss Cox was in severely informal new sports attire. Like most of the other young women, low-salaried office workers upon whom the self-sufficiency, the independence of city work and city living had narrowed their inestimable pressures of loneliness and of spiritual fear, she set a greater value of anticipation upon this cruise than she could dare tell herself. For this short leisure among new faces she had invested heavily in costume, in fear, in hope; and like her colleagues she searched among the men as for steamer smoke from an uncharted atoll.

Small and very lonesome in a great space of glassed-in deck, an aging Jew in a light flannel suit gazed sorrowfully at the Atlantic Ocean. A blond young man who resembled an airedale sufficiently intelligent to count to ten, dance fox trots, and graduate from a gentleman's university came briskly to the dining room in sharply pressed slacks and a navy blue sports shirt, read the sign, dashed away, and soon reappeared plus a checkered coat and a plaid tie. The dining saloon opened. Among big white tables glistening with institutional silverware all the white-coated stewards stood in sunlight with nothing yet to do. They were polite, but by no means obsequious; like the room stewards and the rank and file of the crew they had had a good stiff draught of the C.I.O. The headwaiter, a prim Arthur Treacher type, convoyed his guests to their tables with the gestures of an Eton-trained sand-hill crane in flight. His snobbishness rather flattered a number of the passengers.

Mr. and Mrs. B. studied the pretentious menu with admiration and ordered a whale of a breakfast. They may charge you aplenty, but they certainly do give you your money's worth. Mr. L., a bearish Jew, and his wife, the hard, glassy sort of blonde who should even sleep in jodhpurs, tinkered at their fruit and exchanged monosyllables as if they were forced bargains. The airedale pricked up his ears as two girls came in and as quickly drooped them and worried his Krispies, hoping that to two girls already seated he had appeared to establish no relationship with the newcomers, who were not at all his meat. Mr. and Mrs. L., in the manner of the average happily married couple, brightened immediately and genuinely as friends entered. The cool china noise and the chattering thickened in the cheerful room while, with the casualness of concealed excitement, studiously dressed and sharply anticipatory, singly and by twos and threes the shining breakfast faces assembled, looking each other over. The appraisals of clothes, of class, of race, of temperament, and of the opposed sexes met and crossed and flickered in a texture of glances as swift and keen as the leaping closures of electric arcs, and essentially as irrelevant to mercy. These people had come aboard in New York late the evening before, and this was their first real glimpse of each other.

All told, there were a hundred and thirty-two of them aboard. Perhaps twenty of them, mostly Cubans, were using the ship for the normal purpose of getting where they were going, namely, Havana. The others were creatures of a different order. They were representatives of the lower to middle brackets of the American urban middle class and they were on a cruise. Forty of them would stop over a week in Havana; they were on the thirteen-day cruise. Sixty eight of them would spend only eighteen hours in that city. They were on the six-day cruise. Most of them were from the cities of the eastern seaboard; many were from the New York City area. Roughly one in three of them was married, one in three was Jewish, one in three was middle-aged. Most of the middle-aged and married were aboard for a rest; most of the others were aboard for one degree or another of a hell of a big time. The unattached women and girls, who were aboard partly for a good time and partly for the more serious, not to say desperate, purpose of finding a husband, outnumbered the unattached men about four to one going down and about six to one coming back. There were few children. It wasn't a very expensive outing they were taking: most of them spent between $85 and $110 for passage, but $70 was enough to cover every expense except tips for six days, including two conducted tours of Havana. Besides that there were bar expenses; and plenty of the passengers, particularly the younger ones, had invested pretty heavily in new clothes they could feel self-assured in; for most of them had never been on a cruise before, and had rather glamorous ideas of what it would be like. Few of them could swing this expense lightly, and plenty of them knew they should never have afforded it at all. But they were of that vast race whose freedom falls in summer and is short. Leisure, being no part of their natural lives, was precious to them; and they were aboard this ship because they were convinced that this was going to be as pleasurable a way of spending that leisure as they could afford or imagine. What they made of it, of course, and what they failed to make, they made in a beautifully logical image of themselves: of their lifelong environment, of their social and economic class, of their mother, of their civilization. And that includes their strongest and most sorrowful trait: their talent for self-deceit. Already, as their eyes darted and reflexed above the grapefruit and the coffee, they were beginning to find out a little about all that.

The ship these passengers were aboard was the turbo-electric liner *Oriente*, the property of the New York & Cuba Mail Steamship Co., which is more tersely and less gently known as the Ward Line. The T.E.L. *Oriente* is fashioned in the image of her clientele: a sound, young, pleasant, and somehow invincibly comic vessel, the seafaring analogy to a second-string summer resort, a low-priced sedan, or the newest and best hotel in a provincial city. She can accommodate some 400 passengers, and frequently enough carries less than half that many. She makes fifty voyages a year, New York—Havana—New York, carrying freight, mail, and passengers, of whom a strong preponderance are cruising.

All the big lines and plenty of the minor ones run cruises any distance from round-the-world on down and at any toll from $5 to $25 or better per day. Of the passenger traffic of all flags sailing from U.S. ports in 1935 the cruising passengers accounted for 10 per cent. In the same year, according to the Department of Commerce, 83,000 passengers left U.S. ports on cruises. Of these 72,000 were U.S. citizens and 69,000 sailed from New York. Not more than one in four of them shipped on U.S. vessels, and U.S. shipping took only $1,000,000 of the $15,000,000 U.S. citizens spent on cruising. The cruising trade on the whole is sharply on the upswing. For 1936 the Department of Labor estimates a 25 per cent increase in cruising population. For the first half of 1937 as against the first half of the previous year the Italian Line reports an increase of 50 per cent; Cook's an increase of 38.2; Canadian Pacific's *Empress of Britain* an increase of 25 per cent in advance bookings (she was booked solid for 1936). The *Empress* does the biggest world-cruise business; the Italian Line has the Mediterranean trade pretty well sewed up; in 1935 Cunard handled about as many cruise passengers as all U.S. ships lumped together.

The popularity of cruising in general and of the particular cruise naturally depends respectively upon economic and local political conditions. In times answering to the names of peace and prosperity the Mediterranean and the world cruises take the class; and Canada, the Atlantic coastal islands, and the Caribbean the mass trade. During those years when prohibition and depression overlapped, the short cheap cruises "to nowhere" and to Bermuda did a howling business in more senses than one. Bermuda is still the strongest draw for short cruises. Just now people in the cruise business see a future brightening over the coastal cities of South America as it fades over Europe. Both the *Normandie* and the *Rex* will cruise to Rio de Janeiro this winter; by middle July, 500 of the 700 planned for had already booked passage on the

Rex, though American Express travel service had made no promotive gesture beyond publication of an announcement.

By the time the *Rex* and the *Normandie* are cutting south with
their carriage trade the *Oriente* too will once again be carrying
what one officer, speaking in summer, described as "a better class
of people." Winter is always best; late summer is the low. In July
and August the unattached women, most of them schoolteachers,
outnumber the unattached men ten and even twelve to one. On
the trip we are talking about, which occurred in early summer,
she carried what was in every respect just a good average crowd;
and their cruise, accordingly, was going to be a good average
cruise. It was that from the moment when the first pair of strang-
ers nodded and shyly smiled; it was that all through breakfast; it
kept right on being that as they changed to sneakers and took
their sun-tan oil and moved up to the sports deck. It continued to
same straight through the trip.

Up on the sports deck in bright sun a gay plump woman in
white shied rubber rings at a numbered board and chattered at
her somber female companion. The gay lady was from Washington and had friends at the Embassy in Havana. She admired Noel
Coward almost fatuously and sat at the Captain's table. She was
the godsend-of-the-week to the Captain, a dickensian-built Swede
who enjoyed gallantry and wit and whom even the stewards
liked. A slender Jew made a few listless passes at shuffleboard and
then settled down to obstacle putting. The airedale and a duplicate appeared in naughty trunks, laid towels aside from their
pretty shoulders, oiled themselves, and, after a brief warm-up,
began to play deck tennis furiously before the gradually assembling girls. Some of the girls wore brand-new sports clothes, others wore brand-new slacks or beach combinations. Some of them
traveled in teams, most of the others teamed up as quickly as
they could. They strolled against the wind, they stood at the
white rail with wind in their waved hair, they swung their new
shoes from primly crossed knees, they lay back with shaded eyes,
their crisp white skirts tucked beneath them in the flippant air,
they somewhat shyly laid their slacks back from their pale thighs,
they lay supine, skull-eyed in goggles; their cruel vermilion nails
caught at the sunlight. They examined each other quietly but

sharply, and from behind dark white-rimmed lenses affected to read drugstore fiction and watched those beautiful bouncing blond boys' bodies and indulged the long, long thoughts of youth. The airedales were fast and skillful, and explosive with such Anglo-Saxonisms as Sorry, Tough, Nice Work, Too Bad, Nice Going. Later they were joined by a couple of other bipeds who had the same somehow suspect unself-consciousness about their torsos, and the exclamations of good sportsmanship came to resemble an endless string of firecrackers set off under a dishpan and the innocent childlike abandon of the exhibitionism acquired almost Polynesian proportions in everything except perhaps sincerity and results. To come to the quick of the ulcer, it is generously estimated that the sexual adventures of the entire cruise did not exceed two dozen in number and most nearly approached their crises not in staterooms but aboveboard; that in no case was the farthest north more extreme than a rumpling hand or teeth industriously forced open; that in 70 per cent of these cases the gentleman felt it obligatory to fake or even to feel true love and the lady murmured either "please" or "please don't" or "yes I like you very much but I don't feel That Way about you," or all three; and that the man, in every case, took it bravely on the chin, sincerely adopted the attitude of a Big Brother, and went to his own bunk tired but happy.

Mr. and Mrs. L. sat quietly in the heightening sun. Mr. L. leaned far forward to let the sun fight its way through the black hair on his back and swapped business anecdotes with a man with epaulets of red hair; Mrs. L. incisively read *I Can Get It For You Wholesale* until the strong sun slowed her and she slept. Miss Cox, conversing with two young men, tried with her eyes to sharpen competition between them and to indicate that she was whichever they might prefer: good fun or an incipient good wife. Each of the men tried to establish excitement in her and jotted her on his mental cuff as useful if worst came to worst. Miss Box sat in the shade and read *Lost Ecstasy*. In the writing room Mrs. C. wrote a lot of postcards for herself and her sister who hadn't the energy. She wrote all morning and then wondered how to mail them back to Connecticut. On the promenade deck Mr. B. was saying, "When I retire my wife and I just want to travel from one end of the United States to the other." Mrs. B. was telling of an adventure her nephew had had in Yellowstone National Park when his car broke down. A stocky smiling blonde in an alarming cobalt bathing suit sank into her chair and disposed all that was lawful of her body before the sun. The airedales wagged their tails and did their gentlemanly best to lose themselves in good clean exercise. In the cool shadow of the empty lounge a tall nurse with an extraordinarily pure forehead lazily laid out self-taught breaks on the shallow-toned grand piano. On the shady side of the ship a torpid husband sat under five fathom of the Sunday *Times* and stuffed in the state of the world without appetite while wife caught a beauty sleep with her nostrils inverted, her goggles cockeyed, and her mouth open. People went past him and then more people and he knew something must be going on. He shoveled his way out and followed, in his new, brilliantly white sneakers, into the glassed-in dance floor.

Nearly everyone was on hand in folding chairs and the place was rustling, curiously subdued under one voice, with occasional pigeon-like rushes of shy and uncertain laughter. The Cruise Director, whose name was Earle M. Wilkens, was staging the Get-Together. He gave out information about landing cards and shopping and the good times ahead, introduced the deck steward, a professionally Cute Character whose popularity is significant of the whole nature of the cruise, and spent his best efforts trying as tactfully as possible to tell his charges not to be utter fools, not to be afraid of each other, that it was perfectly sound etiquette to speak to whom you pleased here without introduction. The audience remained amiable and embarrassed. Nine out of ten of them, much against their wishes, retained their onshore inhibitions to the somewhat bitter end; few individuals got to know more than four or five others better than faintly well.

The lunch bugle ended the meeting. A few men and fewer girls sloped into the modernistic bar; the rest went below to dope out some more costumes they could feel secure in. The drinks were cheap, a quarter for cocktails and thirty cents for highballs, and were weak out of all proportion even to that price. Though plenty of the passengers had anticipated Drinking quite as much as Sex, few of them drank much during cruise; apparently because few others drank much. Not even the trip's topers spent more than $20 or so.

There were a number of shifts of table assignments at lunch as new acquaintances got together. It was standard, sterile, turgid, summer-hotel type food, turkey, duck, the sort of stuffing that tastes like kitchen soap, fancy U.S. salads, and so on, and served with a pomp and circumstance that would have sufficed for the body and blood of Brillat-Savarin. The average passenger behaved a little as if this were his regular Thursday evening at the Tour d'Argent, and staggered upstairs to digest at the horse racing.

The horse racing was done with dice and varied with handicaps and gag races. The betting unit was a quarter. Two-thirds of the passengers were on hand; about half of them bet steadily. On the outskirts a small neatly made girl in blue slacks who had operated a horse race in a summer hotel was wondering how profitably the ship jockeyed the odds in its favor. It broke up in about an hour: and the sports deck filled, and the passengers disposed themselves once again among the diversions and facilities of the morning.

Mrs. C., her sister, and a pleasant younger woman sat and passed the time of day. Mrs. C. said: "The water in the thermos bottle in our stateroom is not as cool as the water in the cooler in the corridor." The younger woman said that hers seemed to be. Mrs. C. said to her sister: "She says the water in the thermos bottle in *her* stateroom *is* as cool as the water in the cooler in the corridor." A mean-eyed freckled young woman whose mahogany hair shone with black lights spoke to a new male acquaintance in the remarkable language of Arthur Kober: "I hate mountains; somehow they don't cope with my life." Mr. B. was saying that he and his wife both loved to see new places and try out new drinks, not really getting drunk of course but just seeing what they tasted like. It certainly was a lot of fun. Having Wonderful Time was saying "I don't mind my freckles any more but I used to be terribly sentimental about them; used to cry all the time when people teased me." Mr. B., whose wife was below resting, struck the ash from his popular-priced cigar and said, secure and happy: "Well if I should die tonight I'd leave my wife four-teen hundred dollars, but matter of fact I hope to make that more before I'm done." The younger woman said to Mrs. C., "I noticed you were reading

News-Week this morning. How do you like it?" Mrs. C. replied that she thought it was awful cute.

There was a fire drill, with everyone looking sheepish in life belts and a few cracks about the *Morro Castle* and for that sinking feeling, travel on the Ward Line, and after the drill a rather pompous tea, with dancing, to the spiritless commercial rhythms of a hard-working four-man band, and then the dinner horn, at whose command dressing was for the third to fifth time that day unanimously resumed.

The redressing for the evening ran the whole range—formal, semiformal, informal, with every variant that open insecurity or pretended sophistication could give it. There was a good deal of glancing around and checking up during dinner and quite a few made immediate revisions. After dinner *John Meade's Woman* was shown, with breaks between reels, to a packed house that received it with polite apathy. The floor was cleared of chairs, the tables filled, blue and green bulbs went on among the leaves of the dwarf tubbed trees, the weak drinks were ordered, and the band redistributed the platitudes of the afternoon among warmer colors in a warmer light.

Some of the married couples sat alone; others had found each one other married couple. The latter swapped among their foursome, the former danced together all evening. The four airedales scampered about with two pink girls who looked like George Washington, the cobalt bathing suit and a couple of other blondes, and once in a while, with a face-saving air gracefully combined of wild oats and democracy, swung the more attractive Jewesses around the floor. The inevitable Ship's Card, a roguish fellow of forty, did burlesque rumbas and under protection of parody achieved unusual physical contacts amid squeals of laughter. An earnest and charming young Jew, brows bent, did better dancing than the music would support. The seconds among the girls fell to the elder of the unattached men and most of them (along with the men) got stuck there. The third run sat and smiled and smiled until their mouths ached and their cheeks went numb, while the men passed them with suddenly unfocused eyes. Six Cuban college boys sat at a ringside table drinking and looking very young and not dancing at all. The wow of the evening was a blonde who was born out of her time: her glad and perpetually surprised face was that which appears in eighteenth-century pornographic engravings wherein the chore boy tumbles the milkmaid in an explosion of hens and alfalfa. Her dress was cut with considerable extra *élan* to set off her uncommonly beautiful breasts, which in the more extreme centrifuges of the dance swung almost entirely free of ambush. She had a howling rush and a grand time. The six Cuban boys watched her constantly and chattered among themselves. Whenever she approached their corner their plum-jelly eyes bugged out with love. Twice, without a trace of anything save naive admiration too great to be restrained, they broke into applause.

The dancing stopped and the bar closed at the ungodly hour of 1:00 a.m. A few couples talked quietly in dark parts of the over-lighted decks, but by two they were all in bed and a gang moved up the darkness grooming the decks and then went below; and the wet decks yielded a tarnish of light and the ship, with a steady throe like that of blood, poured strongly through the shaded water. After a while the morning opened upon the mild stare, the insane musical comedy blue of the Gulf Stream, whereon the *Oriente* crept like a jazzy little toy; the decks dried and brightened in the lifted sun; in those hierarchic depths of a ship that passengers scarcely suspect, the crew and the service crews were waking, like rain-chilled insects that fair weather warms; the passengers were assembling themselves toward consciousness; the breakfast horn laced the ship with its bluff brightness; and another day had begun.

It had precisely the same shape and rhythm. Breakfast brought the passengers together, and cast them forth upon their own resources: sports, flirting, bathing, reading, sleeping, talking, tanning. The lunch horn gave them something to do, they dressed; they ate; they played the wooden ponies; more sports, flirting, bathing, reading, sleeping, talking, tanning; tea dancing brought them together with something to do; they dressed for dinner; they ate it; they played Bingo; they danced; they went to bed; they slept. There were certain variants and certain developments. Mr. L. showed his tremendous sunburn to a young woman but it was all right, his wife was there reading *I Can Get It For You Wholesale*. Two Cubans nearly beat two airedales at deck tennis. Miss Box no longer enjoyed *Lost Ecstasy*, which is a piece

of housewives' problem fiction about the troubles of a sophisticated deb who marries a big clean cowboy; it was too serious.
The head deck steward found still some more passengers to fasci-
nate with his modest account of the *Morro Castle*. A steward and
a passenger talked enthusiastically about Spain and the C.I.O. A
girl won three straight pots at Bingo. Earle Wilkens skillfully disposed of a heckler. There were gag dances with inexpensive
prizes, an elimination number dance, a musical-chair dance. Two
contest dances were announced but were not staged; there weren't
many good dancers. The high point of gayety for the cruise was
reached at the rough climax of the musical-chairs game. After the
dancing was over quite a crowd lingered on deck in the obscenely
ticklish darkness and drank stiff Scotches and rums. One of the
Cuban boys played a trumpet very softly; another played the guitar and with extreme quietness, their faces softened, they sang.
First they sang popular Havana tunes whose very banality made
their beauty manifold, then they sang sorrowful romantic ballads,
lyrics of fighting and of homesickness, and dirty songs. The gui-
tarist kept singing straight at a blonde who sat directly in front
of him, her knees withdrawn from touching his. Her partner
touched her shoulder and murmured Let's take a walk around the
deck. She said In a minute, not looking at him. After a little he
leaned above her and murmured When you're ready, let me
know. She did not answer. Her knees relaxed. He poured himself
a steep Scotch and kept his nose in it. The peculiar quality of the
night had everyone as shaky as a well-determined kiss. Far out to
starboard, small, frail, and infrequent, lights walked past. They
denominated the low and bone-white coast of pre-Columbian un-
imagined Florida, and of that dilapidated playground where
wasps whine in hot voids of disheveling stucco, and Townsendites
sit in squealing rockers under the slow fall of their ashes, and
high-school girls are excused from civics class to snap into their
one-piece bathing suits and demonstrate the teasing amenities of
their hot, trite little bodies for the good of the community; and
the trumpet sprang agile gold on the darkness, and the guitar
spoke in the Spanish language, and the eloquent songs continued, and the remote lights thickened and were Miami; and
Miami spread, and sank into the north; and the lights thinned,
and just at this time there was a new feeling through the body of

HAVANA TOURISTS

The *Oriente* tourists "spent their short time ashore . . . streaming at brutal speed through that staggering variety and counterpoint of detail whose sum makes a city as individual as a soul." But their desire to truly know the city could not be satisfied: they had neither the time nor the instinct to be anything other than timorous intruders. Photographs by Walker Evans, courtesy of John Hill and the Estate of Walker Evans.

the ship that could not at first be analyzed; then a couple guessed that the ship was changing her course, and silently detaching themselves from their companions, strolled back to the stern. The faint wake, spuming with phosphorus, trailed abruptly bent behind them, and straightened even as they watched, and their guess had been right. The ship had left the shelf of the continent behind and had directed herself upon the world's deep water. Not very far ahead now, beyond a bulge and world shape of this water, tumescent beneath the shade of the summer planet, her whole sleep stirred and streamed in music such as this, Havana lay.

The passengers saw their best of Havana before they set foot in it. The instant they landed they submitted themselves to the guidance of a spectacled brown-uniformed hog with a loud retching voice who stuffed them into a noisy flotilla of open cars and took them on two tours, called the City Tour and the Night Tour. On the City Tour they saw the Church of Our Lady of Mercy, a cigar factory, the Maine Monument, and a cemetery. On the Night Tour they saw a game of jai alai, Sloppy Joe's, the Sans Souci, and the Casino. Between tours the *Oriente* served a goose dinner for those who mistrusted the dirty foreign food.

At the church they saw a number of bruiselike Italianate paintings, an assortment of wax martyrs under glass among shriveled real and fresh wax flowers, and the high altar with all the electric lights on. A collection was taken as they went out. At the cigar factory they saw a dozen men with bad eyesight working overtime for their benefit in bad light, handmaking highgrade cigars for British clubmen. Cigars were on sale as they went out. At the Maine Monument, which is capstoned by the quaint word Liberty, the hog reminded his little charges how the U.S. gave Cuba Hobson's (not by any chance Iscariot's) Kiss and made our little brown boy friend safe for the canebrake, the sugar mill, and the riding boss, and his island a safe place for decent American citizens to do business in. At the cemetery he pointed out the $197,000 black marble modernistic mausoleum of a lady in high society who had died in Paris; a monument to certain students who had desecrated a general's grave and been shot for it; and the monument to the American Legion.

Some of the men liked the jai alai and placed bets but a lot of the girls were bored and the general impression was it was a queer sort of a game. At Sloppy Joe's, the Grant's Tomb of bars, at which no self-respecting Cuban would be caught dead, the tourists themselves seemed a little embarrassed. They huddled rather silent at the bar and few of them ordered more than one drink. Night life in one of the whoriest cities of the Western Hemisphere was represented by the Sans Souci, meaning CareFree, and the Casino, meaning Casino. Lowing gently, the tourists stepped out of their vans. The marble floors were absolutely beautiful. The trees were just exquisite. The music was every bit as smooth as Wayne King and even the native Cubans that went there seemed an awfully nice, refined class of people. Everyone had such a good time they didn't get back to the ship till nearly four o'clock in the morning.

An heroic majority wrenched themselves up from four hours' sleep and spent the morning buying cigars, perfumes, rum, and souvenirs. Later they hung at the rail and talked of Havana, and watched men and boys dive for coins in the foul olive water. Of those who liked Havana the elder spoke of it as quaint, the more youthful as cute. Most of the passengers disliked Havana and were glad to be leaving it. One man raised his voice among a group and, in one of those mental dialects that are perpetually surprising by virtue of their genuine existence, summed up: "Well, I'm telling you. When you see the Statue of Liberty you're going to say this is the country for me." The group nodded as one. Someone threw another Cuban penny in the sewage.

Slowly, regretted by few, Havana shrank in the lunchtime sun and faded. All afternoon the exhausted passengers slept; and awakening, came slowly to realize that somehow the best of their cruise was over. Only a few of the middle-aged, those who desired and demanded least, those who feared each other least, those innocent and gentle and guileless whom little can harm, seemed to escape the blight that, as the next two days dragged on, fastened upon the others more and more pitilessly. All novelty was gone out of the ship, her facilities, her entertainments. Married couples, used to spending their long days apart, were wearing on each other. New acquaintances had run out of small talk and had no other and did not know how to get rid of each other. The girls knew now that none of them was going to find a husband or even any excitement to speak of. There were even fewer men coming back than had gone down. Only one airedale was left and his nose was hot all the way home. The new passengers were no help. Most of them were families of Cuban bourgeois on their way north for the summer. One new American, a brutal spinster whose life seemed to have been spent on cruises for the sole satisfaction of snotting everything she saw, was soon left to her own cruelly lonely devices. Two moderately but genuinely smart couples, one German, one American, caused some excitement at first. They talked like Frederick Lonsdale first acts and looked like a page out of the late *Vanity Fair*, and accordingly represented the average passenger's most cherished dream of a cruise and of what he himself would be on one. But they turned out to be worse than useless for they kept hermetically to themselves and made visible wit about the passengers.

Friday was worst of all. The Gulf Stream was gone, the water was cold and gray, the weather was cold and gray and rather windy, and by afternoon the ship was traveling very slowly in a deathening absence of engine pulsation, for it had been decided to delay docking until Saturday morning. The passengers were depressed beyond even appetite, and a majority of them stayed below. The tea dancing was notably gelid and when the dressing horn flared through the corridors everyone got stiffly and gratefully from his rumpled bunk and took a very hot bath and put on what crowning creation, if any, he or she had managed to hold in reserve for the last evening aboard.

At the last supper, with its tasseled menus, its signal flags, hats, and noisemakers, things picked up. As each latecomer entered everyone made noises, yelled Yaaay, and applauded. There was a sudden blast of music and everyone took up Happy Birthday To You (slurring the name) dear Whosis, We're Glad to See You, and peering around to make out who it was they were glad to see. A waiter brought in a large cake flaming like a Catholic shrine and set it before an old woman, who was totally astonished. Everyone cheered and her tablemates urged her to get up. Reluctantly and with difficulty she helped her aged body half erect and sat quickly down again blushing and swallowing back tears. The lights went out and a baby spot went on and balloons fell from the balcony in a slow bouncing shower while the band played Bubbles.

Customs thickened around the bar that evening stronger than

ever before. This was the last night now, the last few hours. Nobody had anything to lose and something, perhaps, to gain. Inhibitions began to drop off like the clothes at a Norman Rockwell
swimming hole. Several of the girls to whom a good time meant
most and who were in that proportion the most cruelly disappointed members of the cruise, began to get pretty drunk and
pretty loud. People who had thus far only nodded and smiled began to order each other drinks and to put hands on each other's
shoulders. An amateur photographer got busy with flash bulbs.
He made friends with three drunken girls and sat them on the
bar and made a picture. A ripe redhead with hot warlike eyes
came up and stood very close to him and asked him would he
make a pitcher at her table. One of the girls said, "Would you
mind going away from here?" She replied yes, she certainly would
mind. Another of the girls said, "Would you kindly move off our
territory before I break your jaw?" The amateur, who had probably never before overheard himself described as territory, became very careful. The girl moved away. One of the girls said in a
narrowed murderous voice: "*If you take a picture of that bitch
I'll never speak to you again.*" He overheard another say to her
friend, glaring at him meanwhile, "Let him go ahead. Let him
take her pitcher. *She'll* sleep with him." He put up his camera.

By now the band was playing and somewhat lit couples were
making use of it. Many more than usual of the middle-aged sat
smiling on the sidelines, indirectly lighted by the good fun the
young people seemed to be having, and very cautiously trying to
learn from each other how much to tip whom. A hitherto shy
young man volubly told a girl who had at no time been shy that
like all American girls she was disgracefully inhibited about her
dancing and that there were a number of other things he could
teach her and would be delighted to. He showed her how the
knee is used in pivoting and she cried: "That's it! Pivot! Pivot!
Pivot!" After a great deal too much persuasive applause one of
the Vanity Fair couples took the floor alone and executed a 3.2
rumba. A bald, heavy man palmed coins and did handkerchief
tricks at the bar. A lot of people became fond of him and he set
them up to drinks and they set him and his girl up to drinks. The
more amorous of the ship's officers were working four and five
girls each, in a somewhat nerve-racking synchronization of duty

and pleasure.* The Vanity Fair foursome, in a mood for scornful parody, ordered champagne—a thing no one else had thought of doing. They drank a toast and smashed their glasses. A wife and husband sat in a dark corner talking intensely: two phrases kept re-emerging with almost liturgical monotony: keep your voice down, and god damn you. And god damn you too you god damned. Quite suddenly she struck her full glass of planter's punch into his lap and they left the table walking stiffly, their whole bodies fists. The International Smart Set broke some more glasses. A waiter asked them please not to break glasses and set them down some more. They broke them immediately and ordered that a bottle from the next table, whose occupants were dancing, be put on their table. The waiter refused as politely as possible. They ordered it again as if they had not heard him. He slammed it down in front of them as hard as he could. Everyone craned at the noise. In an icy rage they told him they would take this matter up with the Line, and left their table. The pleasant young Jew who danced well went around getting names signed on a petition stating that the service had been excellent and that the waiter had been provoked beyond human endurance. The husband came back with his suit nearly dry and drank two Scotches rapidly and danced unskillfully but viciously with a blonde girl. The band played Good Night Sweetheart and packed up their instruments. He quickly ordered four more Scotches and retired to a dark corner. The bar shut down. It was one o'clock. Everyone was troubled and frozen in the sudden silence. Life had warmed up a good deal during the evening but not enough to get on under its own steam. Tentative pacts had been hinted at but not strongly enough. The bafflement sank into embarrassment, the embarrassment into straight tiredness, and very soon nearly everyone, muted and obscurely disappointed, drained off to bed. At one table around a diminishing bottle several girls, two male passengers, and two officers hung on. They were determined, they kept telling each other, to stay up till four, when the passengers would be called and breakfast would be served. Their talk and

*The officer's duty: cheering up disappointed girls. His pleasure: flirtation, one way out of his boredom, which in time becomes titanic. The operation is nerve-racking because no better than any steward can he afford to provoke the least conceivable complaint from a passenger on any sexual ground.

sidelong looks, their flirtation and their frustration, ground along like a crankcase without oil. The damp husband finished the last of his whiskeys, wove over, hung above the table like a lame dirigible, with thanks refused an invitation to sit in, and went to bed. They cherished their liquor but it was running low. Each of the girls wanted a man but had to abide his leisure. Each of the men wanted a girl but they were concentrated on two girls and on the others only as second-best stopgaps. Each of the prettier girls had developed loyalties toward a homelier girl. Everyone was playing the hopeless game of waiting everyone else out. About two-thirty, half nauseated with liquor and fatigue and frustration, they all gave it up at once and went alone to their respective bunks.

At four the cornetist blasted up and down the corridors. He played The Sidewalks of New York and Home, Sweet Home. A Spanish steward knocked on a friendly door, leaned in, and said, "Better wake op: see Statch."

The passenger was too tired to care to catch the toastmistress of Bedloe Island, but after a little he went to his porthole and looked out. The ship was riding in silence softly past the foot of the island. The water lifted and relaxed in one slow floor of glass. The city lifted, it seemed, a mile above it, and very near; and smokeless behind the city, morning, the mutilation of honey. The city stood appareled in the sober purple and silver of supreme glory, no foal of nature, nor intention of man, but one sublime organism, singular and uncreated; and it stretched upward from its stone roots in the water as if it were lifted on a dream. Nor yet was it soft, nor immaterial. Every window, every wheatlike stone, was distinct in the eye as a razor and serenely, lost, somnambulists, the buildings turned one past another upon the bias of the ship's ghostly movement, not unlike those apostolic figures who parade with the clock's noon in Strasbourg.

U.S. AT WAR: "A SOLDIER DIED TODAY"

I n Chungking the spring dawn was milky when an MP on the graveyard shift picked up the ringing phone in U.S. Army Headquarters. At first he heard no voice on the other end; then a San Francisco broadcast coming over the phone line made clear to him why his informant could find no words. A colonel came in. The MP just stared at him. The colonel stared back. After a moment the MP blurted two words. The colonel's jaw dropped; he hesitated; then without a word he walked away.

It was fresh daylight on Okinawa. Officers and men of the amphibious fleet were at breakfast when the broadcast told them. By noon the news was known to the men at the front, at the far sharp edges of the world's struggle. With no time for grief, they went on with their work; but there, while they worked, many a soldier wept.

At home, the news came to people in the hot soft light of the afternoon, in taxicabs, along the streets, in offices and bars and factories. In a Cleveland barbershop, 60-year-old Sam Katz was giving a customer a shave when the radio stabbed out the news. Sam Katz walked over to the water cooler, took a long, slow drink, sat down and stared into space for nearly ten minutes. Finally he got up and painted a sign on his window: "Roosevelt Is Dead." Then he finished the shave. In an Omaha poolhall, men racked up their cues without finishing their games, walked out. In a Manhattan taxicab, a fare told the driver, who pulled over to the curb, sat with his head bowed, and after two minutes resumed his driving.

Everywhere, to almost everyone, the news came with the

force of a personal shock. The realization was expressed in the messages of the eminent; it was expressed in the stammering and wordlessness of the humble. A woman in Detroit said: "It doesn't seem possible. It seems to me that he will be back on the radio tomorrow, reassuring us all that it was just a mistake."

It was the same through that evening, and the next day, and the next; the darkened restaurants, the shuttered nightclubs, the hand-lettered signs in the windows of stores: "Closed out of Reverence for F.D.R."; the unbroken, 85-hour dirge of the nation's radio; the typical tributes of typical Americans in the death-notice columns of their newspapers (said one signed by Samuel and Al Gordon: "A Soldier Died Today").

It was the same on the cotton fields and in the stunned cities between Warm Springs and Washington, while the train, at funeral pace, bore the coffin up April's glowing South in re-enactment of Whitman's great threnody.

It was the same in Washington, in the thousands on thousands of grief-wrung faces which walled the caisson's grim progression with prayers and with tears. It was the same on Sunday morning in the gentle landscape at Hyde Park, when the burial service of the Episcopal Church spoke its old, strong, quiet words of farewell; and it was the same at that later moment when all save the gravemen were withdrawn and reporters, in awe-felt hiding, saw how a brave woman, a widow, returned, and watched over the grave alone, until the grave was filled.

VICTORY: THE PEACE

The greatest and most terrible of wars was ending, this week, in the echoes of an enormous event—an event so much more enormous that, relative to it, the war itself shrank to minor significance. The knowledge of victory was as charged with sorrow and doubt as with joy and gratitude. More fearful responsibilities, more crucial liabilities rested on the victors even than on the vanquished.

In what they said and did, men were still, as in the aftershock of a great wound, bemused and only semi-articulate, whether they were soldiers or scientists, or great statesmen, or the simplest of men. But in the dark depths of their minds and hearts, huge forms moved and silently arrayed themselves: Titans, arranging out of the chaos an age in which victory was already only the shout of a child in the street.

With the controlled splitting of the atom, humanity, already profoundly perplexed and disunified, was brought inescapably into a new age in which all thoughts and things were split—and far from controlled. As most men realized, the first atomic bomb was a merely pregnant threat, a merely infinitesimal promise.

All thoughts and things were split. The sudden achievement of victory was a mercy, to the Japanese no less than to the United Nations; but mercy born of a ruthless force beyond anything in human chronicle. The race had been won, the weapon had been used by those on whom civilization could best hope to depend; but the demonstration of power against living creatures instead of dead matter created a bottomless wound in the living conscience of the race. The rational mind had won the most Promethean of its conquests over nature, and had put into the hands of common man the fire and force of the sun itself.

Was man equal to the challenge? In an instant, without warn-ing, the present had become the unthinkable future. Was there hope in that future, and if so, where did hope lie?

Even as men saluted the greatest and most grimly Pyrrhic of victories in all the gratitude and good spirit they could muster, they recognized that the discovery which had done most to end the worst of wars might also, quite conceivably, end all wars—if only man could learn its control and use.

The promise of good and of evil bordered alike on the in-finite—with this further, terrible split in the fact: that upon a people already so nearly drowned in materialism even in peace-time, the good uses of this power might easily bring disaster as prodigious as the evil. The bomb rendered all decisions made so far, at Yalta and at Potsdam, mere trivial dams across tributary rivulets. When the bomb split open the universe and revealed the prospect of the infinitely extraordinary, it also revealed the oldest, simplest, commonest, most neglected and most impor-tant of facts: that each man is eternally and above all else respon-sible for his own soul, and, in the terrible words of the Psalmist, that no man may deliver his brother, nor make agreement unto God for him.

Man's fate has forever been shaped between the hands of rea-son and spirit, now in collaboration, again in conflict. Now reason and spirit meet on final ground. If either or anything is to sur-vive, they must find a way to create an indissoluble partnership.

NEW YORK,
A LITTLE RAIN

In Manhattan, Sept. 18 was a rotten day; but it was also the anniversary of that day in 1931 when, in Mukden, a garrison of Japanese soldiers struck the first, low blow of World War II. That fact meant incomparably more to thousands of men, women & children crowding the streets of Manhattan's Chinatown. With love, skill and patience they had worked for days perfecting their delicately ferocious and gay paper dragons, their butterfly-cheerful costumes, their happy floats.

When the Mayor's office suggested that they postpone their victory parade, their organizer and spokesman T. W. Chu, chairman of the Chinese Benevolent Association, pleasantly replied: "Our people fought for fourteen years in all kinds of weather, and a little rain could hardly dampen (our) spirits . . . on this anniversary."

By a little after noon some 12,000 Chinese poured out of the heart of their town and started their three-hour march from Chinatown up Fifth Avenue. The women and children mostly had raincoats and umbrellas; men, wearing the uniform of the U.S. Army, marched wholly unprotected, imperturbably drenched. Wherever the rumpled weather had even a little pity, people massed the sidewalks.

On the stand in front of the Public Library, to salute the marchers, waited Major General Claire Chennault and Dr. Chen Chi Mai, Counsellor of the Chinese Embassy; Dr. Frank Lee, former Chinese Minister to Portugal, and Mrs. Lee; former Ambassador Dr. Hu Shih; Dr. Tsune-chi Yu, Chinese Consul General in New York; Author Lin Yutang. By the time paraders approached the stand, rain had reduced their pretty dragons to big plaster grins trailing a skeletal pulp. But they gave the standees the best show they had.

An immense revolving disc displayed alternately the face of Chiang Kai-shek and the legend GOD BLESS AMERICA. Following the high-kneed, fancy twirling majorettes, some 30 bands gave out, in the simple-hearted braveries of Western brass and the intricate Oriental din of bells, cymbals and gongs. Fifteen floats embodied scenes from Chinese history. There were seven lion dancers. The half-dozen drabbled dragons pranced and writhed and reared proudly. Painted players and acrobats on stilts—designed by their ancestors for high visibility in crowded market places—enacted bits of traditional drama. The band of the 22nd Regiment of the New York National Guard played *San Min Chu I*, China's National Anthem.

The weather got still worse, but by the time the end was reached at 62nd Street, it was clear to everyone that the occasion was far less pathetic than joyful. The world has never known a more gallant and admirable people than the Chinese; Manhattan has never had a more gallant and admirable parade.

EUROPE:
AUTUMN STORY

T he fall of the year shone gently upon the broken cities and the exhausted fields of Europe. On Berlin's Kreuzberg, frost stiffened upon the worm-wrought, illegible features of an exhumed, Gestapo-killed cadaver to which someone had attached a tag reading, *Homo sapiens*.

Of the unrecounted millions of Europeans who survived him, few could greet the season with anything of its own tenderness. It was the first autumn of liberation, the first since the end of the war. It was the first autumn of the atomic age.

In the steep forests of Norway, German guerrillas still skulked and fought. In Denmark, for want of transportation, practically the only food surpluses in Europe were near standstill. Only butter, eggs, meat moved, thinly, to England, Norway, the U.S. Army.

By millions, in transverse migrations, Germans struggled westward out of New Poland, northward out of the Sudetenland and Austria, to swell a nation already overpopulated and reduced in size; while Russians struggled eastward, some out of slavery and some out of voluntary servitude, towards home and an uncertain welcome.

In Hamburg, hundreds of looted bells awaited restoration to the belfries of nations with bell-like names. Poland, The Netherlands, Belgium; provided, of course, that those belfries, and their churches, still existed.

In the Sudeten, those Germans who remained wore identifying armbands. In Berlin, Jews were entitled to extra rations. In the British zone, on behalf of Jews, the British commandeered clothes from Germans. Thanks to presidential demand, the first of many Jews in the American zone were removed from behind barbed wire and were installed in houses requisitioned from Germans. Into Germany, fleeing a new paroxysm of pogroms in New Poland, wandered still more Jews.

Mysteriously planted placards warned fraternizing Bavarian girls: "O God, if it depends on us, you will pay for it!" Daily, the snowline crept a little farther down the mountains of Bavaria, hideout of SS men. A Sudeten German asked whether it was true that Americans were now fighting the Russians.

In Switzerland, Belgium's Leopold bowed to temporary exile, but by no means to permanent renunciation of his throne.

In The Netherlands, underfueled pumps sucked at flooded farmlands which for years to come would be sterile as salt.

The scraped Danubian plain blazed like brass: Hungary, one of the bounteous nations of Europe, would this year require six million quintals of wheat. Allied authorities started a vast woodcutting campaign in the Vienna woods, to supplement the capital's inadequate coal stocks.

In all the nations of eastern Europe, free and secret elections were still promised. Angered and fearful, a group of Bulgarian peasants told an American correspondent how an armed 23-year-old Communist mayor had lumped their long-held acreages and plowed the boundaries under.

National Actionists in Greece went armed and carried British Army passes certifying their "confidential work." The enemies, the hunted men of EAM, live in peril of arrest and beatings. In Rome, the first Italian democrats to meet in parliamentary Assembly since the murder of Matteotti set themselves to restore integrity and hope to a broken nation. The withdrawal of A.M.G. from Italy was indefinitely postponed; in liberal opinion, to protect Rightists and Monarchists.

In Paris a man's suit cost $500. A correspondent stopped to get his jeep repaired in Neufchâteau. The garage operator, a brawny Frenchwoman, immediately questioned him about American soldiers sleeping with German girls. "*C'est incroyable,*" she mourned. "Yes, some French girls slept with Germans when they were here. But only bad girls. We do not understand why you Americans do it. You are not bad but you still sleep with Germans." An American sergeant lounged at a nearby corner watching the thin traffic in Neufchâteau's one big street; he turned loose barbaric French at passing girls; they giggled, and swept on. Wearily he jerked his thumb towards the hilltop graveyard on the edge of town. He said: "My division liberated this joint. A lot of the boys from the 79th are lying up there. And for what? To have these people spit on us now?"

French nuns and children sifted garbage against the lean chance of bits of food fit for children or nuns or pigs to eat.

Even in Marseilles, the sky muted its Mediterranean blare. Along the wide streets the plane trees turned pale yellow. In the still unmended tenements of Madrid, before long now, a people whom victory had passed by would be shuddering.

Man's hope, man's fate contested in the subtle autumn light. Winter stood just at the shoulder of the gentlest of seasons.

Europe had emerged from history's most terrible war, into history's most terrifying peace. Europeans said, again & again, that their aspirations were for liberty. They showed, again & again, their desperately seasoned respect for security. Now the struggle between liberty and security was engaged.

In London the Council of Foreign Ministers achieved only the disconsolation of all in the world who desired peace, not power. Eastern Europe was a Russian bastion; western Europe coalesced towards a "family" which, to the Russians, would be a bastion against the Soviet Union. Within nations, as among them, political forces jockeyed for power.

The totalitarian socialists, by far the most astute professionals in the field, moved toward their goals by methods which equally disturbed scoundrels and honorable men. The democratic socialists, maintaining that full liberty and full security can be combined and made enduring, were embarrassed by their new responsibilities in Britain, and by those problems of relative inefficiency which confront all democrats. Only in Czechoslovakia, one of the less unhappy nations in Europe, were socialist prospects very promising. But that country's fortunes depended chiefly on friendly relations with the Soviet Union; and democratic and totalitarian socialists are not notable for lifelong friendships.

Europe's peasants continued to be peasants. Materialists in a sense more primal than that of Adam Smith or Marx, politically inert and purchasable, they served less as anchorage than as ballast. As for Europe's conservatives, it seemed unlikely at the moment that ordinary people would ever trust them again.

In whom was man to put his hope? In himself? A Frenchwoman, remembering the magnificent selflessness of war and the millennial hours of the liberation of Paris, sorrowfully said: "We have returned to our own egos."

As winter moved down through Norway and, along the Gulf of Finland, rusted the dark green, springlike grass which heavy summer had never touched, many Europeans were preoccupied with matters even more primitive than the ego. When winter came, they knew, it would trap a hundred million of them with less food for each, or little more, than American soldiers got last year in Japanese prison camps. They would be severely short of fuel, of shelter, of clothing. Millions of homes—and, in Berlin, hospitals—were without windowglass. Tuberculosis was rampant among adolescents and common among small children. Bubonic plague nuzzled at the ports of the Mediterranean.

Many would die. Many more would survive. They were no braver than other men; they could be expected, in sufficient anguish and embitterment and desolation, to turn to those stronger than themselves who offered both a will and a way.

They could also be expected, as winter tightened its vise, to confirm an enduring opinion of that nation which, in the unalterable conviction of Europeans, might have prevented much of the anguish and so might have prevented political dereliction. That nation was the U.S.

Countless millions of Europeans had all their lives seen in the U.S. a dream of liberty and security, of democratic generosity and efficiency. With the American armies had come the American reality, and it was not—it could not have been—the stuff of the dream.

The people of Europe had seen, and had not failed to value, the vigor and promise and individual generosity of the American soldier. They had also seen, with the deadly discernment of peoples experienced in disaster and disillusion, how ill-raised to understand this most sophisticated of wars, and how timidly briefed in its meanings, were these same Americans. Now, in France and the Lowlands, in Germany and Austria and Italy, the people saw Americans, homesick and purposeless and often misbehaved, affronting all around them and under them with their abundance amid want, their altogether human and altogether brutal longing to get the hell out of those ruined lands, and to go home.

The offenses were not universal, nor were they solely American. By a Dutch roadside stood a sign embossed with the Maple Leaf of the Canadian Army: REMEMBER! THE DUTCH ARE OUR ALLIES! But the Americans, in their overwhelming number and voice and strength, had made Europe supremely conscious of them, and of the country from which they came. In the end, and in this autumn of unfilled need, it was not the Americans, but America, that Europe judged.

THE NATION

Out on the Montana range, rattlesnakes were unusually plentiful, and the old men predicted a long warm fall and a short easy winter.

In Chatsworth, Ill. First Lieut. Billie Wittler, an Army nurse, made Page One of the weekly *Plaindealer* when she got back home: "She has seen much front-line active duty in the European sector, including Italy and Germany. She was able to see the Alps in all their beauty and says Switzerland, especially, is beautiful."

In Manhattan, a nobly decorated veteran of the Pacific was passed along by a junior executive, who was unfavorably impressed by his willingness to take "anything," to a junior executive who told him, kindly, "You know, I don't think this is exactly the job for you." Upon hearing this, the young hero burst into tears.

Happy days, more or less, were here again. Despite prodigious achievements at home & abroad, the nation had not been essentially changed by war. Now, returning to peace rather than struggling through to it nine-tenths dead, the U.S. was more like itself than ever—in a world which would never again be remotely the same.

Butter pats were served again at Schrafft's and Henrici's; cases against cigaret blackmarketers were dropped. Along the highways, in whatever cars they had, people were blowing out tires and bumping into each other again; the city traffic tie-ups were something awful. Other moral equivalents to war were the fall's football games—which drew record crowds—and a shooting season so trigger-happy that Colorado's game department recommended manslaughter laws for hunters.

Army deaths were totaled 216,966, the Navy's 55,896; the National Safety Council announced that on the home front, since Pearl Harbor, 355,000 had been killed through accident, and 36,000,000 injured.

The great hit songs of the season were *Till the End of Time*, *I'll Buy That Dream*, *On the Atchison, Topeka & the Santa Fe*. Bestselling novels were *The Black Rose* and *Forever Amber*. A big movie hit was *Love Letters*, a romance about amnesia. A psychologist claimed that *Superman* provided a beneficent Aristotelian catharsis; a Jesuit saw in him a fascist archetype. Young girls tried to look like Bacall with a dash of Hepburn. Their elders went in for cosmetics with manic names like Fatal Apple and Havoc. They also favored detachable daintiness features and phantom crotches. In ads as expressive as dreams, fathers forfeited their children's love because of denture breath, and women exclaimed: "Don't expect *me* to marry *you* with a mouthful of cavities!"

A Navy doctor, soon to come home, wrote warning his wife rather sadly that he had gotten bald and heavy. She wrote back gently: "You will find that three years has done quite a bit to me, too."

A partially paralyzed ex-defense worker gave his six-year-old daughter a doll, his nine-year-old son a pack of cards, told them to shut their eyes because more was coming, and shot them through their heads.

The war was over. The postwar world was born. Everywhere the returning traveler saw signs of change, signs of no change at all, signs of change but too fast, signs of change but not fast enough: signs by the millions.

In Seattle a 25-year-old veteran was sore about the skimpiness of his civilian shirttails. All over the U.S., businessmen read a brochure: *Among Convention Leaders Who Know—It's Chicago 81 to 65*. In New Haven a CIOrganizer told ralliers: "We want full employment and if free enterprise must go, let it go. The manufacturers want to return to normalcy—the normalcy of no labor movement."

In the window of a gas station-soda fountain in McFarland, Calif. (pop. 605), appeared a wobbly handmade sign: "Colored Trade Not Solisited at Fountain."

In New Orleans white housewives, proud for the first time in their lives of doing their own housework, said "those niggers all want $12 or $15 a week and they're no good at that." The editor of the Laurel, Miss. *Leader-Call* listened to servicemen on train en route to mustering-out camp, talking of sports, and home, and their tremendous desire to get back to the joys of civilian life. He wrote: "I wonder if they aren't going to get a great jolt."

In Kansas City, which calls itself the heart of America, a veteran of the Pacific observed: "Over there in the line we talked about life and death, and who was going to get it next. So what happens when I get home? I no more get into the house the old man begins to tell me about his God-damned lawn mower."

A twelve-year-old delinquent phoned home at 3 a.m.: "Mom! Guess where I am? In jail again."

At the height of a historic, nationwide housing shortage, such classified ads as this were common in the *Star*: "Desperate. No place to go. Veteran, wife and two children need home immediately."

In Davey Markowitz' place two veterans, former friends and schoolmates, met for the first time in four years. The ex-sergeant gave his boyhood friend, an ex-lieutenant, only a perfunctory greeting: "I hate lieutenants," he snarled.

Over in Byers, Kans. Wayne Fisk came back from the Navy and said that a long rest would sure look good to him. But a day of loafing was enough. So while he was resting he painted his father's house.

In its own quiet way, it was a period as madly chaotic in the relatively unscathed U.S. as in the shattered rest of the world. Nobody seemed able to see much beyond the end of his nose. Business tossed on the greatest wave of labor unrest since the middle '30s. In vast numbers ex-war workers, some unwilling and some unable to live on reduced postwar wages, floated along on war savings or on unemployment compensation while, in vast numbers, jobs went begging. Veterans too wanted time to rest up and to enjoy themselves and to get readjusted, and they didn't want to be hurried about it either. Many were jealous of the high wages paid in wartime and paid no longer; many others, who took back their old jobs, left them within a few weeks.

Everywhere, people had expected an immediate, dreamlike postwar flow of the autos and refrigerators and radios and washing machines and farm machines and nylons and plumbing and good clothes which had been promised all through the war to the most machine-dependent and comfort-loving of nations. Everywhere, such hopes were sorely disappointed.

Underneath all the pleasure-bending, elbow-bending and tongue-bending (reflected perhaps—and perhaps not—in increased church attendance) lay a more mature awareness, a profound, bewildered foreboding, a tragic and justified uneasiness, a still more disturbing fatalism. Many Americans assumed that the nation's interracial troubles were barely beginning; that another great depression and another great war were dead certainties; that the next opponent was Russia; that nothing whatever could be done about such matters.

Almost without exception Americans realized that they might not like the neighbors but they had to live with them. Almost without exception they talked a good deal about the atomic bomb; many had it on their minds even more than they talked about it. But almost without exception they were so thoroughly absorbed in immediate troubles, pleasures, hopes, angers and disappointments—and perhaps so essentially far-gone in the basic kind of hope which holds human beings upright—that they were virtually incapable of even trying to take fate into their own hands.

The general attitude about atomic control got no farther than the first primitive reflex of greed and terror; the unkeepable secret must be kept. The general attitude toward racial problems was most sadly expressed by the more thoughtful Southerners, who said they only wished they could spend the next few years where there weren't any Negroes. The general attitude toward Europe was in the first place insufficiently informed, in the second place wearily or even scornfully indifferent.

Isolationism, in its old, simple, scarehead sense, was somewhere near being a thing of the past. But unconscious isolationism, far more insidious, was an all-powerful and increasing phenomenon of the present and future. If civilization, or time itself in the provincial, planetary sense, was to last more than another few decades, the responsibility rested chiefly on the

American people. But for wholly understandable, nonetheless tragic reasons, the American people were not very responsible toward any major responsibility. If this troubled season was any indication, they would be too busy trying to buy that wholly un-purchasable dream.

VOICE OF REASON

o the English writer whom Anatole France once called the greatest intellectual force in the English-speaking world, death came last week. Herbert G. (for George) Wells had described himself to a friend just a few weeks before as having "one foot in the grave and the other waving about." The last time Wells left his house alive was to vote in the 1945 general election. When he left it for the last time one day last week, the London *Daily Herald* observed that, more than any other one man, H. G. Wells was responsible for Socialist England.

He had looked like, and was, the quintessence of the Common Man. It was as a common man, and through the convictions and aspirations which history made available to common men in his generation, that he grew to stature.

Wells was possibly the greatest British journalist since Defoe. To the respectful Henry James he once said that he had no interest in being a literary artist; but three of Wells's novels (*Kipps, Mr. Polly, Tono Bungay*) are considered the best pieces of genre comedy since Dickens. His scientific romances were immensely entertaining and often clairvoyant in their view of the future. His realistic novels are pretty certain to live. His novels of sex propaganda (*Ann Veronica, et al.*), in their time, were notable liberating forces. His *Science of Life* (written with his son G. P. Wells and Julian Huxley) may come to be recognized as an achievement still more remarkable than his world famous *Outline of History*.

When he was 19, Wells wrote an essay called *The Past and Future of the Human Race*. Seldom thereafter did he tackle a less ambitious subject in a spirit less sanguine. He disliked and soon left the evangelistic Protestantism in which he was brought up;

but he always remained the most passionate of Protestants, the most eloquent of evangelists.

He worked his way through London University by writing digests of textbooks for lazy classmates; he worked his way through the rest of his life by doing just about the same thing. His courage and intelligence, activated rather than stunted by a drab, lower-middle-class childhood were touched off by the kind of illumination most characteristic of his day—rationalism.

He early became aware that the forces and skills which scientific research was turning loose on the world could possibly liberate, and might destroy it. Wells believed that in order to cope with these forces and with himself, man had only to embrace all that a scientist would call reasonable, and reject all that a scientist would call unreasonable.

This belief was the essence of his gospel. For five decades, in most of his 76 volumes, Wells preached it with the intense passion and reckless zeal of a religious fanatic.

Much of the world was already starving for such a gospel. So gifted and disarming a preacher was all that was needed. But it was not enough, as it turned out, to help the world to save itself from disaster.

It was H. G. Wells's tragedy that he lived long enough to have a second thought. All his life he had worked to warn and teach the human race and, within the limits of thought, to save it. At the end, he was forced to realize that his work and his hopes were vain; that either he or the human race were somehow, dreadfully wrong. Characteristically, with the last of the valiant, innocent optimism which had always sustained him, he blamed it all on the human race.

Some people found his last bitter utterances offensive, even cracked. Others found them unbearably pathetic, for there is no anguish to compare with that of a man who has lived on a faith of any kind and found it wanting. H. G. Wells was such a man, a great pietistic writer set on fire by reason, not by God; but in his era, among the most devoted, eloquent and honest.

GREAT BRITAIN: BEYOND SILENCE

One evening last week Britain's No. 1 test pilot shut himself into what was probably the most advanced piece of air machinery ever to get beyond the blue-printing stage, and took off into the darkening sky. The pilot was Captain Geoffrey De Havilland, 37, crown prince of one of aviation's few dynasties. His father, Sir Geoffrey, heads the De Havilland Aircraft Co.; his younger brother John was killed (1943) in the collision of two planes. Since 1938, Captain Geoffrey had made every first flying test of De Havilland's aircraft.

The new plane was the DH-108, a jet-propelled, tailless aircraft shaped like a sting ray. Captain De Havilland's purpose was: (1) to study problems of control in aircraft with swept-back wings (in preparation for a transatlantic airliner which is being built by his father's company); (2) to advance Britain's supremacy in aircraftsmanship by breaking the British-held world's speed record (616 m.p.h.).

The last anyone saw of this adventure was the strange machine's magnificent trajectory into the dusk—as if a match had been swept across a hot stovelid. That same evening a plane exploded above the Thames estuary with such violence that neither pilot nor much of the wreckage was found. But R.A.F. flyers concluded that scraps of wreckage they found had once belonged to the DH-108. It was possible that Captain De Havilland had made his new record (unofficially); and that for one fearful moment, he had experienced more of the new problems of aeronautics than is known to any living man.

One conjecture: his speed may have passed the dreaded limit of "compressibility" when the air streams pass the wing or control surfaces at the speed of sound. A "standing sound wave" may have formed, clung like a yammering banshee, and torn the plane to shreds. Perhaps Captain De Havilland crossed that sonic threshold only to discover, in Hamlet's soaring words:

> *The undiscovered country from whose bourn*
> *No traveler returns.*

A STAR
IN THE DARKNESS

I n the year 529, the civilization of Rome was a fainting glimmer. That year Saint Benedict of Nursia, founder of the Benedictine Order, established its abbey on Monte Cassino—a steady light, on a steep hill, which was ultimately to illuminate all Western Europe. In February 1944, seeking out a German observation post, U.S. bombers demolished the abbey, and put out the light.

The light had shone from one of history's great treasure houses, which was a library and a school as well. In the school, the oldest in Christendom, Saint Thomas Aquinas was once a pupil. In the library, which included unique manuscripts of Tacitus, Apuleius and Varro, such Renaissance scholars as Giovanni Boccaccio browsed and pilfered. Adalhard, Charlemagne's cousin, became a monk at Monte Cassino. So did Paul the Deacon, to whom Charlemagne wrote, in a letter, a phrase which epitomizes the abbey: *Est nam certa quies fessis venientibus illuc*—"For there is certain rest for the weary who come there."

From the abbey had gone forth the Benedictine monks who had mainly converted and civilized all Western Europe but Ireland. By the beginning of the 14th Century the Benedictines had given to their church 15,000 bishops, 7,000 archbishops, 200 cardinals, 24 popes. And they had become schoolmasters to the world. They preserved and taught handicrafts and the rudiments of science; Monte Cassino itself was second only to Salerno as a seat of medical learning. The Benedictines kept and copied poetry and letters and the Scriptures; they kept and developed the art of music. For century upon dark century, all men and women who possessed minds and hearts awake enough to hold learning and beauty in high regard had only one sure refuge and one sure lifework: in the monasteries and the convents.

Much of the Abbey of Monte Cassino, at the time the bombers destroyed it, dated only from the 17th Century; for it had suffered already, through more than a millennium, under the Lombards and the Saracens, and the Napoleonic French, and by earthquake as well. But some remained from the 11th Century; and a little from the 6th. Virtually all of the stone palimpsest was rendered forever illegible by the bombers. But the irreplaceable possessions of the library, its 1,200 MSS. and 40,000 records, were removed by the Hermann Göring Division. Monte Cassino's librarian and archivist, Don Mauro Inquanez rescued the ashes of Shelley and the holographs of Keats's last miseries in Rome, smuggling them out among his personal papers in a German military car.

Last week Don Mauro was back in Europe after six months in the U.S., setting afoot a campaign to restore Monte Cassino. Fortnight ago, on the 1,400th anniversary of Saint Benedict's death, Pope Pius XII issued an encyclical commending the study of the saint's life and work, and pleading for the restoration of the abbey. Saint Benedict, the Pope said, had kept alive the flame of religion and culture as "a star in the darkness of night."

Immediately after the destruction of the abbey, a group of U.S. sponsors had organized as the Friends of Monte Cassino. They included Swarthmore's ex-President Dr. Frank Aydelotte, Harvard's classicist Professor E. K. Rand, Princeton's medievalist Dr. E. A. Lowe (who had studied at Monte Cassino) and Morgan Librarian Dr. Belle da Costa Greene. They had issued a statement, conveying "to the Abbot and monks of Monte Cassino, now in exile, the expression of our sorrow and sympathy in this hour of tragedy and trial. We . . . ardently wish to contribute our mite to hasten the day of its reconstruction."

Washington suggested that the group postpone its activities: they amounted to a criticism of the U.S. Army.

BIBLIOGRAPHY

Agee, James. *Agee on Film.* 2 vols. New York: McDowell, Obolensky, 1958, 1960.
————. *The Collected Short Prose of James Agee.* Ed. Robert Fitzgerald. Boston: Houghton Mifflin, 1971.
————. *A Death in the Family.* New York: McDowell, Obolensky, 1957.
————. *Letters of James Agee to Father Flye.* 2nd ed. Boston: Houghton Mifflin, 1971.
————. *The Morning Watch.* Boston: Houghton Mifflin, 1950.
————. *Permit Me Voyage.* New Haven: Yale Univ. Press, 1934.
Allen, Frederick Lewis. *Since Yesterday.* New York: Harper, 1940.
Baker, Carlos. *Ernest Hemingway, A Life Story.* New York: Scribner's, 1969.
Barson, Alfred T. *A Way of Seeing.* Amherst: Univ. of Massachusetts Press, 1972.
Bergreen, Lawrence. *James Agee: A Life.* New York: Dutton, 1984.
Bingham, Robert. "Short of a Distant Goal." *The Reporter,* 25 Oct. 1962, pp. 55–58.
The Book of Common Prayer. New York: Thomas Nelson, 1944.
Brewer, Carson. "Town's History Rises Through Waters of TVA." *Knoxville News-Sentinel,* 15 May 1983.
Bruccoli, Matthew J. *James Gould Cozzens, A Life Apart.* New York: Harcourt Brace Jovanovich, 1983.
Elson, Robert T. *The Intimate History of a Publishing Enterprise 1923–1941.* New York: Atheneum, 1968.
Fabre, Genevieve. "A Bibliography of the Works of James Agee." *Bulletin of Bibliography,* 24 May–Aug. 1965, pp. 148, 163–65.
Flye, Father James Harold, photographer. *Through the Eyes of a Teacher.* Ed. Donald Dietz and David Herwaldt. St. Andrew's, Tenn.: n.p., 1980.
Huse, Nancy Lyman. *John Hersey and James Agee, A Reference Guide.* Boston: G. K. Hall, 1978.

Joyce, James. *Dubliners*. New York: Modern Library, 1971.

Little, Michael Vincent. "Sacramental Realism in James Agee's Major Prose." Diss. Univ. of Delaware 1974.

Macdonald, Dwight. *Against the American Grain*. New York: Random House, 1962.

Madden, David, ed. *Remembering James Agee*. Baton Rouge: Louisiana State Univ. Press, 1974.

Moreau, Genevieve. *The Restless Journey of James Agee*. New York: William Morrow, 1977.

Muggeridge, Malcolm. *Things Past*. Ed. Ian Hunter. New York: William Morrow, 1979.

Raines, Howell. "Let Us Now Revisit Famous Folk." *New York Times Magazine*, 25 May 1980.

Rowell, Geoffrey. *The Vision Glorious*. New York: Oxford Univ. Press, 1983.

Swanberg, W. A. *Luce and His Empire*. New York: Scribner's, 1972.

Thomas, Martha Skinner. "James Agee: A Bio-Bibliography." Thesis, Univ. of Tennessee, 1967.

Updike, John. "No Use Talking." *New Republic*, 13 Aug. 1962, pp. 23–24.

Young, Thomas Daniel. *Tennessee Writers*. Knoxville: Univ. Of Tennessee Press, 1981.

TIME AND FORTUNE ARTICLES

"Housing," *Fortune*, 6 (Sept. 1932), 74.

"Sheep and Shuttleworth," *Fortune*, 7 (Jan. 1933), 43–81.

"Strawberries," *Fortune*, 7 (Apr. 1933), 64–69.

"$100,000 Worth," *Fortune*, 7 (May 1933), 58–66.

"Cincinnati Terminal," *Fortune*, 7 (June 1933), 72–76, 125.

"Baldness," *Fortune*, 8 (July 1933), 52–55, 79–82.

"T.V.A.," *Fortune*, 8 (Oct. 1933), 81–97.

"Steel Rails," *Fortune*, 8 (Dec. 1933), 42–47, 153.

"Quinine to You," *Fortune*, 9 (Feb. 1934), 76–86.

"Butler's Ball," *Fortune*, 9 (Mar. 1934), 68–69.

"Cockfighting," *Fortune*, 9 (Mar. 1934), 90–95, 146.

"U.S. Ambassadors," *Fortune*, 9 (April 1934), 108–122.

"Arbitrage," *Fortune*, 9 (June 1934), 93–97, 150–160.

"Roman Society," *Fortune*, 10 (July 1934), 68–71, 144–150.

"Cabinet Changes" (on Mussolini), *Fortune*, 10 (July 1934), 126–127.

"The American Roadside," *Fortune*, 10 (Sept. 1934), 53–63, 172–177.

"Drought," *Fortune*, 10 (Oct. 1934), 76–83.

"Illuminated Manuscripts," *Fortune* 10 (Dec. 1934), 90–98.

"Glass," *Fortune*, 11 (Jan. 1935), 48.

"T.V.A.," *Fortune*, 11 (May 1935), 93–98, 140–153.

"The Normandie," *Fortune*, 11 (June 1935), 84–88.

"Williamsburg Restored," *Fortune*, 12 (July 1935), 69–73.

"Saratoga," *Fortune*, 12 (Aug. 1935), 63–69, 96–100.

"Hercules Powder," *Fortune*, 12 (Sept. 1935), 57–62, 110–125.

"The Modern Interior," *Fortune*, 12 (Nov. 1935), 97–103, 164.

"U.S. Art: 1935," *Fortune*, 12 (Dec. 1935), 68–75.

"U.S. Commercial Orchids," *Fortune*, 12 (Dec. 1935), 108–114, 126–129.

"Jewel Spread," *Fortune*, 14 (Aug. 1936), 70.

"Posters by Cassandra," *Fortune*, 15 (May 1937), 120.

"Smoke," *Fortune*, 15 (June 1937), 100–102, 130.

"Havana Cruise," *Fortune*, 16 (Sept. 1937), 117–120, 210–220.

"U.S. at War" (on F. Roosevelt's death), *Time*, 45 (23 April 1945), 1.

"Victory: The Peace," *Time*, 46 (20 Aug. 1945), 19–21.

"New York, a Little Rain" (National Affairs), *Time*, 46 (1 Oct. 1945), 22–23.

"Europe: Autumn Story" (Foreign News), *Time*, 46 (15 Oct. 1945), 24–25.

"Godless Götterdämmerung" (Religion), *Time*, 46 (15 Oct. 1945), 62–64.

"The Nation" (National Affairs), *Time*, 46 (5 Nov. 1945), 22–24.

"Average Man" (The Press), *Time*, 46 (26 Nov. 1945), 58–60, 64.

"Voice of Reason" (Foreign News), *Time*, 48 (26 Aug. 1946), 28.

"Syria: Triumph of Civilization," *Time*, 48 (9 Sept. 1946), 34.

"Russia: Last Mile" (Foreign News), *Time*, 48 (9 Sept. 1946), 34.

"Food—Harvest Home" (International), *Time*, 48 (23 Sept. 1946), 30.

"Great Britain" (Foreign News), *Time*, 48 (23 Sept. 1946), 32–33.

"Great Britain: Beyond Silence" (Foreign News), *Time*, 48 (7 Oct. 1946), 31.

"A Star in the Darkness" (Education), *Time*, 49 (7 April 1947), 55–56.

James Agee: Selected Journalism has been set into type in ten point Caledonia with two points spacing between the lines. Graphique (shaded outline characters) and Gill Sans Book capitals were selected for display. The book was designed by Sandra Strother Hudson, composed by G & S Typesetters, Inc., printed offset by Thomson-Shore, Inc., and bound by John H. Dekker & Sons. The acid-free paper on which the book is printed is designed for an effective life of at least three hundred years.

THE UNIVERSITY OF TENNESSEE PRESS
KNOXVILLE